THE ATLANTIC BLUE RIBAND

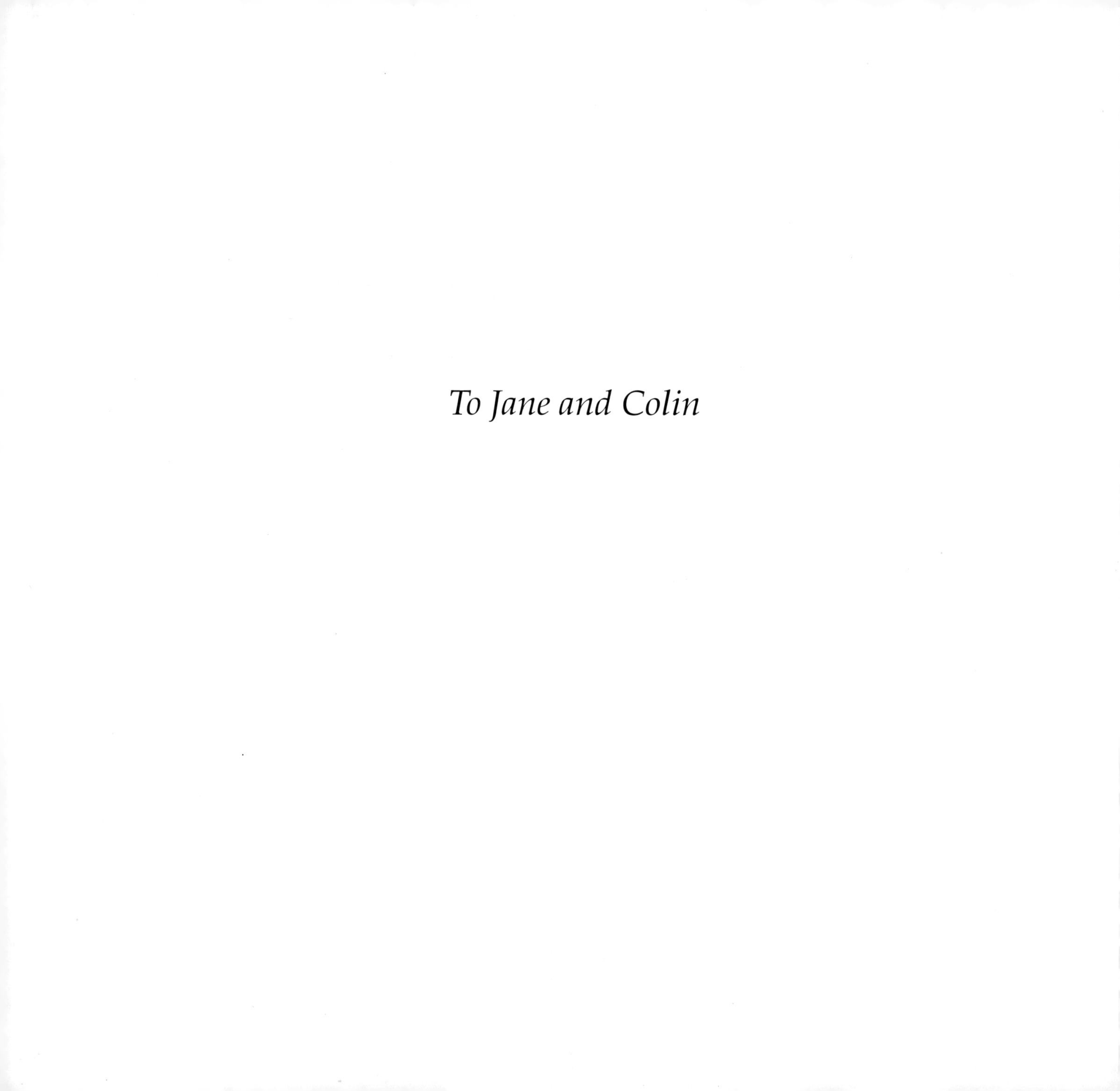

To Jane and Colin

The Atlantic Blue Riband

Evolution of the Express Liner

by

C. Mackenzie-Kennedy

William Sessions Limited
York, England

ISBN 1 85072 133 5

Printed in 10 on 11 point Palatino Typeface
by William Sessions Limited
The Ebor Press
York, England

Preface

THE TERM 'BLUE RIBAND' (or 'Blue Ribbon') has always been considered a symbol of honour and high esteem associated with achievement and therefore denotes a mark of greatest distinction in various walks of life. ('Blue Ribbon – Ribbon of the Garter, greatest honour in any sphere, sign of teetotalism' ibid: *The Concise Oxford Dictionary*).

Although it is not actually known when the legendary term 'Blue Riband of the Atlantic' was first introduced to denote the fastest passage between Europe and America by a merchant ship, this notional publicity honour was apparently invented for their aggrandisement by Shipping Companies (Cunard – Inman – White Star) around 1860-1870, with each particular record claimant qualifying to fly a long blue pennant from the topmast until such time as a rival managed a faster crossing, thus becoming eligible to claim the honour.

Maritime history could well assume that in sense the term 'Blue Riband' should retrospectively date back to the first steam powered passenger crossing of the Atlantic in May 1838 by the 703-ton wooden paddle steamer *Sirius* in 18 days 10 hours from Cork in Ireland to New York, averaging 6.7 knots and back to Falmouth in 18 days at 6.9 knots. This two-way passage was then 'competitively' bettered by the larger paddler *Great Western* also in May 1838, at averages of 8.7 and 8.0 knots, respectively, her original journey between Avonmouth and New York having been completed in 15 days 10½ hours.

Following these pioneering passages a 'competition' for fastest Atlantic crossings tended to develop and consequently the term 'Blue Riband' could be assumed to have become the international distinction applicable to a particular steamer (and to a relevant shipping company) achieving the feat of fastest single or round trip, thus qualifying for the designation as the world's fastest ship of the period.

Needless to say period media of participating countries, even in the earliest days consisting of diverse newspapers and magazines, did not waste much time catching on to this chance of spectacular and chauvinistic reportage. Highly imaginative and enthusiastic articles and illustrations provided much scope for filling the pages of the popular press and created much encouragement to shipowners and operators.

In 1933 the Member of Parliament for Hanley, Harold K. Hales, donated a most impressive and decorative, 4-foot tall 'Hales Trophy' as tangible recognition prize for temporary allocation to the latest successful Blue Riband record claimant.

Although all shipowners operating the Atlantic run took great interest in the Blue Riband, it was never recognised as a formal competition ruled by diverse regulations, need for prior application or adjudication by official referees; it was left to ships' officers, on basis of ships' logs, to work out average speeds from certain starting to finishing points as agreed by shipping companies. Right up to the turn of the century the predominantly British and American steamers involved sailed via Liverpool to New York, with the exception of some of the earliest Cunarders, prior to 1847-50, making landfall at Halifax. Later it suited agreement between ship-owners to use regular departure and arrival termini, such as Queenstown in Ireland and New York entry (Sandy Hook and later Ambrose Lightship) to work out crossing averages.

After the turn of the century, with Continental shipping companies becoming involved and the increasing use of south-coast and European ports, Cherbourg, Eddystone and Bishop's Rock were accepted as European termini. In the case of Italian ships, Gibraltar (Tarifa Point) was recognised.

Distances between these various points could differ appreciably, hence the crossing record was always claimed by the ship achieving the best average speed for the whole journey.

Shipping companies were usually reluctant to publish their intention to compete for the Blue Riband by building special record breakers because of possibility that considerable commitment of company funds could be rendered ineffective by a failure to achieve the record, thus creating considerable embarrassment to all concerned.

Politically, maritime nations began to face each other as contestants for the possession of the notional 'Atlantic Blue Riband' which began to represent a high national honour, bringing with it considerable publicity and invariably attracting maximum prestige and volume of passenger traffic besides creating increased business for all steamers of the shipping company concerned and even for the state. Shipowners of major maritime nations were encouraged to create, usually with large state subsidies, liners capable of achieving such distinction but had to exercise considerable discretion until such time as the record was ratified.

Express liners built for the glamour of the North Atlantic were, needless to say, conceived with reference to past experience and extensive research into the ultimate in ship design and all machinery in order to introduce the latest technology and safety features of the period. Promotion of developments in engineering, metallurgy and fuels, as well as passenger accommodation was greatly encouraged and accelerated by the competitive urge on the Atlantic. One has but to consider the Cunard evolution within one century, from the 1840 *Britannia* to *Queen Mary*.

Since the achievement of 35.59 knot average by the American liner *United States* in 1952, there has been no further commercial competition for the Blue Riband mainly because only a few years after the *United States* record, jet aircraft began to come into their own, rapidly monopolising scheduled transatlantic passenger services. Thus the passenger liner as created for the Atlantic and other long distance journeys in the past, was rapidly relegated to the role of a tourist cruising vessel.

The Hales Trophy

The trophy was presented in 1933 for international Blue Riband competition by Harold Keates Hales, Member of Parliament for Hanley, Stoke-on-Trent, to be temporarily held by the ship making the fastest crossing between Europe and America.

The donor collaborated with Henry Pidduck and Sons, Silversmiths of Hanley, to create this imposing trophy designed to symbolise evolution of the sailing ship to the modern record-breaking Atlantic liner.

The trophy made in heavily gilt solid silver, weighing ca 28 lbs (12.8 kg) rested upon a solid onyx plinth and the total height including the plinth was nearly 4 ft (1.22 m). The design features two finely modelled figures surmounting the globe, with the uppermost figure symbolising speed overcoming the forces of the Atlantic and urging forward a modern liner. The Atlantic on the globe is depicted in pale blue enamel with the route from the Fastnet to New York indicated by a red line, also in enamel.

Four winds are symbolised by four sailing ships, as copied from old prints illustrating the squadron of Columbus. A girdle encircling the globe contains enamelled panels portraying the evolution of steamships from the *Great Western* (1838) to *United States* (1952). Two figures of *Victory* standing back to back, support the Blue Riband and two additional seated figures represent Father Neptune and Amphitrite. Names of past record-holding steamers since 1838 are engraved at the base of the trophy, with provision for future record breakers. The first panel of the trophy contains a hand-painted photograph of the donor.

The first presentation was made in 1934 to the owners of the Italian record breaker *Rex* and in 1935 it was passed on to Cie Gle Transatlantique, owners of *Normandie*, until the outbreak of the war in 1939. During the war the trophy was in the safekeeping of Henry Pidduck & Son in Hanley and in 1952 presented to the record breaker *United States*.

As decreed by the Chairman of Cunard, Sir Percy Bates, the trophy was not claimed as recognition of achievement by the liner *Queen Mary* which held the Blue Riband for 14 years, between 1938 and 1952.

The Hales Trophy.

Acknowledgements

THE AUTHOR GREATLY APPRECIATES the help rendered by various individuals, organisations and authorities as listed below in the compilation of this book. Permissions granted to reproduce illustrations referred to by markings of page numbers are also gratefully recognised.

Archive Administrator, Long Beach, Cal., USA, p. vii.

Blohm & Voss, Hamburg (1945-46) (Herren Dir R. Blohm and H. Berendt), pp. 85, 89, 94.

Bristol Museum and Art Gallery, Bristol, pp. 6, 8.

City Museum and Art Gallery, Hanley.

Cie Generale Maritime, Le Havre.

Cunard Archive, Liverpool University, pp. 12, 14, 15, 30, 32, 63, 115, 116, 119, 121.

Deschimag Bremen (1945) (Herrn Dr Gustav Bauer), pp. 85, 95.

Deutsches Schiffahrtsmuseum, Bremerhaven, pp. 96, 147, 166.

A. Duncan, Esq., p 54.

The Engineer, pp. 75, 76, 79, 87, 93.

HAPAG/Lloyd AG, pp. 84, 86, 88, 96, 101.

Harland & Wolff Ltd., Belfast.

Illustrated London News library, pp. 5, 6, 7, 8, 12, 13, 16, 17, 18, 22, 23, 25, 28, 30, 33, 38, 46, 61, 65, 66, 67, 71, 72, 163, 164.

Italia di Navigazione, Societa p. A., Genoa, pp. 131.

Kempe's Yearbook (1964), pp. 179, 197.

Marine Publications International Ltd., Basingstoke.

Merseyside Maritime Museum, Liverpool, p. 7.

National Lending Library, Boston Spa, Yorks.

National Maritime Museum, Greenwich, p. 24.

Henry Pidduck & Son, Hanley.

Riva Calzoni, SPA., Milan, pp. 158.

Science Museum, London, p. 165.

Sea Containers Ltd., pp. 157, 159, 160.

Shipbuilder, pp. 167, 177, 178, 179, 190, 191, 196.

Shipbuilding & Shipping Record, pp. 117, 123, 124, 132, 140, 168, 169, 180, 181, 2032, 204.

Shipbuilder & Marine Engine Builder, pp. 104, 105, 108, 120, 137, 138, 139, 141, 142, 143, 144, 145, 170, 171, 175, 176.

Shipping World, pp. 125, 126, 148, 150, 152, 153, 182, 185, 189, 193, 196, 200, 201.

Herrn Rainer Tiemann, pp. 19, 28, 52, 58, 63, 74, 83, 91, 103, 108.

VDI Nachrichten, p. 113.

Virgin Atlantic, p. 155.

World Ship Society Library, pp. 36, 47, 49, 51, 70, 74, 133, 151.

Contents

Introduction

TRANSATLANTIC STEAMSHIPS COMMISSIONED in the course of just over a century within context of the 'Blue Riband' accolade, were instrumental in greatly boosting development of the Merchant Marine to enable ever increasing safe average speeds and profitability to be achieved in the course of catering for greater numbers of passengers and quantities of merchandise.

This book portrays the general history related to each record breaking steamship of its particular period on the Atlantic within scope of the pertinent shipping company's commercial and political aspects while emphasising contemporary developments in facilities for ever growing numbers of travellers. Introduced is also abridged technical information applicable to ships and their performance.

The aim is to enable the interested, possibly non-technical reader to appreciate and understand achievements of progress made during the 112 years or so of the Blue Riband period with concurrent influence upon the Merchant Marine as such, without being overwhelmed by detail nor swamped in 'chatty travel experiences'.

Illustrated chapters deal chronologically with evolution in the generation of steam as primary driving medium and its conversion into mechanical forces capable of propelling the ever growing sizes of steamships in order to cross oceans in safety and with competitive urge to attain greater efficiency than their rivals, at the same time ensuring that the very important commercial viability is not forefeited.

Chapters dealing with interpretation of mensuration and terminology are included.

C. MACKENZIE-KENNEDY

Blue Riband in the 19th Century

The Pioneers: Steamships *Sirius, Great Western* and *Great Britain*

EARLY IN THE 19TH CENTURY various individual journeys originating with North American pioneers, were made across the Atlantic by virtually steam engine assisted sailing ships and it was becoming obvious that sail was bound to be eventually supplanted by steam as the definite primary propulsion medium, offering positive and reliable performance to ensure Atlantic crossings catering for an ever increasing number of prospective passengers, mail and quantities of merchandise.

In 1835 the Great Western Railway Company was urged by their eminent engineer, Isombard Kingdom Brunel, to extend the new railway service between London and Bristol to New York by transferring intending passengers to an ocean steamship at the port of Bristol, thus enabling them to continue the journey to America with the least bother and inconvenience. As a result of these ideas and with appropriate financial backing, the 'Great Western Steamship Company' was formed and it was planned to provide two steamships of ca 1200 tons (gross) and 300 HP in order to perform 12 round trips each year between Bristol and New York. Before the laying of the first keel the directors decided to build initially only one vessel, leaving the construction of further ships to be decided from experience with the new venture.

In July 1837 the ship's hull of the steamship *Great Western* to Brunel's very advanced designs, was launched at W. Patterson's shipyard in Bristol. This vessel of 1,340 gross tons, was built expressly for transatlantic service and featured a specially reinforced timber hull which proved exceptionally strong and impervious to Atlantic weather. Overall dimensions of the *Great Western* were a length of 236 ft x 35 ft 4 ins beam x 23 ft depth. During winter 1839/40 some alterations to accommodation added deck space, extended her length by 16 ft and created additional berths. Gross tonnage thus increased to 1,700.

The 28 ft 9 in diameter paddles were driven by a two-cylinder side-lever steam engine to Brunel's specification, capable of developing 740 Indicated HP, with cylinders of 73½in in diameter and 7 ft stroke, in order to deliver some 450 HP to drive the paddles. Steam was generated at a pressure of 5 psi in four 3-furnace iron 'box' boilers supplied by Maudslay, Son & Field, who also built the engine plant as their to-date largest contribution to marine engineering. Re-boilering in June 1844 introduced three coupled tubed boilers developing steam at 12 psi constructed by the Great Western Steamship Company.

Pioneering steamer Great Western *of 1838. From contemporary painting by J. Walters:* Great Western *at mooring at Broad Pill in the River Avon.*

One hundred and twenty to 140 First Class travellers were accommodated in comparative luxury but the 20 or so Second Class berths, usually intended for servants of First Class passengers, offered rather more utilitarian quarters.

The new Atlantic enterprise created much interest in shipping circles and an upsurge of competition materialised. Whilst *Great Western* was being fitted out, one of the newly formed rival enterprises, 'British and American Steam Navigation Company' founded by the American Junius Smith, was completing a similar steamship, the 2,000 ton *British Queen*, 275 ft in overall length and 40.5 ft beam, to be equipped with a 2-cylinder side-lever engine capable of developing ca 800 IHP, to compete with the *Great Western*.

Due to delays in construction, *British Queen* was unable to go into service until July 1839 and could therefore not compete with the proposed inaugural departure date of *Great Western*, set for the spring of 1838. The new company chartered a small Irish coastal steamer *Sirius* from their associated St George Steam Packet Company in 1838 in order to achieve the first steam-powered crossing to New York. *Sirius*, a comparatively new paddler built in 1837 by Menzies of Leith, had a gross tonnage of 703 and was 178 ft in overall length and 26 ft wide. *Sirius* was powered by a 2-cylinder side-lever steam engine capable of developing some 450 IHP with steam at 5 psi generated in time-honoured 'box' boilers and equipped with surface condenser.

On 4th April 1838, *Sirius* with 40 fare paying passengers set out from Cork in Ireland for New York, three days before *Great Western*, delayed by a minor fire, could leave Bristol and completed the 2,961 nautical mile journey in 18 days 10 hours, at an average speed of 6.7 knots. It was rumoured that the *Sirius*, having used up all its coal from the bunkers, had to stoke the boilers with ship's furniture and other odds and ends in order to make port after a particularly rough passage.

Great Western, leaving on 8th April with only seven passengers, caught up and arrived in New York only some 4 hours after *Sirius* dropped anchor, averaging 8.7 knots between Avonmouth and New York, having completed the crossing of 3,223 nautical miles in 15 days 10 hours and 30 minutes, presumably just in time to share the reception celebration.

The inaugural westward crossing was later improved upon by *Great Western* on numerous occasions and in May 1843 a journey of 12 days 18 hours was achieved.

In the course of the pioneering return leg, in May 1838, *Great Western* averaged 8.6 knots between New York and Avonmouth. Her quickest subsequent transatlantic journey from New York to Avonmouth, in May 1842, took 12 days 7½ hours, with a mean of around 10 knots.

Paddle steamer Sirius *of 1838. First British powered passenger carrier on the Atlantic.*

Great Western *negotiating Atlantic waves. Contemporary painting by J. Walters:* Great Western *at sea in storm during her fifth crossing to New York.*

Contemporary artist's impression of Sirius *battling with the Atlantic during her service in 1838.*

Sirius made only one more return trip to America in 1838 before returning to her original commitments in Ireland where in 1847 she finished her career on the rocks in Ballycotton Bay. Subsequent reports mentioned the fact that some 20 passengers lost their lives because of the inadequacy of the lifeboat. Others managed to scramble ashore and had to walk the 5 miles or so to the village of Cloyne. The wreck was meanwhile plundered in the time-honoured manner.

However, the small paddler could claim the honour of being the first to cross the Atlantic westward, with steam as primary motive power.

As far as the *British Queen* of the British and American Company was concerned, following the maiden voyage from Portsmouth in July 1839 she completed a few years' transatlantic trading but could not better the crossing times of the *Great Western* nor was she as reliable. Following the loss at sea in March 1841, of the company's newest, 1840 built, 2,366 ton steamer *President*, the *British Queen* was sold in 1841 to Belgian interests and the British and American Navigation Company went into liquidation. *British Queen* returned on the transatlantic service but was broken up in 1844.

Sirius *on the rocks at Ballycotton, as left by the tide.*

Great Western proved to be an exceptionally reliable and robust ship. Between 1838 and 1845 she crossed the Atlantic some 90 times and when considering the size of ship, dependence upon sails to complement the primitive engine and vagaries of North Atlantic conditions, she maintained reasonably consistent crossing times of 13 to 19 days in the course of her career. In 1847 the *Great Western* was sold to the Royal Mail Steam Packet Company and in the course of the next eight years traded on the West Indian and South American routes. Subsequently two years were spent trooping in Government service and she was broken up in 1857.

The Great Western Steamship Company did not prove financially viable without subsidies, in spite of Brunel's revolutionary second new steamer, the 3,270 ton iron-hulled, screw propelled *Great Britain* with accommodation for 360 First Class passengers, being introduced on the Atlantic in 1845. Apart from being the first ocean going vessel with screw propulsion, it had other features, such as watertight bulkheads, a double bottom and a balanced rudder. *Great Britain* could be considered the first genuine ocean liner.

Propulsion machinery for this very latest Atlantic steamship comprised two pairs of 88in bore inverted cylinders inclined at ca 60° to each other and with pistons travelling a 6ft-0in stroke to rotate an

Great Western Steamship Company's revolutionary Atlantic liner Great Britain, *commissioned in 1845.*

enormous, 17ft-0in long crankshaft, located at high level. The 15ft-0in diameter, 7-ton propeller having to revolve at 50-60 RMP for the ship's designed speed of 9-10 knots, the engine speed of ca 18 RPM had to be stepped up in order to drive the propeller shaft at the requisite revolutions. This was achieved by means of a chain transmission system using a quadruple pitched chain with links having teeth to suitably engage an 18ft-3in diameter 'sprocket' wheel/drum in the centre of the overhead crankshaft, to transmit drive to a second drum, 6ft-6in in diameter, keyed on to the inboard end of the propeller shaft. (Also see page 163.)

The size and weight of this, by present-day standards 'Heath Robinson' transmission, were not inconsiderable, the chain alone tipping the scales at 7 tons. The primemover and drive tended to give a fair amount of trouble, much detail redesign and alterations having to take place. However it must be admitted that numerous realistic and useful inventions and innovations materialised for incorporation.

Whereas sea trials produced reasonably satisfactory results with speeds up to 13 knots being achieved, the steamer's subsequent trans-atlantic behaviour between Liverpool and New York tended to be moderate with the capricious powerplant behaving in an erratic maner and the vessel having to rely more and more upon the good offices of the 1,700 or so square yards of sail gracing the six masts.

Unfortunately, with teething troubles just beginning to get ironed out and with the sixth mast removed, the pioneering liner had a short life in the service of the Great Western Steamship Company on the Atlantic. Becoming stranded off the Irish coast in

Steamship Great Britain *of 1845. Promenade deck with roof lights and doors on both sides to cabin accommodation.*

Steamship Great Britain *of 1845. The Saloon with roof lights and doors on both sides to cabin accommodation.*

Dimensionally rather optimistic contemporary sketches of accommodation on the Great Britain *indicating typical passenger facilities on steamers of the period.*

1846 she did not have a chance to offer competition to the crossing speeds of the period. In August 1847 complicated salvage operations finally brought success and *Great Britain* was floated for towage to Liverpool where it was ascertained that the ship was reasonably sound and re-usable. By the end of 1850 *Great Britain* was sold to Gibbs, Bright & Co., who completely refurbished and re-engined the ship for further service on the Atlantic and from November 1852 until 1876 for the Australian run. Later, under new management, *Great Britain* saw service on the South Atlantic until 1886, when much damage caused by heavy weather brought about her abandonment as coal hulk off the Falklands. In 1970 *Great Britain* was returned to Bristol, where she was refurbished and is kept in her original building dock as a historic relic.

The cost of salvage of the *Great Britain* as well as the unsuccessful tender for the new Admiralty Atlantic Mail Contract, contributed to the Great Western Steamship Company having to sell *Great Western* prior to winding up in 1852.

Another typical shipping enterprise with pioneering ambitions, 'Transatlantic Steamship Company' of Liverpool, arrived on the scene around 1838 and following the fashion of the 'British and American' also chartered an Irish coastal steamer, the *Royal William*, (not to be confused with Canadian namesake of 1832) in anticipation to acquisition of a more suitable and larger passenger carrier, the *Liverpool*, a small but well appointed paddler sporting two funnels. However success did not crown this venture and no records were achieved. The enterprise became a financial failure in 1840 after a few years' 'shoestring' operation.

Cunard Line Pioneering

The Company

SAMUEL CUNARD, BORN IN 1787 in Canada, developed during the period 1819 to 1838 his retired father's shipping business under the title 'Samuel Cunard and Company' and by 1838 owned some 40 sailing vessels trading between North American and Canadian ports.

Cunard was also involved in the new Quebec and Halifax Steam Navigation Company whose only steamer, the 1831 built *Royal William* of 800 tons, operated the Quebec and Halifax run.

In 1833 *Royal William* also made the journey from Quebec to England in some 21 days and this crossing strengthened Cunard's profound ambition to create a transatlantic shipping venture operating steam propelled ships capable of undertaking a scheduled service between the 'Old World' and North America.

In 1838, *Great Western* and *Sirius* as well as other steamers having pioneered Atlantic passenger travel by steam propelled ships, the British Admiralty recognised the desirability for a regular transatlantic mail service by passenger carrying steamships sailing to Halifax (Nova Scotia) and New York and advertised for tenders from shipowners, on the basis of favourable mail contracts.

In competition with other pioneering companies, Samuel Cunard obtained financial backing in partnership with the engine builder R. Napier and the Scottish shipping businessmen Burns and McIver, to submit tenders for fortnightly sailings from Liverpool to Halifax with feeder services to Quebec and Boston, operating three steamships of ca 900 tons. Cunard was awarded a 10-year contract in May 1839.

The newly formed shipping enterprise was named 'The British and North American Royal Mail Steam Packet Company', subsequently officially called the 'Cunard Steamship Company'.

Cunard and his partners were advised by Robert Napier that the proposed vessels would be too small for the service because they would not have the space for adequate coal bunkerage and furthermore, in order to obviate possible operational problems provision of a fourth vessel would be most desirable. Further financial assistance was obtained from various business concerns and following relevant approaches to the Admiralty, orders were placed for the construction of Cunard's first four mail steamers, paddle propelled wooden vessels of around 1,100 tons, amply provided with auxiliary sails.

Contracts for the pioneering paddle steamers during the period 1839 to ca 1852 were all placed with

Robert Napier, who built the side-lever engines while sub-contracting the wooden hulls to various affiliated Clydeside shipbuilders.

The First Cunard Mail Steamers

In order to fulfill conditions of the contract while the new mail steamships were being built, Cunard chartered a small coastal steamer, *Unicorn* from the Burns concern, to ensure dispatch of the first mail contingent from Liverpool to Halifax and Boston, subsequently placing the steamer on the branch run between Quebec and Halifax.

The first Cunard Atlantic mail carrier, the wooden paddle steamer *Britannia*, launched in February 1840 at the yard of Robert Duncan & Company of Greenock, departed on the inaugural voyage for Halifax on 4th July 1840 carrying some 65 passengers. *Britannia* arrived off Halifax on 17th July and at Boston on 19th July, averaging 8¼ knots (not beating the time taken by the *Great Western*). On the return journey from Halifax to Liverpool the average for 2,573 nautical miles was 10.72 knots, easily improving upon the previous best crossing. *Britannia* thus became the pioneer of a new era of passenger steamship services and the carriage of mails to schedule across the Atlantic.

Britannia and her near-sisterships *Acadia*, *Caledonia* and *Columbia*, commissioned between August 1840 and 1841, were each of ca 1,156 GRtons and 207 ft in overall length by 34 ft beam. *Acadia* was built by John Wood of Glasgow, *Caledonia* came from the yard of Robert Duncan & Co., Greenock and *Columbia* was completed by Robert Steele & Son of Greenock.

The four inaugural steamers were equipped with 2-cylinder side-lever steam engines capable of developing 740 IHP with steam at 9 psi generated in four iron smoke-flue boilers, in order to drive 28 ft diameter paddles at 16 RPM. If wind was favourable, the barque-rigged sails rendered a certain amount of welcome assistance.

In 1843/45 two larger but very similar versions of the original quartet, named *Hibernia* and *Cambria*, joined the Halifax/Boston run. The two new steamers were built by R. Steele of Greenock and had a GR tonnage of 1,422 with an overall length of 219 ft by 37¾ ft beam. The paddles were driven by larger versions of the *Britannia* power plant, rated at 1,040 Indicated Horsepower.

These six original Cunarders operated successfully the initially planned fortnightly service from Liverpool to Halifax/Boston, which only experienced minor revisions to suit winter conditions in Canada.

The two newer vessels provided cabin accommodation for some 200 passengers as compared with the capacity for 115 as offered by the original *Britannia* class. Accommodation and catering on these pioneering paddlers were, to say the least, primitive, with each of the tiny, ca 6 ft-6 in x 8 ft-0 in, two berth cabins being provided with a semi-upholstered box-settee, a small cupboard and a double washbasin.

The long dismal dining saloon-cum-lounge was lit by candle-lanterns, heated by means of a wood stove and the central table was equipped with two rows of semi-upholstered benches. Toilets were located on deck, not far from the cowshed housing the provider of fresh milk for essential users.

In accordance with a new negotiated contract, the *Hibernia* introduced a new service to New York in 1847 and this was complemented in 1848 by the commissioning of four larger paddlers of the 'America' class,

Britannia – *the first of four wooden paddle mail steamers built in 1840-41 to inaugurate scheduled transatlantic service between Liverpool and Boston via Halifax for the British and North American Royal Mail Steam Packet Company (Cunard Line).*

Cunard mail steamer Hibernia *taken into service between Liverpool and Halifax/Boston in 1843. In 1847* Hibernia *bettered all eastward crossing records, averaging 11.6 knots and in the same year inaugurated the service to New York. In 1850* Hibernia *was sold to the Spanish Navy.*

Wreck of the Cunard Mail Steamer Columbia.

Cunard wooden steamship Columbia *of 1,175 tons, was one of the original quartet of pioneering mail ships built in 1840 by R. Steele & Son of Greenock.* Columbia *was the first steamer to better the original crossing times of* Britannia, *by achieving 9.8 knots westward and 10.9 knots eastward on the Liverpool to Halifax run. In July 1948* Columbia *went aground on the Black Ledge reef near Seal Island off Townsend Bay at the SW coast of Nova Scotia, while steaming for Halifax. All her 95 passengers and 73 crew landed safely on Seal Island before the ship broke up. All mails were also saved. Captain Shannon of the* Columbia *was acquitted of all blame for the loss of the steamer and the master of Seal Island Light was complimented and compensated for the help he rendered and for his hospitality to the passengers. Apart from this mishap and the loss in 1886 of* Oregon *(also without loss of life) the only Cunard losses at sea have been ascribed to hostile action during the two world wars.*

with *America, Niagara* and *Canada* built by Robert Steele & Son, Greenock, and the fourth, *Europa* coming off the stocks at the yard of John Wood of Port Glasgow.

This quartet were of 1,825 to 1,925 GR tons, equipped with 2-cylinder jet-condensing engines developing up to 1,800 IHP with steam generated at 18 psi in four time-honoured iron 'box' flue boilers. With an overall length of 251 ft by 38 ft beam, the ships were barque-rigged three-masters.

The 'America' class were the first on the Atlantic to have navigation lights and the passenger accommodation, although still comparatively spartan, introduced a notable degree of improvement with additional rooms to make the 140 or so travellers more comfortable.

In 1850 a further enlarged and improved mutation of the wooden paddler was introduced on the Boston and New York run. Also built by Robert Steele, the two sisterships *Asia* and *Africa* were each of 2,226 GR

Cunard wooden mail steamer Europa *of 1,834 tons, commissioned in 1845. With accommodation for 140 'cabin' passengers she was one of the first Cunarders on the New York run.*

Europa *bettered the westbound Atlantic record of the* Columbia *in September 1848 by averaging 11.5 knots between Liverpool and New York.*

After a period of trooping in 1854, during the Crimean War, she returned to Atlantic service in 1858 and was sold in 1867 for conversion to sail.

Cunard mail steamer Canada *of 1,830 tons, built by R. Steele and Son of Greenock and commissioned in 1848. A sister ship to* Europa, *she also had accommodation for 140 passengers and was put on the Liverpool to New York/Boston run.*

In July 1949 Canada *made a record journey eastward, averaging 12.23 knots. She was sold for conversion to sail in 1867 and was broken up in 1883.*

tons and 267 ft in length by 40 ft beam. Their 36 ft-10 in diameter paddles were driven at 15-17 RPM by very large side-lever jet-condensing engines having two cylinders, each 98 in in diameter with a stroke of 9 ft and capable of developing 2,150 IHP with steam at 18 psi generated in four large iron 'box' boilers stoked by a team of 32 men. Catering for consumption of ca 75-80 tons daily, the coal bunkers had a capacity of 890 tons. The three masts were barquentine rigged.

Although the accommodation and catering were quite a bit superior to these of the earlier Cunarders, it was still much less sumptuous than offered by the newly emerging Collins rivals. In all there were cabin berths for 150 First Class travellers and 30 were allocated to 'Second Cabin'. State-rooms and cabins showed a notable improvement on earlier rather spartan Cunard facilities but still tended to be cramped.

Saloon and lounges were reasonably spacious as were the ladies' rooms and contained much highly polished woodwork, gilt framed mirrors and a large collection of paintings in papier-mache depicting scenes at different notable parts of the world.

A crew of 112 including 38 engine room staff attended to operational requirements. On the deck there was a mess-room for 2nd Class passengers and a similar room for the crew. As in the case of earlier Cunarders, a cow was housed on the deck in order to provide fresh milk.

There being no outside competition at the time, the Cunard steamers more or less vied against each other for the honour of the fastest crossing and during their monopoly between 1840 and 1850, crossing times were progressively reduced, with *Asia* in May 1850 averaging a record 12.12 knots between Liverpool and Halifax (8 days 17 hours) and in October 1850, 12.36 knots from New York to Liverpool in 10 days 7 hours.

The early Cunard paddlers were robust and reasonably reliable, operating the transatlantic services for anything from 8 to 15 years prior to being sold for other duties in different parts of the world and for conversion for other purposes.

Only one of the pioneering steamers was wrecked while in Cunard service; the *Columbia* struck a reef off Nova Scotia while being carried off her course, but there was no loss of life and the mails were saved although the ship became a total loss. This safety record must be considered quite extraordinary in the days when crossing the Atlantic was a hazardous achievement amounting to some 10 to 15 days' battle against the elements and unforeseen perils by tiny ships relying upon fairly crude machinery and sails

The 2,226 ton wooden paddle steamer Asia *built in 1850 by R. Steele & Son of Greenock and engined by R. Napier of Glasgow, was the first of a pair of Cunard mail steamers commissioned to offer serious competition to the new American Collins Line, but also specially reinforced for eventual Naval conversion.*

Asia *achieved record crossings both ways in 1850 but these were bettered a few months later by Collins' mail-boats which won the comfort and luxury stakes.*

Asia *sailed the Cunard transatlantic run until 1867. She was then sold for conversion to sail and was burnt out in India in 1877.*

Brigantine-rigged wooden mail steamer Africa *built for the Cunard Line by R. Steele & Son and commissioned in 1850 for the New York service.* Africa *was an identical sister ship to the* Asia *and equipped with similar machinery and boiler plant, also accommodated 180 passengers.*

The two steamers were built to special Admiralty requirements and had reinforced hulls to carry cannon for easy conversion to wartime auxiliaries.

Although like her sister Asia, *the* Africa *maintained high Atlantic crossing averages around 12 knots, she did not manage to achieve records which at the time became the prerogative of the Collins Line.*

Africa *was in Cunard service between Liverpool and New York, sometimes also Halifax and Boston, until 1867. A period of use as a depot ship followed and she was sold in 1868 for conversion to sail only.*

for propulsion and equipped with only very basic navigational aids and primitive safety facilities.

Needless to say, shipwrecks, fires and other losses at sea, invariably with considerable loss of life, were frequent occurences during these early days on the Atlantic.

As a typical example of longevity, the original *Britannia,* having completed some 50 transatlantic journeys, was sold to the German Reich-Navy in 1849, to be renamed *Barbarossa* and converted to a frigate for eventual warlike activities against the Danes. In 1852 *Barbarossa* was passed on to Prussia and used for Naval accommodation duties prior to demolition in 1880. (Also see pages 77-78.)

Britannia's sistership *Acadia* was also acquired by the Reich-Navy in 1849 for conversion to a frigate renamed *Erzherzog Johann.* In 1853 she was sold to W. Fritze & Co. of Bremen and renamed *Germania* for transatlantic service between Bremen and New York. In 1855 she was chartered for transportation of troops in the Crimean War and in 1857 the paddler was wrecked on the Thames.

In 1850 Cunard lost his Atlantic monopoly and the westbound and eastbound crossing records to steamers of the newly-formed United States Mail Steamship Company (Collins Line), which introduced the mail service subsidised by the American Congress.

As an answer to Collins, in 1852 Cunard placed an order with Robert Steele for a pair of to-date largest additions to his fleet, to be named *Arabia* and *Persia*. The 2,402 ton steamers were to be equipped with the largest and most powerful engines of the period and were intended to achieve record speeds. In the course of construction it was decided to sell *Arabia* to the Royal Mail West India Company, while retaining the second ship (*Persia*) and renaming it *Arabia* (2).

Arabia, the last Cunarder to be built of wood, was of 2,402 GR tons, 285ft in length and 41 ft wide. She was brig-rigged and equipped with powerful machinery comprising a 2-cylinder side-lever engine having 103 in diameter cylinders and a 9 ft piston stroke. The engine was capable of developing ca 3,000 IHP with a steam pressure of 18 psi created in four tubed flue-box boilers each having six furnaces, and drove the 36 ft diameter paddle wheels at 15-17 RPM.

Arabia catered for 160-180 First Class passengers in much greater comfort and luxury than the previous Cunard paddlers. She was the first Cunarder to be equipped with steam heating and an ornate saloon capable of seating 160 diners formed an unbroken apartment richly carpeted and elegantly panelled; there being no mizzenmast, a stained glass cupola crowned the room.

Although *Arabia* achieved crossings averaging around 13 knots, thus very nearly maintaining same travel times as contemporary Collins rivals, she

Arabia (2) *commissioned by Cunard Line in January 1853 was intended to compete with the latest Collins mail steamers on the Atlantic run, both on terms of speed and luxury of travel.*

never quite qualified for Atlantic records, possibly because the engine was too powerful for the wooden hull and at higher speeds considerable vibrations were experienced with much deterioration of seagoing qualities.

Arabia served on the Atlantic run until late in 1854 and then became a troop transport during the Crimean War. In 1856 she returned for service on the Atlantic but was sold in 1864 for conversion to sail. *Arabia*, with a coal consumption of over 120 tons per day, was not an economical nor successful passenger carrier in Cunard service.

During the Crimean War of 1854-56 most of the Cunard Atlantic mail steamers were requisitioned by the Admiralty for transportation of troops. On the Atlantic the new American mail steamers reigned supreme with none of the remaining contemporary Cunard boats capable of offering competition, until in accordance with some 'forward planning' and positive encouragement by the Admiralty, a pair of even larger iron built Cunard paddlers appeared on the scene in 1856 and 1862.

Friendly rivals: Collins mail steamer Pacific *and Cunarder* Asia.

United States Mail Steamship Company – The Collins Line

The Company

ALTHOUGH DURING THE EARLY days of the 19th Century it was in the New World that the first steps were being taken by various shapes and sizes of steam propelled coastal vessels, there always existed a strong lobby of owners of sailing packets for their highly developed ships to operate passenger and mail services on the Atlantic ocean. The magnificent sailing packets were equipped with passenger accommodation and facilities of utmost luxury and they were famous for their cuisine with all kinds of culinary masterpieces to tempt intending travellers to 'Sail American'.

Unfortunately the crossing times, completely dependent upon trade winds and Atlantic weather conditions, were erratic and journeys were unreliable as well as having a dubious safety record.

The rapidly developing steam monopoly by Cunard on the Atlantic since introduction in 1847 of scheduled, punctual and safe crossings on the Liverpool, Boston and New York run, indicated that the day of the clipper with all its luxuries and profitability, was coming to a close.

Introduction of weekly sailings during the summer months, with more or less regular crossing times of 11-13 days, as compared with 20-30 days by sailing packets, brushed aside all competition and Cunard steamers dominated the Atlantic.

Growing concern at the British reign over the sea routes gave birth to chauvenistic sentiments with political repercussions and American public demands for the government to create positive competition to the success of the Cunard enterprise. As a result in 1848 Congress allocated appropriate funds and American shipowners were invited to submit tenders for a mail contract on the basis of generous subsidies, to initiate a fortnightly mail/passenger service between New York and Liverpool with large and most modern steam propelled ships capable of higher crossing speeds than the Cunarders. The general idea was that American maritime superiority would eventually drive Cunard from the Atlantic.

Edward Knight Collins, the prosperous owner of the Dramatic Line of Sail Packets, appreciated at the time of Cunard incursion that the future lay with steam completely superseding sail and that American ocean shipping had become obsolescent. In 1846 Collins created the 'United States Mail Steamship Company' and by 1848 he was awarded the Government mail contract, originally initiated on the strength of his own lobbying.

With Congress subsidies, four large, solid oak-built paddle steamers *Atlantic, Baltic, Arctic* and *Pacific* were commissioned in 1850-51. Although iron hull construction had already proved its worth in other countries, at the particular time iron was not available in sufficient quantities in the United States and shipyards had insufficient experience with its use for the construction of such large ships as required for Atlantic service. Collins would have preferred iron built steamers but had to be satisfied with the excellent oak and other timbers available in great profusion.

Record Breakers of the Collins Line

The four new steamships, each of 2,710 to 2,860 GR tons, were built at the shipyards of W. H. Brown and G. Steers, both of New York, in 1848-1850 and were 282 ft in overall length with a 45 ft beam. Thirty-six feet diameter paddles were driven at 18-20 RPM by twin cylinder side-lever machinery manufactured by Stillman, Allen of New York. With a cylinder diameter of 96 in and a piston stroke of 9 ft, engine output was in the region of 2,500 IHP with steam at 17 psi generated in four large iron water tubed 'box' boilers consuming 85 to 95 tons of coal daily.

As a comparison, the smaller Cunarders, depending upon size, used 40-60 tons daily; however Collins' ships were 1½ to 2 knots faster and with a ca 100% greater capacity for passengers, maintained Atlantic record speeds as long as the company existed. In May 1851 the *Pacific* claimed the distinction of achieving the Atlantic crossing in less than 10 days and the regular journeys at around 13 knots introduced the first serious competition to the Cunard dominance. Furthermore, much in accordance with standards set by American sailing packets, the Collins' steamers were much more luxuriously appointed and more comfortable than the Cunard ships and offered splendid cuisine and services.

Superb accommodation had elegant interior fittings in highest grades of combined woodwork in white holly, satinwood and rosewood with the finish presenting a rich and sumptuous appearance. Drawing rooms, saloons and ladies' room were equipped with very large mirrors to emphasise spaciousness, elaborate bronzework, stained glass and many paintings framed in bronze. Heavy pile carpets covered the floors and all furniture was richly upholstered. Even the ceilings were elaborately wrought, carved and gilded. Staterooms located in the ship's stern had stained glass windows with pictorial reproductions of American cities and all cabins, although still rather cramped, had elegant sofas and berth frames in satinwood with damask curtains.

Ample light, ventilation and steam heating featured on all three decks and the steamers were the first to be provided with bathrooms, a barber's shop, telegraph communication between bridge and engine room and a so-called, 'Annunciator', an arrangement by which passengers could immediately summon a steward if his services are required. The five lifeboats were of galvanised iron, supposedly superior to traditional wooden ones as used by other ships of the period.

It soon became obvious that much passenger trade was gained by Collins at the expense of Cunard.

In September 1850 *Pacific* steamed from Liverpool to New York in 10 days 4 hours at an average of 12.5 knots, improving upon the previous record of 12.12 knots held by the Cunarder *Asia*.

In August 1851, *Baltic* bettered this westward passage of the *Pacific* with a crossing in 9 days 18 hours, at a mean of 13.17 knots. This record remained valid until July 1857, when the latest Cunarder *Persia* managed a quicker journey.

Eastbound, in July 1850, *Atlantic* beat the record set by *Canada* of Cunard Line, by averaging 12.29 knots between New York and Liverpool and completing the

Collins Line mail steamer Atlantic *entering the Mersey on the 10th May 1850. The first of four sisterships built to compete with the Cunard dominance on the North Atlantic. At the time it was the largest steamship in the world.*

The elegant 67 ft x 20 ft Grand Saloon of the Collins steamer Atlantic. *Interior decor featured large mirrors, stained glass, rich pile carpets and elegant upholstered period furniture.*

voyage in 10 days 8 hours. In the same year the Cunarder *Asia* averaged 12.36 knots but the record went back to Collins in May 1851, with *Pacific* breaking the 10-day 'barrier' by crossing to Liverpool in 9 days 20 hours at a mean speed of 13.1 knots.

In May 1852, *Arctic* improved upon the eastward journey of *Pacific* by averaging 13.25 knots and steaming from New York to Liverpool in 9 days 17 hours 12 minutes. This achievement was only bettered in May 1856 by the new Cunarder *Persia*.

End of the Collins Line

In addition to the fact that Collins was operating at a great financial loss because the large and uneconomical steamers never paid their way, to a great extent due to excessive maintenance and repairs necessitated by enforced speeds to achieve record passages overloading the engines, in September 1854 the *Arctic* foundered after a collision, giving rise to a tragic loss of life, and in January 1856 *Pacific* disappeared without trace with all hands. It was assumed that she had sailed into an icefield.

Following the loss of the two Atlantic record breakers, Collins took the belated delivery in 1857 of a new, larger and more luxurious paddle steamer, the 4,140 ton *Adriatic* which was urgently required to replace the *Arctic* and take over from the small replacement steamers unable to cope with the firm's commitments.

The firm's financial position became precarious and the American Government reduced subsidies to

Collins Line mail steamer Arctic. *Eastbound Atlantic record from May 1852 to May 1856.* Arctic *foundered in September 1854 with the loss of 346 lives.*

Collins Line record breaker Pacific *of 1851. Copy of engraving showing* Pacific *rescuing the crew of barque* Jessie Stevens.

Collins Line record breaker Baltic.

Collins Superliner that did not quite make it.

Wooden paddle-driven mail steamship Adriatic *of 1857. The last and largest Collins newbuild* Adriatic *was commissioned a year late in 1857; this possibly contributed to the failure of the Collins Line.*

Adriatic *with a GR tonnage of 4,140, an overall length of 355 ft and a 50 ft beam, was one of the largest, fastest and most luxurious liners on the Atlantic run of the period. Propulsion machinery, built by Novelty Ironworks of New York, featured a powerful engine with twin oscillating cylinders, each 100 in in diameter and with a piston stroke of 12 ft, capable of developing some 3,500 IHP to drive 40 ft diameter paddles at 17 RPM. Eight rectangular flue boilers contained vertical iron water tubes and developed steam at 25 psi by averaging a coal consumption of some 90 tons daily. Superior passenger accommodation catered for 300 travellers in the First Class and ca 100 in the Second.*

On her first voyage from New York to Liverpool in conditions of gale force winds, the journey apparently took 10 days 8 hours, occasionally logging 15 knots. Adriatic *could without a doubt have eventually achieved the coveted crossing records; unfortunately shortly after this maiden voyage the Collins Line was wound up.*

such an extent that the Collins Line had to be wound up in 1858. Apparently the sixth luxury liner originally planned and to be named *Antarctic,* never materialised. The remaining ships, *Atlantic, Baltic* and the new *Adriatic* had to be sold to meet the creditors' claims.

The three steamers were acquired by a newly created but short-lived 'North Atlantic Steamship Company' (American) for service between New York and Panama, although in 1960 the *Adriatic* was also put on the transatlantic run. In 1861, during the American Civil War, *Baltic* and *Atlantic* were taken over as Federal transport and *Adriatic* was sold to the Irish Galway Line. In the service of the new owners, the *Adriatic* completed a few transatlantic voyages, sometimes averaging over 13 knots between Galway and St Johns, Newfoundland, but because of the comparatively short distance involved, the journeys did not qualify as Atlantic records. The large elegant paddler had a short life, being sold again around 1862/63, to finish her life in the late sixties as a hulk off the African coast.

Following some further service to the Central Americas, *Atlantic* and *Baltic* were sold in 1866 and operated by small short-lived shipowners, completed some 6-7 transatlantic trips during the next two years. They were scrapped around 1870.

Although Edward K. Collins' enterprise collapsed, his competition with Samuel Cunard contributed greatly to the Merchant Marine by stimulating extensively future development of Atlantic travel by accelerating considerably the design and construction of ships' hulls, machinery and propulsion as well as operation and administration of shipping.

Cunard Line – 1856 to 1869

Record Breakers of the Period

Persia

FOLLOWING A SERIES OF amalgamations with other shipping interests and expansion of trade to different areas of operation as well as with cessation of Crimean War hostilities, Cunard began modernising his fleet with particular emphasis on the Atlantic trade. Since 1851 new smaller ships, mainly destined for the Mediterranean traffic, were experiencing a change in hull construction from wood to iron, but only in 1856, one of the more important vessels in the new series, the 3,300 GR ton paddle steamer *Persia,* built by R. Napier of Glasgow, became the first iron steamer to join the regular Cunard transatlantic service.

Persia was commissioned to compete with the Collins Line's predominance of the period and with its overall length of 390 ft and 45 ft beam became the longest liner on the New York run. As a complete departure from traditional wooden construction the hull was built in riveted iron plates and it was stated at the time that the weight of iron in the ship when launched, was 2,200 tons and upon completion the deadweight tonnage was 5,400. *Persia* also featured numerous constructional improvements such as seven watertight compartments with freight storage tanks forming what amounted to a double bottom. Coal capacity of bunkers was 1,400 tons and in addition 1,200 tons of cargo was carried.

Persia was a handsome vessel, luxuriously appointed for the 250 First Class passengers in order to win back the travelling public originally lost to the Collins' mailboats. As things worked out this 'competition' did not really materialise.

The iron construction of the hull proved its worth in January 1856, when *Persia,* on her way from Liverpool to New York, steamed at some 10 knots into an icefield and although extensively damaged, reached New York safely. At the time it was assumed that the Collins Line's wooden hulled steamer *Pacific,* which left Liverpool the previous day and disappeared without trace, was lost in the same icefield.

Persia was equipped with a traditional jet-condensing 2-cylinder side-lever engine with 8 ft-4 in diameter cylinders and 12 ft stroke, capable of developing some 4,600 IHP with a steam pressure of 20 psi generated in eight five-furnace tubular-flue boilers and consuming over 145 tons of coal daily in order to drive 40 ft diameter paddle-wheels at 18 RMP.

Persia took the Blue Riband from the *Arctic* of the Collins Line in May 1856 with an eastbound crossing average of 13.49 knots (New York to Liverpool in 9 days 12 hours) and improved this achievement to 13.88 in August 1856.

In 1856 the magnificent Cunard paddle driven mail steamer Persia *was introduced on the New York run to compete on equal terms with the contemporary dominance by American mailboats of Collins Line.*

Illustration shows Persia *as she was commissioned with three masts. The mizzen-mast was removed after the maiden voyage.*

Cunard record breaker Persia *at speed. The two-masted version.*

Westbound in July 1856 *Persia* broke the record held by *Baltic* of Collins Line by averaging 13.82 knots and completing the journey from Queenstown to New York in 9 days 1 hour.

Persia held the eastward record until December 1863 and the westbound one until July 1866, losing both to her newer sister *Scotia*.

Persia operated the transatlantic service for some 12 years and was then sold in 1868 to other interests. She was broken up in 1872.

Scotia

In 1862 the Cunard Company put into service their last Atlantic paddle steamer, the iron hulled vessel *Scotia* of 3,871 GR tons, also built by R. Napier of Glasgow. At the time considered the largest liner on the scheduled Atlantic run, *Scotia* was 397 ft in overall length by 47 ft-8 in beam. The liner was equipped with a 2-cylinder side-lever engine, similar to that of the *Persia* but capable of developing 4,900 IHP while consuming daily some 160 tons of coal, in order to achieve as uneconomically as possible her speed of 14 knots. *Scotia* was intended originally as the running mate to *Persia* to help deal with American competition. Possibly because of demise of the Collins Line, completion of *Scotia* lost some urgency and this enabled greater attention to be paid to various points of design and passenger facilities.

Scotia could accommodate some 275 travellers in the First Class but in addition there were berths for 300 in the Second Class and the steamer was also intended for rapid conversion to troop carrier.

For Cunard *Scotia* was an expensive luxury, more designed for record speeds than paying her way. Her exceptionally comfortable and luxurious accommodation catered for the most discriminating passengers by whom she was greatly liked. The steamship could have been considered an extravagant 'loss-leader' and obsolete as a concept, but also very popular.

Scotia could carry 1,500 tons of cargo and the bunker capacity for 1,800 tons of coal was apparently fully justified by her fuel consumption in the course of record-breaking journeys.

During her career *Scotia* acquired the eastbound Blue Riband from her sistership *Persia* in December 1863 averaging 14.02 knots between New York to Queenstown in 8 days 3 hours. She retained the honour until July 1869, when the speed was bettered by the first screw-propelled Cunarder *Russia*.

Westward *Scotia* also broke the record in July 1866 achieving an average of 14.51 knots from Queenstown to New York in 8 days 4 hours 35 minutes. This record was lost to the White Star steamer *Adriatic* in May 1872.

Scotia remained in Cunard service until 1878 when she was sold for conversion to cable layer. This last Cunard paddler was wrecked in 1904.

Cunard Line Developments

Although the Cunard Company introduced the principle of screw propulsion around 1852 for various short-haul smallish slow-speed steamships as used for coastal trading and on the Mediterranean service as well as for occasional Atlantic trips, this latest mode of propulsion was not acceptable for the prestigious Atlantic mail service catering for express First Class travel until full technical and commercial implications could be fully proven and suitable reliable machinery was developed. In the main Cunard policy was also subject to the fact that it took the Admiralty some time to accept evidence that screw propulsion may well be superior to paddles for express mail ships on the Atlantic.

1862 Mail Steamship Scotia. *The largest and last paddle driven liner built for the Cunard Line by Robert Napier & Sons, Glasgow. Intended as a running mate to* Persia *to offer competition to the liners of Collins Line.*

Scotia – *Works scale model.*

The birth of screw propulsion belonged mainly to the Victorian era. Around 1837 virtually all steamships were driven by paddle wheels and although the screw was beginning to receive some attention, it was not till some years later that the paddle wheel became superseded in sea-going vessels. Developments of engines from lumbering single-cylinder slow-speed monoliths to multi-cylinder reciprocating high speed primemovers, boiler pressure increases much above these associated with paddlers, combined with screw propulsion, resulted in very large reductions in weight and space required for given power with the crowning achievement of considerable savings in fuel consumption and greatly improved reliability.

Many prejudices had to be overcome before the paddle was finally abandoned for sea-going ships. Even after some 50 years of experimentation there were still many differences of opinion regarding the system with 'eminent' scientific men evolving theories on the function of the propeller which often contradicted each other with sometimes weird designs featuring in the course of early 19th century manifestations giving rise to disappointing practical results. However around 1836 to 1840 patents and designs of the American/Swede Ericcsen and Pettit Smith, a London farmer, resulted in the formation of the 'Ship Propeller Company' and the construction of a small Bristol steamer *Archimedes* on which successful tests were carried out and suitably impressed various investing parties in the USA and Britain including Isombard K. Brunel, who promptly altered his designs for *Great Britain* making it the first ever Atlantic liner to be equipped for screw propulsion in 1845.

With ever growing Atlantic competition by many other shipowners who abandoned paddles much earlier than Cunard, the company finally introduced a series of larger screw-propelled Atlantic steamships such as the 12-13 knot, 2,529 ton *China* in 1862, which also gave birth to a new company policy of providing accommodation for emigrants. With Admiralty dispensation to finally abolish paddle drive in favour of the screw, the company initiated a programme of newbuilds featuring the new mode of propulsion for the Atlantic mail service.

Russia

The largest steamer of this new series, intended specifically for the New York express mail service, was the iron-hulled, screw propelled *Russia* of 2,960 GR tons, built in 1867 by J. & G. Thomson of Glasgow and equipped with elegant accommodation for 460 'Cabin' class travellers. *Russia* was a handsome three-masted barque-rigged ship, 358 ft in length by 43 ft beam and was one of the last Cunarders with a 'clipper' stem. Propulsion was by means of a simple expansion two-cylinder engine developing ca 2,800 IHP with steam at 25 psi generated in four iron tubed smoke-flue boilers. A service speed of 14 knots was achieved with a daily [illegible] consumption of 90 tons.

In favour of screw propulsion a comparison with the slightly larger paddle driven previous record holder *Scotia* can be mentioned. For a marginally lower service speed, *Scotia's* boilers consumed ca 160 tons of coal daily. The hull space of *Russia* not being cluttered by the vast propulsion unit as required for paddle drive, could accommodate an approximately 25% greater payload than *Scotia*.

Russia achieved the eastbound, New York to Queenstown record in July 1869 at an average of 14.19 knots only to relinquish it in favour of the Inman Line steamer *City of Brussels*, in December 1869. However *Russia* was the first screw propelled Cunarder to break an Atlantic crossing record.

Russia proved a reliable and well liked passenger carrier for the Cunard Line, having completed some 100 return journeys between Liverpool and New York over a period of some 12 years. In 1880 she was lengthened to 435 ft and in 1881 sold to the Red Star Line. Renamed *Waesland* she returned on the Atlantic run. In 1889 the liner was equipped with a triple expansion engine and boilers developing 160 psi. *Waesland* was transferred to the American Line in 1895. In 1902 she was lost at sea as a result of a collision.

Russia *of 2,960 GR tons, built in 1867 was the first screw-propelled Cunarder to win the Blue Riband.*

Race across the Atlantic between the Russia *and the* City of Paris.

Atlantic Steamship Race in 1869

On 29th February 1869 much interest and excitement was created in Liverpool by the conclusion of a 'Race' across the Atlantic between two very similar, propeller driven mail steamers built in 1866/67, the Cunarder *Russia* and the Inman Line's *City of Paris* (1), both having left New York within an hour of each other and both claiming to be the fastest on the Atlantic.

The two ships kept strictly to their companies' safety regulations and especially steam pressures were not allowed to exceed permissible margins.

The two steamers virtually kept within sight of each other throughout most of the 8 days 18 hours journey. Although *City of Paris* is supposed to have arrived at Liverpool 35 minutes before *Russia*, many claims,counterclaims and excuses followed and one can but conclude that there was a draw!

Inman Line – Inman & International Steamship Company

The Company

In 1850 a Liverpool to Philadelphia service was inaugurated by the newly formed 'Liverpool and Philadelphia Steamship Company', created by the Liverpool ship chandlers, Richardson Brothers & Co., to cater primarily for the emigrant trade. The third partner, William Inman, arranged the purchase of the first steamship, the screw-propelled vessel *City of Glasgow* of 1,600 tons, from the builders Tod & McGregor of Glasgow, with which the first Atlantic crossing from Liverpool to Philadelphia was undertaken, carrying some 400 emigrants as well as other passengers.

The success of the service led to the acquisition of the next steamer *City of Manchester* in 1851 and by 1854 some six similar vessels were operational, mainly carrying emigrants. These pioneering steamers had a chequered career, *City of Glasgow* and *City of Philadelphia* being lost at sea in 1854. Also in 1854 the Crimean War broke out and virtually the balance of the Inman fleet were chartered to carry troops at the initiation of Inman. The two Richardson brothers being Quakers, left the company because it did not suit their religious anti-war sentiments to endorse such duties for the fleet.

William Inman, by now the senior partner, bought the ships which had brought in a good profit from the charter. He reorganised the company which was renamed 'The Inman Line', and acquired a couple of new steamers to supplement the ones returning from trooping.

By 1856 the Philadelphia service was resumed and included New York in the itinerary, later to become the principal terminus with Philadelphia relegated as secondary port of call. In 1858 the company title was duly changed to 'Liverpool, New York and Philadelphia Steamship Company'.

Inman created great improvements to emigrant facilities in his ships and virtually became the pioneer of reasonably tenable steerage accommodation which actually provided him with most of his profits.

In the early sixties additional tonnage was acquired in order to create a gainful weekly service but then two further ships were lost at sea. However in 1866 some consolation was created by the new ship *City of Paris* (1) crossing the Atlantic at 13.5 knots thus nearly achieving the Blue Riband.

Around 1865 following the American Civil War, there was an upsurge in business followed by a recession in 1867. Meanwhile, the Cunard Line's Halifax mail contract with the Admiralty having expired, Inman managed to obtain a subsidy for a fortnightly mail service between Queenstown and Halifax and he also secured a United States mail contract for the New

York, Queenstown and Liverpool run, which in 1869 was changed to an annual subsidy for a weekly service.

On the strength of such financial assistance the new 3,750 ton iron steamer *City of Brussels* was acquired and she became Inman's first Blue Riband contender. However in 1871 the company's jinx struck again, *City of Boston* being lost with all hands.

1871 also saw the emergence of White Star Line as a serious contender on the Atlantic with the result that additional new tonnage of equivalent quality had to be commissioned mainly with an eye to carriage of emigrants rather than achievement of record speeds. By 1875 a degree of reorganisation took place initiating some cooperation with White Star and a new company title 'Inman Steamship Company' materialised. The new flagship *City of Berlin* of 5,491 tons designed to compete in the Atlantic express service, was commissioned.

The First Inman Record Breakers

City of Brussels

In 1869 Inman Line's first record breaker, *City of Brussels,* built by Tod & Mcgregor of Glasgow, was taken into service on the Liverpool, Queenstown and New York run. She was an iron vessel of 3,750 tons, 390ft in length and 36ft wide, representing the Harland & Wolff 'Longship' principle of hull length to beam ratio of more than 10 instead of the universally accepted figure of less than 8. The liner was powered by a horizontal direct acting simple expansion engine developing 3,200 IHP with steam at 30 psi generated in tubed flue boilers consuming ca 110 tons of coal daily. Accommodation was provided for 120 'Saloon' passengers and over 1,000 emigrants in steerage.

In December 1869 *City of Brussels* crossed eastward from New York to Queenstown in 7 days 22 hours, averaging 14.66 knots, improving upon the record held by *Russia* of Cunard Line. The Inman steamer's achievement was valid until January 1873 when it was bettered by the *Baltic* of White Star Line.

In 1876 the *City of Brussels* was re-engined and equipped with 4-cylinder Compound machinery, steam pressure being increased to 60 psi. However no further Atlantic records materialised.

In 1883 *City of Brussels* was lost after a collision in Liverpool bay.

City of Berlin

In 1875 the 'new look' Inman Steamship Company commissioned the new liner *City of Berlin*, designed specifically to compete for the Blue Riband. *City of Berlin* was an iron vessel of 5,420 tons, 513ft in overall length and 43ft width; one of the 'longships' produced by Cairds of Greenock. Propulsion machinery consisted of a 2-cylinder vertical Compound engine of ca 4,800 IHP with steam at 75 psi driving the single screw. At the time she was the longest steamer on the Atlantic run.

Passenger accommodation maintained the Inman policy of offering maximum space for emigrants and *City of Berlin* could take some 1,500 travellers in the Third (ex-steerage) Class, although excellent facilities, including an elegant midships saloon, were also provided in the First Class for 200 passengers. Around 1879 *City of Berlin* was equipped with a pioneering installation of electrical illumination by six arc-lamps in the dining saloon and machinery rooms.

In September 1875 *City of Berlin* broke the westbound Atlantic record held by the White Star steamship *Adriatic,* by averaging 15.21 knots between

1869 Inman Line steamer City of Brussels, *built by Tod & McGregor.*

City of Berlin *built in 1875 for the Inman Line by Cairds of Greenock.*

Queenstown and New York, in 7 days 18 hours and kept the record until it was bettered in November 1876 by the *Britannic* of White Star Line.

In October 1875, crossing from New York to Queenstown *City of Berlin* captured the Blue Riband from the *Baltic* of White Star by achieving a mean of 15.37 knots while completing the journey in 7 days 7½ hours. She relinquished this honour to the White Star Line's *Germanic* in February 1876.

In order to reduce fuel consumption, the original Compound engine was replaced by Triple-Expansion machinery in 1887.

1893 saw *City of Berlin* renamed *Berlin*, in service of the new owners the American Line, and in 1898 she was converted as troop transport for the US Government, renamed *Meade*. Subsequently the steamer was used as a training ship until 1918 and finally sold to breakers in 1921.

City of Rome

The Inman Super-liner that did not quite make it. Flagship of the Inman Line, was built in 1881 at the Barrow Shipbuilding Company and intended to regain the Blue Riband from the current record holders, the White Star Line and to compete with the Guion and other 'Ocean Greyhounds' on the Atlantic.

The 8,453 GR ton, 586 ft long by 52 ft wide liner represented the latest technical developments and was equipped with a tandem 6-cylinder, 3-crank Compound engine, designed to develop 8,000-10,000 IHP with steam at 90 psi, and driving a 24 ft diameter propeller in order to achieve a speed of 18 knots thus reducing the crossing times between Liverpool and New York to well below 7 days.

The appointments of the *City of Rome* were of utmost luxury with First Class accommodation comprising large decorative saloons, drawing rooms and a lofty dining room equipped with separate tables and revolving armchairs. Staterooms with pullmann berths catered for 300 discriminating passengers. One thousand five hundred emigrants (Third Class) were accommodated on a 'specially enlarged' scale of comfort, light and ventilation on forward and aft ends of the main deck and on the lower deck.

Unfortunately this elegant and well proportioned liner was unable to achieve speeds in excess of 14-15 knots, did not possess the requisite capacity for cargo and therefore not being able to compete with its contemporaries, became a commercial failure. This was partly blamed on her heavy construction in iron instead of steel which happened to be in short supply at the time.

After a few voyages Inman Line returned the ship to the builders, who carried out various modifications which still did not help to comply with requirements.

The builder could not sell *City of Rome*, which was then registered with 'Barrow Steamship Company' for operation by the Anchor Line on the Liverpool and Glasgow to New York service. In 1898 *City of Rome* was used by the US Government to repatriate prisoners after the Spanish-American War. In 1902 the Barrow Steamship Company was wound up and *City of Rome* sold to shipbreakers.

Reorganisation of the Inman Steamship Company

As a result of much reduction in transatlantic business around 1879, many of the smaller uneconomical ships were sold. Additional major operational problems were created with the company having to return to the builders in 1882 the prestigious and elegant new liner *City of Rome*, designed as a record breaker but unable to achieve its destiny and the loss in 1883 of *City of Brussels* following a collision. By 1886 serious

Inman liner City of Rome.

financial difficulties gave rise to capital shortage; the company had to go into liquidation and the fleet with other assets were acquired by the American International Navigation Company, owners of the American Line and the Red Star Line.

The company was renamed Inman and International Steamship Company and became financed entirely by American capital. In 1888-1889 the two large luxurious liners, at the time the largest in the world, *City of New York* (3) and *City of Paris* (2) were commissioned.

In spite of being entirely American funded, all ships remained under the British flag until 1892/93 when a US mail contract stipulated the proviso that all steamers were to sail under the US flag and in 1889 the whole fleet was transferred to American registry. The head office moved to New York and even the ships' names were changed, omitting the prefix 'City'. 1893 was also the year when the Inman name disappeared from the Atlantic, the International Navigation Company having finally assimilated all commitments.

In 1902 the International Navigation Company changed its name to International Maritime Marine Company, under the aegis of J. P. Morgan.

The Last Inman Record Breakers

In 1888 and 1889 respectively, the two new express liners, *City of New York* (3) of 10,500 tons and *City of Paris* (2) of 10,669 tons, designed and built by J. & G. Thomson of Clydebank, were commissioned by the American-financed Inman International Steamship Company, for luxury transatlantic service and the Blue Riband.

The two liners were iron-hulled sister ships, 560 ft in overall length by 63 ft-2 in beam and, apart from being at the time the longest transatlantic steamships, were luxuriously appointed in order to surpass anything the competition had to offer.

The liners were first on the Atlantic to have twin-screw propulsion with machinery comprising two 3-cylinder triple-expansion engines rated at ca 18,000 IHP with cylinder bores of 45 in for HP, 71 in for IP and 113 in LP with a 60 in stroke. Arrangement of internal bulkheads allowed each engine to virtually occupy its own compartment. Steam was generated at 150 psi in nine double-ended tubular boilers with combustion air supplied by forced draught into closed stokehold.

The steamers were the first on the Atlantic not to be provided for sails and square rigging on masts and attempts were made to reduce rolling by patented water ballast tanks. As a major safety feature, the hull was divided into 15 watertight compartments with transverse bulkheads reaching from keel to saloon deck.

Overall electric illumination comprising some 1,000 fittings was provided and in addition electric fans greatly improved ventilation in the main passenger accommodation. Ammonia refrigeration plant catered for food storage.

Great attention had been paid to interior appointments and furnishing of accommodation for 540 First Class travellers, 200 in the Second and ca 1,000 by Steerage. In the First Class the staterooms and suites were spacious, well ventilated and supplied with hot and cold running water, with call-buttons for stewards and tasteful electric illumination. The amidships dining saloon was ostentatiously decorated and had a 20 ft high arched dome as part of the roof. In addition to the usual long tables, there were small ones located in alcoves and fixed revolving armchairs catered for diners. Lavishly appointed smoking rooms and library also catered for passengers needs. Second Class cabins, dining room as well as the promenade deck were located aft. Even Steerage facilities including the usual dormitories, occupied 'a generous space'.

City of Paris

In May 1889 *City of Paris* took the Blue Riband from the Cunarder *Etruria* at a westbound average of 19.95 knots, crossing from Queenstown to New York in 5 days 23 hours and returning to Queenstown in the same month in 6 days 29 minutes at 20.03 knots, again improving upon the *Etruria* record. In September 1889 *City of Paris* bettered the westward journey to 20.01 knots. This record was lost to the White Star liner *Majestic* in July 1891.

However, in October 1892 *City of Paris* crossed westward at a mean of 20.7 knots (5 days 14 hours 24 minutes), this time taking the record from *Teutonic* of White Star. She kept this record until October 1893, when it was bettered by the new Cunarder *Lucania*.

After being renamed *Paris* (in the service of the American Line) in 1893, the liner remained on the Atlantic run for a further five years prior to being chartered to the US Government and being renamed *Yale*. After her return to passenger service, again as *Paris*, she became stranded off Cornwall in 1899. Following salvage, *Paris* was brought to Harland & Wolff, Belfast, to be rebuilt and re-engined with quadruple expansion machinery, losing one funnel in the process and again rechristened, *Philadelphia* by the American Line. Further Atlantic service followed between 1901 and 1917, and then came another charter to the US Government as armed troop transport, this time named *Harrisburg*. In 1919 the liner returned to the American Line, again as *Philadelphia* and in 1922 she was sold for

Italian service. The former record breaker was finally broken up in 1923.

City of New York

In August 1892 *City of New York* improved upon her sistership's eastbound achievement by averaging 20.11 knots between New York and Queenstown in 5 days 20 hours and kept the record until it was bettered by the Cunarder *Campania* in May 1893.

Renamed *New York* in 1893 and following a refit during which Second and Third Class accommodation was greatly improved, the liner saw a further five years' service with the American Line (after the demise of Inman Line) prior to being chartered to the Government in 1898 and renamed *Harvard* as an auxiliary cruiser. By 1903 again as *New York*, with new quadruple expansion engines, she re-entered the Atlantic service with the American Line, this time sporting only two funnels. In 1917 she was requisitioned by the US Government to serve as an armed troop transport, this time named *Plattsburg*. In 1921 the liner was sold to Poland after a short spell of service with the American Line, again named *New York*. In 1923 this last of the classic Blue Riband liners was sold to the breakers.

Twin-Screw liner City of Paris *commissioned by Inman and International Steamship Company in 1889 to compete for the Blue Riband against White Star liners of the period.*

Inman and International record breaker City of New York.

Express Liner New York *serving the New York-Cherbourg-Southampton route of the American Line (IMMC) in 1903. The liner was originally built in 1889 as record breaker* City of New York *for the Inman International Steamship Company; it experienced a major refit during 1901-1903.*

Oceanic Steam Navigation Company – White Star Line

The Company

THE ORIGIN OF THE White Star Line dates back to 1845, when the ship brokers Pilkington & Wilson operated sailing ships to Boston, New York and New Orleans and later to Australia during the Gold Rush; the enterprise was named 'The White Star Line of Packets'. By 1856 the management of the company changed and the concern was renamed H. T. Wilson & Chambers. In 1865, after a partnership crisis, a new partner joined the firm and the organisation was again renamed, this time Wilson & Cunningham as managers of the White Star Line of Packets.

By 1868 the partnership was in serious financial difficulties and forced into liquidation. Following the sale of the firm's assets, Thomas Ismay acquired the name 'White Star' and the house-flag with its white star, as well as all goodwill. Ismay already operated a fleet of sailing ships and was a director of the National Steam Navigation Company; he also wanted to create his own fleet of modern passenger steamships to sail the North Atlantic route under the White Star house flag.

Ismay co-operated in his ideas with the shipbuilding yard of Harland & Wolff in Belfast, completing an agreement to have all his steamers designed and built by the firm. At the same time, in exchange Harland & Wolff offered not to build ships liable to seriously compete with current White Star services.

In 1869 Ismay registered his firm as the 'Oceanic Steam Navigation Company' with headquarters in Liverpool. The company's official title still remained 'White Star Line'. In 1870 William Imrie joined the concern and the management agents became Ismay, Imrie & Co., continuing operation of steamers to Australia in addition to the transatlantic trade.

Thomas Ismay aimed at forcing a major entry into the highly competitive but very lucrative North American market with sailings from Liverpool and in 1870-1872 four new sister ships, *Oceanic, Atlantic, Baltic* and *Republic*, as well as a pair of improved, slightly larger liners, *Adriatic* and *Celtic* were completed by Harland & Wolff of Belfast and introduced on the Liverpool to New York service, also with an eye to competing for the Blue Riband. This first batch of White Star steamships revolutionised ocean travel by introducing hitherto unknown standards of comfort with the First Class accommodation located amidships, clear of machinery and propeller vibration, instead of at the usual after end of the ship, thus superseding the tradition of a bygone era created in Atlantic paddle steamers.

Standards of comfort and luxury included well appointed roomy cabins with running hot and cold water, oil lamps instead of candles, bathrooms and efficient steam heating. All cabins were provided with outside portholes.

The First Class dining saloon located amidships, was 80 ft long by 40 ft wide, thus occupying the full width of the ship and was provided with separate upholstered chairs for individual passengers. Other elegantly appointed public rooms offered ample space, comfort and ventilation.

Even the 1,000 or so 'bread and butter' emigrants' quarters, featuring four-berth cabins and good-sized public rooms, showed notable improvements as compared with other contemporary ships.

Both *Adriatic* and *Celtic* were originally provided with a Harland & Wolff designed system of gas lighting, comprising some 300 burners in the First Class and staff rooms. The gas was generated from oil in three special retorts and a 'gasometer' was installed in the engine room. The system was, however, not a success because of frequent leaks and had to be dismantled after a few journeys.

The original plans for a regular weekly service between Liverpool and New York were difficult to implement because of cut-throat competition and the foundering of *Atlantic* off Nova Scotia in 1873, with considerable loss of life, but with *Adriatic* and *Baltic* achieving record crossings, travellers began to appreciate the fast and well appointed liners.

Experience with the operation of the first six transatlantic steamers, led to development of a larger version to a similar specification and in 1874 White Star took delivery from Harland & Wolff of the iron-hulled steamships *Britannic* and *Germanic*, of 5,004 and 5,008 tons respectively.

Each liner offered accommodation for 220 travellers in the First Class and ca 1,500 by Third. The standards of decor and facilities for the comfort of passengers were to a great extent an improved up-to-date development of those in the earlier liners.

Britannic and *Germanic* were the fastest, most popular and successful liners in the White Star fleet and contributed greatly to the company's reputation and prosperity, especially as both became record breakers and virtually monopolised the Atlantic Blue Riband during the period between 1876 and 1882.

After the outburst of Blue Riband ambitions between 1870 and 1880, White Star Line concentrated upon economical operation, comfort of passengers and provision of efficient cargo space to maximise trading profits in their services to America, Far East, New Zealand, Australia and the Pacific, thus developing a second-to-none reputation for steady, well equipped ships travelling at reasonable speeds.

However, encouraged by the British Government and duly subsidised in 1889, White Star commissioned a pair of twin-screw prestige liners capable of competing with the latest Cunarders and Inman express steamers on the Atlantic run.

The sister ships *Teutonic* and *Majestic* of ca 10,000 tons, were delivered by Harland & Wolff in 1889 and 1890 respectively, for the Liverpool to New York service and were the first White Star liners designed specifically for rapid conversion to armed merchant cruisers in time of war and capable of a turn of speed to suit Naval operation.

The two liners were the last White Star contenders for the Blue Riband, achieving it for a short period in 1891 and 1892. Whether the 1899 commissioned, also Government subsidised, 17,274 ton, twin-screw mail liner *Oceanic* (2), also built for conversion to Admiralty requirements and designed for a service speed of possibly over 20 knots, was capable of indulging in speed contests, is not clear, but her operation did not appear to have manifested record breaking ambitions. An originally planned sistership to this magnificent liner was seemingly cancelled. *Oceanic* (2) had a short period distinction of being the world's largest liner and developed a reputation for exceptionally luxurious and relaxed carriage of passengers. White Star Line having decided against uneconomical high speeds in favour of maximum comfort and reliability, scheduled the *Oceanic* and her running mates on six-day crossings of the Liverpool to New York run and this became the determining factor for future company policy.

Early 20th century, however, saw the start of the company's rather chequered future developments. In 1902 a major shareholding of the White Star Line was acquired by J. P. Morgan's giant combine, 'International Mercantile Marine Company', in the course of assimilation of numerous other American and British shipping ventures. Within the combine, the White Star Line played the major role in the North Atlantic passenger services in addition to its other world-wide trading routes. Although American owned, financed and operated, the company's ships, which included famous premier luxury liners, remained under British registry.

Early in the 20th century, White Star also experienced the greatest ever maritime disaster on 14th April 1912, when the company's latest and largest luxury liner *Titanic* of 46,328 GR tons, struck an iceberg 300 miles south of Newfoundland and foundered inside three hours with a loss of 1,500 lives.

Titanic was the second of three giant liners built by Harland & Wolff for the White Star express service between Southampton and New York. Whereas the first of the giant trio, the *Olympic* had a highly successful career, the third and last, named *Britannic* (2) of 48,158 tons, commissioned during the war in 1915 as a hospital ship, was victim of a German mine in the Aegean Sea in November 1916. *Britannic* was the largest British merchant ship to be lost during the war.

Most of the White Star liners were requisitioned by the Government as Naval auxiliaries during the period 1914-1918 and although some five liners were lost through enemy action, the company had an excellent record of trooping and carriage of freight during the period of hostilities.

After the war the Liverpool and Southampton as well as the Mediterranean services to New York were resumed and some of the lost tonnage was replaced by ex-German liners taken over as reparations. These included the *Majestic* (2) (ex-*Bismarck*) of 56,500 tons, the *Homeric* (ex-*Columbus*) of 34,400 tons and the 16,800 ton *Arabic* (ex-*Berlin*). Together with the 1912 *Olympic* these liners established the luxury express service between Southampton and New York.

In combination with the Dominion and Leyland Lines, White Star Canadian services were introduced in 1921-1925.

It is hardly necessary to enlarge upon the subsequent early 20th century reputation of the White Star Line as a prestigious and efficient passenger carrier with her giant luxury liners, however by 1926 Morgan's IMMC was feeling the strain of operating the many uneconomical old steamships on the Atlantic and managed to dispose of the White Star Line to the Royal Mail Steam Navigation Company. White Star thus again came into British ownership.

The American trade slump of 1929 was followed by the European depression of the 1930's and the financial position of White Star Line with her aged fleet became precarious. The slump also greatly affected the Canadian services and even with the larger, more luxurious liners being employed cruising, more lay-offs followed.

Even the introduction of two successful and economical diesel-engined 27,000 ton liners *Britannic* (3) and *Georgic* in 1931/32 on the Liverpool and later London, services, left no alternative to disposal of many older ships.

1934 saw the Government initiating an amalgamation with the Cunard Line, thus creating the new title 'Cunard-White Star Ltd' for the combine in which Cunard owned some 62%. The White Star contribution amounted to eight liners, five of which were disposed by 1935 and these included the aged and uneconomical *Olympic, Majestic* (2) and *Homeric*.

By the outbreak of the Second World War only three remaining liners were flying the White Star flag and in 1945 the motorships *Britannic* and *Georgic* remained as the only representatives of the company; after post-war repairs and refits, the two liners saw commercial service under various guises until 1960 and 1956, respectively, prior to demolition.

In 1949 Cunard Line had assimilated full control of the partnership and the name 'White Star Line' ceased to exist.

Record Breaking Mail Liners of the Oceanic Steam Navigation Company

The inaugural steamships of 1871/1872

The first four iron-built White Star steamships *Oceanic, Atlantic, Baltic* and *Republic,* designed and constructed by Harland & Wolff of Belfast, were introduced on the Liverpool to New York run in 1871/72. They were identical sisterships of 3,707 GR tons, 470 ft-4 in in overall length and 40 ft-10 in beam. The passenger capacity catered for 160 in the First Class and some 1,000 in Third. The steamers pioneered First Class amidships, greatly improving the layout for more effective utilisation of space.

In 1872 two further very similar vessels of improved design, the sisterships *Adriatic* and *Celtic,* of 3,888 tons and 452 ft-6 in by 41 ft beam, joined the fleet, with a weekly New York service in mind.

These six single-screw steamers were equipped with compound steam primemovers each consisting of two sets of Maudslay vertical 2-cylinder tandem engines operating two cranks in order to develop 3,200 IHP for the rotation of a 22 ft-6 in steel four-bladed propeller at 50 RPM. Each engine's cylinders were 41 in in diameter (high pressure) and 78 in for the low pressure mode, with a piston stroke of 5 ft. Steam was generated at 65 psi in 12 twin-furnace tubular boilers and this was considered a notably high pressure by contemporary practice.

These White Star ships virtually pioneered the compound engine on the Atlantic run and proved its superiority over the simple expansion machinery of the period. The White Star steamers' coal consumption averaging at 65 to 75 tons daily compared with 90 to 100 tons experienced with similar sized rivals of the period meant that with the requisite power generated by comparatively smaller machinery, coal bunker capacity could be reduced thus providing the consequent considerable increase in payload space.

The steamers were equipped with four iron masts, three of which were ship-rigged and the fourth, jury-rigged. Without crosstrees the yards were vertically moveable and Harland & Wolff design enabled the movement to be carried out by means of steam winches, which were also used for lifting cargo, setting sail and other heavy duties. Steam operated steering gear was located amidships and a complete standby steering system at the stern was in communication with the bridge by means of 'Gisborne's Telegraph'.

In the course of the earliest journeys the new White Star Atlantic steamships experienced some technical problems but subsequent operational corrections and elimination of various teething troubles, resulted in ensuring reliable and efficient service, especially with the latter vessels of similar type.

The hull design of all White Star Atlantic record breakers beginning with the *Oceanic* (1) of 1871, introduced the Harland & Wolff 'Longship' feature by having the universally adopted maximum Length to Beam ratio of 8:1 increased to more than 10:1. Presumably the idea was to create a graceful hull capable of reducing water resistance in order to improve speed and fuel consumption. Whether this ideal was ever achieved is not clear, but the 'Longships' showed a tendency to increased rolling and vibration which did not always please the passengers, especially at high speeds.

This hull form was adopted for all White Star express steamers and was also represented by other contemporary liners but the design was discontinued after 1899, when the second *Oceanic* of 17,274 tons was built as the last of the 'Longships' but was not a Blue Riband contender.

The originally planned weekly service to New York did not at first materialise, especially as the rather optimistically small bunker capacity had to be increased.

Contemporary engraving of Ocean Steam Navigation Company's steamship representing Oceanic *(1),* Baltic *(1),* Atlantic *and* Republic *(1), the inaugural class of sisterships built for White Star Line by Harland & Wolff Ltd of Belfast in order to challenge the established transatlantic shipping services.*

Oceanic

After some engine and bunkerage modifications the liner served the Liverpool to New York run but broke no records.

Atlantic

A short career was terminated in 1873 by foundering near Halifax in heavy weather. There was a loss of 585 lives.

Baltic

Served the New York run until 1883. In 1873 the steamer achieved the eastbound record. Sold to Holland America Line in 1888.

Republic

Spent her life peacefully on the White Star Atlantic run and also sailed on South American commitments. *Republic* broke no records but was considered a successful passenger carrier. She was sold to Holland America Line in 1889.

Adriatic

The *Adriatic* was built in 1872 by Harland & Wolff of Belfast, as an improved and slightly larger version of the original *Oceanic* class and was the first White Star mail steamship to attain an Atlantic record.

In May 1872 *Adriatic* broke the six-year-old westbound record held by the famous paddler *Scotia* of Cunard Line by the smallest of margins but proved

Atlantic record breaker Adriatic *of the White Star.*

Oceanic Steam Navigation Company mail steamship Baltic. *Held Blue Riband (eastward) from January 1873 to October 1875.*

the superiority of screw propulsion to paddles, especially by the fact that her coal consumption was less than half that of the similar sized *Scotia* but at the same time offering a much greater payload capacity.

In the course of her westward record breaking run *Adriatic* averaged 14.52 knots while crossing between Queenstown and New York in 7 days 23 hours 17 minutes and retained this record until September 1875, then relinquishing it to *City of Berlin* of the Inman Line.

Adriatic had a chequered career having by 1880 been involved in four collisions with other ships and still managing to survive and build up a reputation for comfortable and efficient travel.

This successful steamer remained in operational service with the White Star Line until 1899 and was then sold to shipbreakers.

Celtic (1)

The sistership of *Adriatic* was apparently no lagard but never managed to achieve record crossings. *Celtic* was sold to Danish shipowners in 1893 in order to initiate the Copenhagan to New York service, duly renamed *Amerika*. The ex-record breaker was finally broken up in 1898.

Baltic

The 3,707 ton iron hulled steamship *Baltic*, one of the original Atlantic 'Quartet', was put into service between Liverpool and New York in 1871. Her single-screw propulsion machinery was identical to that of the slightly later built sisterships.

In January 1873 *Baltic* took the eastbound record from the *City of Brussels* of the Inman Line by averaging 15.04 knots in completing the 2,840 nautical mile journey from New York to Queenstown in 7 days 20 hours 8 minutes. *Baltic* kept this record until October 1875 and then lost it to the newest Inman liner *City of Berlin*.

Baltic was in regular White Star transatlantic service until 1883 and was then chartered to the Inman Line until 1885 to fill the break in their operational continuity caused by the loss in 1883 of *City of Brussels* and the return to the builders of the unsuccessful *City of Rome*.

In 1888 the then elderly ex-record breaker was sold to the Holland America Line and renamed *Veendam* and served on the Rotterdam to New York emigrant run. *Veendam* foundered in 1898 without loss of life.

Britannic and *Germanic*

In 1874 White Star Line took delivery from Harland & Wolff of a pair of iron-hulled sisterships *Britannic* (1) and *Germanic*, as a larger and more modern development of the original Atlantic steamers of the 'Oceanic' class.

The new liners were of 5,004 and 5,008 GR tons respectively and 455 ft in overall length by 45 ft beam. Propulsion was by two sets of the highly developed and reliable Maudslay, Sons & Field 2-cylinder compound steam engines operating in tandem on two cranks and capable of developing 5,000 IHP with steam generated at 70 psi in eight four-furnace cylindrical tubular boilers.

The two liners were designed for record crossings and these were duly achieved, with the pair becoming the most successful Atlantic passenger carriers of the period.

White Star record breaker Germanic *built in 1874. Achieved Blue Riband crossings in both directions in 1876 and 1877. Illustration portrays the liner in 1895 after extensive modernisation.*

Germanic

Germanic was the first to achieve an Atlantic record by bettering the eastbound crossing of the Inman steamer *City of Berlin* in February 1876 with a mean speed of 15.79 knots and completing the journey between New York and Queenstown in 7 days 15 hours. In December 1876 she lost the record to her sistership *Britannic*.

In April 1877 between Queenstown and New York, *Germanic* took the Blue Riband from *Britannic* at 15.76 knots with a crossing of 7 days 11 hours 35 minutes. *Germanic* retained this record until 1882, losing it to the Guion liner *Alaska*.

Germanic was modernised in 1895 by the addition of one deck and the fitting of new triple expansion engines by her builders.

Germanic was in White Star service until 1903. In 1904 she was transferred first to the American Line (IMMC) and then to the Dominion Line, renamed *Ottawa* for the Canadian service. In 1910 the liner was sold to the Turkish Government and duly rechristened *Gul Djemal*. She was torpedoed and sunk by a British submarine during the First World War in 1915 but was raised and refitted in 1920 for use on the emigrant service to New York. In 1928 the liner's name was again changed, to *Gulcemal*, and by 1949 she became a store ship for the Turkish Navy. She became a floating hotel in 1950 and late in that year she was sold for demolition.

The liner's builders, Harland & Wolff of Belfast are proud of her career spanning 76 years.

Britannic (1)

In November 1876 *Britannic* improved upon the previous best westward journey between Queenstown and New York by the Inman liner *City of Berlin*, by averaging 15.43 knots in 7 days 13 hours 11 minutes. This record was bettered by the sistership *Germanic* in April 1877.

Eastbound in December 1876 *Britannic* wrested the Blue Riband from *Germanic* by crossing from Queenstown in 7 days 13 hours at a mean of 15.94 knots. This record was lost to *Arizona* of the Guion Line in July 1879.

Britannic was in White Star transatlantic service until 1899 during which period, in keeping with White Star 'hoodoo', she survived at least three collisions. She was then transferred to Government service as troop transport during the Boer War. In 1903 *Britannic* was sold to shipbreakers.

The Last Record Breakers of the White Star Line

Teutonic and *Majestic* (1)

The two liners were delivered from the shipyard of Harland & Wolff in 1889 and 1890 respectively and the two very similar steel-hulled steamships became the last Blue Riband contenders for the company.

The pair were the first White Star liners to be equipped with twin screws and driven by triple expansion, 2 x 3-cylinder machinery with steam at 180 psi generated in 12 double-ended cylindrical smoke-tube boilers. The propulsion plant of each liner developed ca 17,000 IHP for a service speed of 20-21 knots.

Teutonic and *Majestic* were rated at 9,984 and 9,965 GR tons, respectively, and were 582 ft in overall length by 58 ft beam, thus also representing the 'longship' hull shape. It is interesting to note that because of the comparatively narrow beam, the two 20 ft diameter propellers overlapped by some 5 ft. The starboard propeller had therefore to be fitted 6 ft beyond the port one. Present-day experience would indicate that this

Steamship Britannic *was commissioned by White Star Line in 1874 and held Blue Riband honours in both directions between 1876 and 1879.*

staggering of the very large screws must have created considerable loss in propulsive efficiency because of cavitation and this was proved by an increase in ships' speeds after change of propellers.

The two liners had very superior accommodation, originally for 300 First Class passengers as well as 190 in the Second and 1,000 in the Third Classes. Having to compete with the best on the Atlantic as offered by the 'greyhounds' of Cunard and Inman, as well as the palatial accommodation and super cuisine available with the French Line, Norddeutscher Lloyd, HAPAG and other new arrivals, the two White Star flagships had to fly the flag with a degree of sophisticated luxury with elegant suites and staterooms as well as other facilities featuring superior decor and finish in costly woodwork, deep pile carpets, velour and brocade upholstery. As an example, the First Class dining saloon had a two-deck high central glass dome supported by decorative pillars and large windows helping to provide natural light. There was also universal utilisation of electric illumination and electric power was used for full ventilation and ample refrigeration plant.

For a period between May 1889 and October 1892 the Blue Riband was alternating between the two White Star sisterships and the *City of Paris* of the Inman Line.

When delivered by the builders, these last two White Star record breakers were looked upon as the epitome of advanced marine engineering.

Twin-screw liner Teutonic *built in 1889 by Messrs. Harland & Wolff of Belfast, was the last Atlantic record breakers of the White Star Line.*

Atlantic record breaker Majestic *(1) of the White Star Line, built in 1890 by Harland & Wolff, Belfast. Illustration shows the steamship after the major refit in 1902-3.*

Majestic (1)

In July 1891 *Majestic* wrested the westward record from the Inman liner *City of Paris* by averaging 20.1 knots in completing the journey between Queenstown and New York in 5 days 18 hours 8 minutes and kept the Blue Riband until it was captured a month later by the sistership *Teutonic*.

Majestic (1) served the Liverpool to New York run until 1899 and was then taken over by the Government as troop transport in the Boer War until 1902. The liner was then returned to the builders, Harland & Wolff of Belfast for major modifications and a refit, which entailed the fitting of new boilers, lengthening of funnels and removal of the mizzenmast. *Majestic* then returned on the Atlantic in 1903 and in 1907 her home port became Southampton for service to New York via Cherbourg. In 1911 she was put into reserve but in 1912 returned on the Atlantic run because of the loss of the *Titanic*. In 1914 *Majestic* (1) was sold to shipbreakers.

Teutonic

In August 1891 the *Teutonic* improved upon her sistership's westward record crossing by averaging 20.35 knots with a journey to New York, taking 5 days 16 hours 30 minutes and kept the Blue Riband until October 1892 when it was again captured by *City of Paris* of Inman International.

In August 1889, just prior to departing upon her maiden voyage, the *Teutonic* in her guise as an armed merchant cruiser, attended the Spithead Naval Review, in the course of which the Prince of Wales demonstrated the possibly aptly named liner to the Kaiser.

In 1897, again because of her Naval qualification, *Teutonic* also took part in the Diamond Jubilee Review at Spithead, at which event Charles Parsons' prognosticative launch *Turbinia* showed her paces at some 34 knots.

Teutonic remained on the Liverpool to New York run until 1907 and together with her sistership was then transferred to Southampton as home port. In 1911 she entered the Canadian service after a refit at Belfast when her decks were enclosed for winter weather and she was converted for Second and Third Class passengers only.

At the outbreak of the First World War, *Teutonic* was taken over for Naval service as an armed merchant cruiser with the 10th cruiser squadron but after 1916 was bought outright by the Admiralty and put on various convoy and trooping duties.

In 1921 *Teutonic* was finally disposed of for demolition.

Oceanic (2)

This last of the White Star Longships, the twin-screw *Oceanic* measuring 17,274 GR tons, was commissioned in 1899 and was also sponsored by the Admiralty. Her two triple expansion engines were capable of 28,000 IHP with steam at 192 psi generated in 15 double-ended boilers and it is possible that she was originally planned with Atlantic records in mind.

A similar liner, to be named *Olympic* apparently never materialised. However this large elegant vessel entered service at a time when the latest Cunard and German express liners were struggling for supremacy at 21-23 knots and *Oceanic* could not achieve competition in terms of pure speed.

Twin screw 17,275 tons White Star liner Oceanic *(2) built in 1899 by Harland & Wolff Ltd., Belfast, was 705ft in overall length and 68ft wide.* Oceanic *was the last of the 'Longships' commissioned by the White Star Line.*

The designed service speed of 19 to 20 knots was apparently comfortably achieved but no Blue Riband ambitions ever materialised.

Passenger accommodation on the Oceanic *was particularly elegant and she was well liked by the passengers. The liner maintained the express service between Southampton and New York until 1914 and was the running mate of the* Teutonic *and* Majestic. *She was then requisitioned by the Admiralty for conversion to an armed merchant cruiser but late in 1914 became victim of a navigational error and ran aground off the Shetlands becoming a total loss.*

National Line –National Steamship Company Ltd

The Company

THE NATIONAL STEAM NAVIGATION Company Ltd (National Line) was founded in 1863 to provide a passenger service from Liverpool to New York with three newly-acquired single-screw propelled iron steamships and by 1866 the fleet grew to 11 passenger steamers, each of some 3,300 tons. Unfortunately also by 1866 two of the newest ships were lost at sea.

The National Line's passenger traffic was at first handled by the shipbrokers Guion & Co., who however started their own shipping enterprise; in 1866 National decided to create their own passenger organisation with emphasis on the emigrant trade. In 1867 the National Line was reorganised and the official name changed to National Steamship Company Ltd, one of the directors being Thomas Ismay, the founder of the White Star Line.

Around 1867-68 the company owned some eight steamships on the Liverpool-Queenstown-New York route and seven of these vessels were among the largest on the North Atlantic but unfortunately rather slow and this precluded competition on equal terms with their rivals. Around 1870-1872 there was some refitting and modernisation of the engines of the better ships and the firm achieved the distinction of operating one of the first compound engined steamers on the Atlantic.

The 1870-1871 vintage saw two new modern steamers capable of 14 knots and this was considered a satisfactory service speed for the 4,670 ton liners although it could not offer competition to the express mailboats of the day. During this period of its history the company prospered, was operating 12 large ships and competed on equal terms with its rivals, Inman, Guion and Cunard Lines, by carrying similar numbers of passengers and quantities of freight. A new service from London to New York was initiated and other destinations were introduced.

The Record Breaker *America*

By 1883 the fleet having become aged the company decided to improve its image by creating a particularly splendid and luxurious liner to achieve the Blue Riband in order to compete on equal footing with the Guion 'flyers' and commissioned the single screw steel-hulled steamer *America* of 5,528 tons and 450 ft in overall length by 51 ft beam.

America was built in 1884 by J. & G. Thomson of Clydebank and was equipped with a 3-cylinder compound engine rated at 10,000 IHP with steam at 95 psi generated in eight double-ended cylindrical boilers. At a designed service speed of 18 knots her coal consumption was to be ca 190 tons per day. She was one of the last brig-rigged steamers on the Atlantic.

The graceful and elegant liner, intended to seriously compete with the current Atlantic 'greyhounds', offered hitherto unknown splendour of travel facilities. Accommodation for 300 Saloon (First) Class passengers was provided in luxurious staterooms and public rooms equipped with every comfort and furnished to standards of utmost elegance. Electric lighting was provided throughout the ship and saloons as well as staterooms were steam heated. Even the Steerage facilities were fitted out 'as never before' with numerous wash-houses, drying closets and lavatories.

The most magnificent accommodation feature of the *America* was the Grand Saloon, extending over the width of the vessel to 51 ft. It was vast and lofty and its height and size were augmented by a magnificent ornamental glass dome. Rising at the centre to 19 ft the dome was supported over the entire length of the saloon by massively carved pillars terminating in a gallery at the end.

Multi-coloured rays of light reflected from the stained glass of the dome, greatly enhanced the effect of handsome fittings and created an ostentatiously palatial impression.

On her maiden voyage in May 1884 *America* won the Blue Riband from the Guion liner *Alaska* by averaging 17.6 knots between Queenstown and New York in 6 days 15 hours 20 minutes. This record was lost to the newest Guion liner *Oregon* in August 1884.

National Line flagship America. *For speed and elegance this liner developed the reputation of a 'floating palace'.*

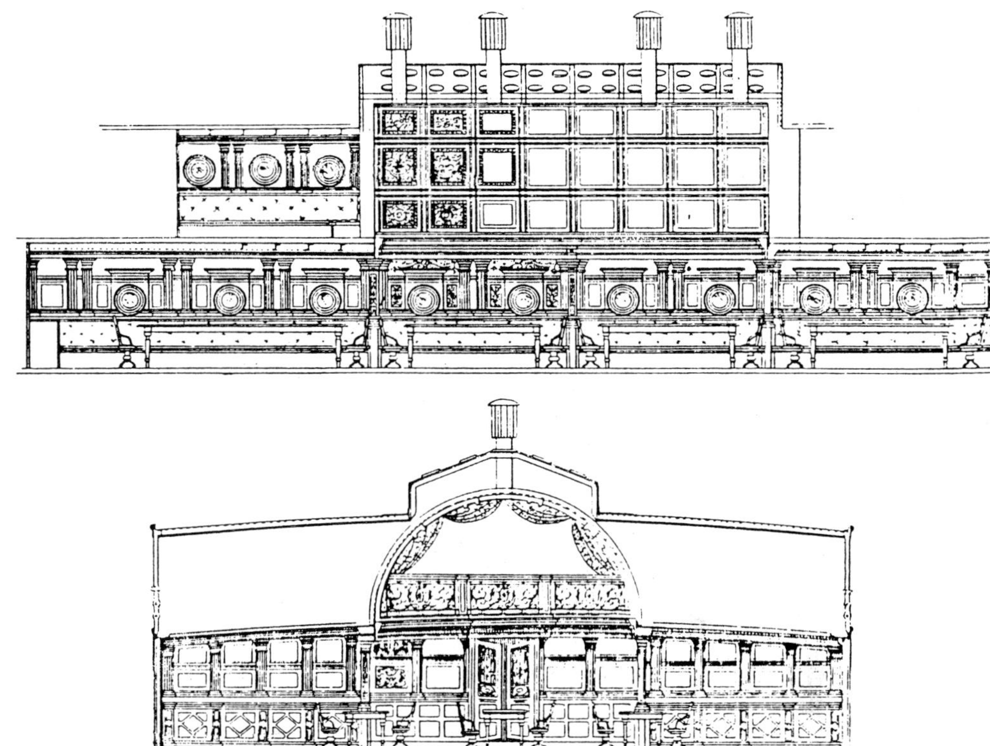

Grand saloon – longitudinal section

Grand saloon – cross-section showing entrance

Eastbound, in June 1884 *America* took the Blue Riband from the *Oregon* at 17.8 knots but had to return the honour to *Oregon*, this time belonging to Cunard Line, in August 1884.

Although *America* was in possession of the Blue Riband for a few months only, the graceful and luxurious liner was well liked by passengers and greatly furthered the standing of the National Line, although it may well have been rather late in the day.

This was the National Line's one and only Atlantic record achievement.

During 1885 *America* was operated as an auxiliary merchant cruiser and by 1886 she returned on the Liverpool to New York run. Fuel consumption becoming uneconomically high, she became expensive to run and in 1887 was sold to Italy for conversion to Naval duties, duly renamed *Trinacria*.

Subsequent History of the Company

After two profitable years in 1886-1887, some of the services had to be discontinued because of trade recession in 1889 and by 1890 the company's financial position became precarious, aggravated by the loss at sea of the 3,300 ton *Erin* and of the 4,700 ton *Egypt* by fire.

The company then discontinued passenger services and concentrated on the carriage of freight and cattle; its 1891 built, 5,000 ton cargo steamers were put on the London to New York run. The rest of the old fleet was sold off and in 1896 the new cargo ships and company goodwill were taken over by the American financed Atlantic Transport Line. By 1914 all ships of the National Line were fully absorbed into the Atlantic Transport Line and the name 'National Steamship Company Limited' ceased to exist.

Competitors en-route: America *(National),* Arizona *and* Alaska *(Guion).*

Guion Line – Liverpool & Great Western Steamship Company

The Company

IN 1866 A NEW SHIPPING enterprise, the Liverpool and Great Western Steamship Company, known as the Guion Line, was founded and although American financed, was based in Liverpool operating under the British flag.

The founder, Stephen Guion, was originally involved in the management of sailing packets transporting emigrants between Liverpool and New York and he later established a branch office in Liverpool to act as passenger agent for different companies. In 1866 he created his own company, the Guion Line, and ordered his first four steamers for the Liverpool to New York service, mainly concentrating on the emigrant traffic. Additional tonnage followed and in 1870 Guion took delivery of the steamship *Wisconsin,* the first to be equipped with a compound engine and this vessel proved a major success.

Guion's ambition to create a fleet of record breaking liners to compete with the Cunard, White Star and Inman greyhounds of the day, resulted in orders being placed in 1871 for a pair of 4,000 ton express steamers *Montana* and *Dakota,* to be equipped with compound engines and 100 psi water-tube boilers. This proved a technical failure; the ships had to be reboilered with the engines downrated and an order for two similar ships was cancelled. During the period 1872 to 1880 disaster struck and four ships were lost at sea.

However, from 1879 onwards, John Elder & Co. (subsequently Fairfield Shipping Company) of Glasgow delivered to the Guion Line three express liners capable of virtually monopolising the Atlantic crossing records between 1879 and 1884. The three vessels were named *Arizona, Alaska* and *Oregon.*

It proved unfortunate for the company that the excellent liners were built mainly with an eye on speed and with much space being occupied by machinery and coal. Considerable commercial capacity was thus forefeited tending to make the ships unprofitable unless loaded to at least 70% capacity. High coal consumption, especially at speed, also made the steamers expensive to operate and interest on capital outlay became excessive. Guion experienced financial difficulties to the extent that the third and latest, 1883-built express liner *Oregon* could not be paid for and had to be sold to Cunard Line after a few journeys.

The sale of *Oregon* was the start of the company's financial decline. The two record breakers *Arizona* and *Alaska*, together with three other ships, maintained the service until 1892 when all the older steamers were sold off.

In 1894 there was no alternative for the company but to go into liquidation.

The Guion Line Record Breakers

Arizona

The first of the Guion record breaking liners, *Arizona* built by J. Elder of Glasgow, was commissioned in 1879. The iron built steamship was of 5,179 GR tons and 450ft long overall by 45ft beam, thus representing the 'longship' design. *Arizona* was equipped with a powerful 3-cylinder compound engine (1 x HP + 2 x LP) driving three cranks and rated at 6,300 IHP with steam at 70 psi developed in six double-ended and one single-ended tubular boilers. Coal consumption was around 125-135 tons daily in order to achieve a service speed of over 16 knots.

Based upon experience with American packets, First Class accommodation and facilities (such as electric illumination) for some 300 passengers were well up to the best in contemporary standards and the steamer was well liked and patronised by better-off travellers.

Unfortunately the very large power plant requiring capacious coal bunkerage, considerably reduced the availability of space for payload such as steerage accommodation, with the result that the rather limited numbers of 'bread and butter' passengers did not experience much comfort nor space.

In July 1879 *Arizona* broke the eastbound crossing record of the White Star liner *Britannic* at an average speed of 15.96 knots, completing the journey from New York to Queenstown in 7 days 8 hours 11 minutes. This record remained valid until June 1882 when it was bettered by the larger sistership *Alaska*.

Although *Arizona* did not manage to accomplish the westbound 'double' she experienced world fame in November 1879 by surviving without loss of life or casualties, a direct collision with an iceberg off Newfoundland in thick fog on her way to New York. Subsequently with her bows crumpled right back to the first collision bulkhead, she made land at St John's, Newfoundland and duly equipped with a provisional wooden bow the liner completed the 1,700 mile journey to Liverpool in 6 days 18 hours. This ability to cope with the most feared peril at sea did much to enhance the reputation for strength of the steamer and she became much sought after by the travelling public.

Following the winding up of the Guion Line in 1894, *Arizona* was laid up but in 1898 experienced a refit and had a triple-expansion engine installed prior to transfer to the US Government, to be renamed *Hancock* for service in the Pacific. During the First World War *Hancock* became a troop transporter and was subsequently laid up in 1918. The record breaking liner was broken up in 1926.

Alaska

The second of Guion liners built for record speeds was *Alaska* of 6,930 GR tons, also originated at J. Elders of Glasgow and put into service in 1881. *Alaska* was a larger sistership to *Arizona* and measured 500ft in overall length by 50ft beam.

The single screw of this iron built steamer was driven by a similar but much larger version of the *Arizona* powerplant, comprising a 3-cylinder (1 x HP + 2 x LP) compound engine acting on three cranks and capable of developing some 8,000 IHP with steam at 90 psi generated in eight double-ended tubular boilers consuming some 230 tons of coal daily for a designed service speed of 17 knots.

Elegant accommodation was provided for ca 350 travellers in the First Class and the most up-to-date facilities showed quite an improvement on those of the smaller sistership. Again, because of the size of the powerplant and large coal bunkerage there was only limited space available for the quarters to accommodate emigrants and cargo.

Guion Line's first Blue Riband liner Arizona, *built in 1879 by J. Elder of Glasgow.*

Alaska *built by J. Elder of Glasgow in 1881 for the Guion Line as a larger version of* Arizona. *Held the Atlantic record in both directions for two years.*

Westbound, in April 1882, *Alaska* took the Blue Riband from the White Star liner *Germanic* with an average of 16.04 knots (Queenstown to New York in 7 days 6 hours 45 minutes). In April 1883 *Alaska* improved this crossing speed to 16.54 knots and kept this record until May 1884, then losing it to *America* of the National Line.

Eastward in June 1882, *Alaska* improved upon the *Arizona* record by achieving 16.8 knots between New York and Queenstown in 6 days 22 hours and later, in September 1882 bettered this average to 17.2 knots. In April 1884 *Alaska* lost the Blue Riband to the newest Guion liner *Oregon*.

Guion Line having ceased to exist in 1894, *Alaska* was laid up for three years and then, renamed *Magellanes*, transferred to the Spanish Transatlantic Company for a short period of service. Subsequently the liner was laid up in Scotland and after 1899 used as an accommodation ship prior to being broken up in 1902.

Oregon

The 7,375 GR ton liner *Oregon* was built in 1883 by J. Elder & Co. of Glasgow to complete the Guion Line trio of record breaking express steamers and based upon the design of *Arizona* and *Alaska*, featured many improvements which made it one of the largest and most up-to-date passenger carriers of the period on the Atlantic run.

The iron hulled steamship of 520 ft in overall length and 54 ft beam, was propelled by a large and powerful 3-cylinder compound engine (1 x HP + 2 x LP) acting on three cranks and capable of developing 12,500 IHP with steam at 110 psi generated in nine double-ended boilers. The designed service speed was 18 knots and this was easily achieved during trials. However, coal consumption during Atlantic crossings averaged at 300 to 330 tons daily and the bunker storage had to cater for this at the expense of such payload as Third Class (Steerage) accommodation.

Facilities for 470 travellers in the First Class were of the highest order and featured some 155 well-appointed staterooms and roomy elegant saloons as well as the latest most modern prerequisites based upon the most advanced American practices. Also the 400 Third Class passengers were offered reasonably appointed berths, a dining saloon and recreational facilities well in accordance with current practice. Although a substantial amount of space was occupied by the machinery and bunkerage for some 2,500 tons of coal, nearly 2,400 tons of cargo could also be carried.

Eastbound in April 1884, *Oregon* took the crossing record from *Alaska* by averaging 17.48 knots and completing the journey from New York to Queenstown in 6 days 17 hours and in August 1884 improved upon this achievement at 18.39 knots, this time flying the colours of the Cunard Line. *Oregon* lost the record to the latest Cunarder *Etruria* in March 1887.

Westbound, this time in the service of Cunard, *Oregon* took the Blue Riband from *America* of National Line in August 1884, by crossing from Queenstown to New York in 6 days 9 hours 42 minutes at an average of 18.14 knots. This record was bettered in May 1885, also by the Cunarder *Etruria*.

Unfortunately, as a result of a collision off Fire Island, New York Bay, in March 1886, this magnificent liner became a total loss. There were no casualties and all the mails were saved.

Record breaking express steamship Oregon *commissioned by Guion Line in 1883.*

Guion liner Oregon *in company with* Campania *of the Cunard Line.*

Cunard Line – 1869 to the Turn of the Century

Period from 1869 to 1884

After losing the Blue Riband to Inman, White Star and Guion Lines during the period from 1869 to 1884, the company tended to make the best possible use of its existing fleet and numerous newbuilds, also catering to a greater extent than before for the remunerative emigrant traffic, especially as the Atlantic competition grew by leaps and bounds with the appearance on the ever more busy ocean of diverse new shipping companies founded in France, Germany, Holland and Belgium. Cunard steamers, however, had an unsurpassed reputation for solid reliability and punctuality, if not undue luxury.

In 1880 the company went 'public' and 'Cunard Steamship Company Ltd' became the new title.

During 1880-1883 a programme of new steamers was implemented and these were also intended for the 'bread and butter' emigrant service to New York and Boston. Most of the new tonnage was equipped with conservatively rated compound engines driving single propellers for speeds around 12-15 knots.

The following pages feature figures 1-5 reproducing a series of 1881 contemporary artist's encouraging impressions of Cunard embarkation activities with passengers joining a New York mail steamer at Liverpool prior to departure, as originally published in the *Illustrated London News* of February 1881.

This illustrated article was possibly intended to counteract the fact that in January 1881 the good ship *Batavia* of 2,550 tons (built in 1870) had just created a minor alarm and consternation by losing her propeller somewhere on the Atlantic. After the *Batavia* had been located, she was towed to the Azores for repairs and all passengers and mails were delivered at Liverpool by other steamers. Such adventure, needless to say, was not an extraordinary occurrence for the period and did not in any way detract from the Cunard historical exemption from disasters at sea.

The illustrations can be covered by the original part-caption from the 1881 magazine, to quote:

> '. . . . The cabs and other vehicles with anxious people inside and with piles of luggage on the roof, continually drive up to the entrance of the landing stage on the Mersey quay where passengers have presently to go aboard the tender by which they are soon conveyed to the noble Cunard steamship lying in the middle of the river. They are received at their coming on board the ship by one of her courteous and attentive officers and are directed to their respective berths, readily obtaining whatever assistance they need . . . . . . when this has been effected to their satisfaction, they can freely enjoy in the spacious and handsome saloon as much

leisurely quiet, with opportunities for undisturbed family or social converse, as in the public room of a first rate hotel on shore. We say nothing of the ample provision of meals and lesser refreshments, or the prompt and agreeable manner in which they are served. In all these respects, as well as in the perfection of the ship's equipment, the skill of her officers and the discipline of her crew (whose preliminary muster for official inspection is shown on one sketch) the Cunard Liner may, at least compare to advantage with any other mail and passenger steamships in the world . . . .'

1. *Passengers arriving at the landing stage.*

2. *Going on board the tender.*

3. *Passengers coming on board.*

4. *Saloon.*

5. *Muster of the crew for inspection.*

Passengers joining a New York mail steamer at Liverpool prior to departure.

Courtesy Illustrated London News *library.*

Company Policy and the Last 19th Century Record Breakers

Up to 1883/84 Cunard services and trade were extended and consolidated but at the same time some technical features as far as propulsion and auxiliary machinery were concerned, tended to become rather outdated. The development of the compound steam engine with increased steam pressures in order to achieve higher power, was slow to materialise but Cunard management found it essential to persevere because to neglect technical developments of the period, was bound to imperil the company's status and reflect upon profitability. As a result of the often repeated exaggerated opinions on dangers of higher steam pressures being uppermost on the minds of the management, extensive debating and arguments as to advantages and safety factors related to compound engines working at pressures above 100 psi, went on for a long time but the influence of competition reflecting upon pure economics finally forced Cunard to try and catch up with the latest ideas and practice.

The modernisation policy was greatly encouraged by and coincided with the acquisition in June 1884 of the ex-Guion 7,375 ton express liner *Oregon* equipped with a 12,500 IHP compound engine working with a steam pressure of 110 psi; this vessel promptly presented Cunard with the Blue Riband in August 1884. The purchase of *Oregon* was complemented by Cunard in commissioning in 1884/85 of a pair of sisterships *Umbria* and *Etruria*, slightly larger than the *Oregon* and with similar but more powerful machinery.

It was a sad blow for Cunard, when on 14th March 1886 *Oregon* was involved in a collision with a sailing vessel and sank east of Long Island. All passengers and crew members were rescued by the German steamer *Fulda*.

The two 8,128 ton single screw steel-hulled express liners *Umbria* and *Etruria* were, at the time the largest in the company fleet and were equipped with enormous 3-cylinder compound engines rated at 14,500 IHP. The engine type, based upon the primemovers of the *Oregon* were of a size and power beyond current practice and the liners became the most powerful single screw vessels built to date. Proof of the fact that the technical limit of power application on to a single shaft commensurate with engineering experience of the period was reached, was provided by the fact that both liners had serious trouble with propeller shafting and both experienced shaft fractures.

Although both *Umbria* and *Etruria* were record breakers and Blue Riband holders, their enormous engines became expensive to operate, with coal consumption at ca 320 tons per day being considered very high. It appears that the liners only became profitable if they carried over 70% of their commercial capacity.

It became appreciated by Cunard management that the size of compound engines as fitted in *Umbria* and *Etruria* signalled more or less the ultimate economical stage of compound development and furthermore, if also introduced in other large liners of the fleet, might well have resulted in considerable financial loss.

By 1886 rivals in the transatlantic trade were already changing to triple expansion steam engines for larger newbuilds in order to solve the problems of improving efficiency of operation with higher boiler pressures. This development in steam machinery proved superior to the compound engine, offering more power with reduced coal consumption and at the same time providing considerable decrease in size and weight of power plant. Subsequent experience, also confirmed by operation of other companies' ships, indicated that the two Cunard record breakers were virtually obsolete soon after they came into service.

To some extent Cunard also lost out to White Star and Inman competition by being slow to introduce twin-screw propulsion and the consequent elimination of auxiliary sails. At the same time Cunard could also have been considered fortunate to be in the position of seeing the rivals ironing out any snags and problems associated with the new propulsion system before deciding in 1893 to start adopting twin screws.

In 1893 the commissioning of the two 12,950 ton express liners *Campania* and *Lucania* introduced such modern technology as triple expansion engines driving twin screws.

Even then some problems such as cavitation and vibration were experienced with the propellers and by 1894 some adjustment and modifications achieved the desired improvements. Both ships became record breakers and Blue Riband holders until challenged in 1897 by *Kaiser Wilhelm der Grosse* of the Norddeutscher Lloyd as well as other German crack liners.

Campania and *Lucania* were the first Cunard express liners to graduate the First Class accommodation from a comfortable hotel to that of palatial stately homes with the luxury and opulence intended to appeal to a well-to-do travelling public expecting their mode of travel to act as a status symbol. Needless to say, the period 1893 to 1898 was reserved to the two Cunarders as far as travel by 'creme-de-la-creme' was concerned.

The appearance on the Atlantic in 1897 of the prestigious German record breaking 'four-stackers' introduced by Norddeutscher Lloyd and Hamburg Amerika Line, all capable of outpacing the best Cunard could offer, brought about a notable loss of business to Cunard, whose fleet thus became rapidly outdated.

The Cunard financial position became such that there materialised a serious threat of the company's shares becoming vulnerable to acquisition by J. Pierpont Morgan's giant American combine, the International Mercantile Marine Company, which by 1902 had gained control of the White Star, Leyland and Dominion Lines as addition to the already purchased Belgian Red Star Line and various American companies.

National prestige and economical considerations necessitating relief from financial pressure exerted by IMMC, brought about a Government agreement with Cunard, for the company to receive a large Government loan in order to remain fully under British management, with shares not being made available to foreign interests. Cunard also obtained a substantial subsidy to build new super-liners capable of overwhelming German predominance on the Atlantic and at the same time being suitable for conversion to Admiralty wartime requirements as Armed Merchant Cruisers, in case of a possible outbreak of hostilities.

Cunard Line in the 20th Century and contemporary development of the fleet are featured in a later chapter.

Blue Riband Achievements between 1884 and 1897

Oregon

Built in 1883 by J. Elder & Co. (Fairfield Yard) of Glasgow, for the Guion Line, the liner was bought by Cunard Line because of financial problems experienced by the original owner.

The liner is described in the chapter dealing with the Guion Line. In April 1884, flying the Guion flag *Oregon* broke the eastbound record with 17.48 knots and by August 1844 lost the honour to *America* of the National Line, changed allegiance to Cunard and wrested the eastbound record back from *America* with an average of 18.4 knots between New York and Queenstown in 6 days 11 hours 9 minutes. This achievement remained valid until it was bettered by the new Cunarder *Etruria* in March 1887.

Westbound *Oregon* improved upon the Queenstown to New York fastest crossing by the National Line's *America* by averaging 18.16 knots in August 1884, and completing the journey in 6 days 9 hours 42 minutes. In May 1885 *Oregon* relinquished this Blue Riband record in favour of the *Etruria*.

In March 1886 *Oregon* foundered as a result of a collision while approaching New York.

Umbria and *Etruria*

The 8,128 ton single screw express liners, built by J. Elder of Fairfield, Glasgow, were brought into service in 1884-85. The steamers were 519 ft in overall length by 57 ft beam and built in steel throughout. The hulls were divided into 10 watertight compartments with most bulkheads being carried to the upper deck and fitted with waterproof and fireproof doors to give access from one part of the ship to the other. In all, the design of the ships allowed full conversion to Admiralty requirements for service as 'mercantile auxiliaries' in times of war.

The single screw propulsion was by means of powerful 3-cylinder compound engines with one HP and two LP pistons operating three cranks, and with steam at 110 psi generated in nine double-ended smoke-tube cylindrical boilers. The engines were of contemporary Fairfield design but with a rated output of 14,500 IHP, just about the largest ever made by the firm.

Umbria and *Etruria* were the last single-screw propelled passenger and mail express steamers operated by the Cunard Line on the Atlantic and were also the last to have auxiliary sails (barquentine rigging).

Cunard Line 1885 liner Etruria – *at Liverpool.*

Record breaking liner Umbria *at the Queens Birthday Naval Review of 1888.*

Cunard Steamship Etruria – *Life on the Ocean Wave*

Right: The elegant Music Saloon.

Left: The palatial entrance to the Dining Saloon.

Right: Gentlemen's Smoking Saloon.

Accommodation for 550 First Class and some 800 Third Class passengers was up to and beyond qualitative standards of the day and particularly the electrical illumination and power were sophisticated by contemporary reckoning. Both liners were appointed to compete, at least on equal terms, with rivals on the Atlantic and consequently passenger facilities were of exceptionally high standard and luxury.

Etruria

Although commissioned a year later than her sistership *Umbria*, the express liner *Etruria* was the first to achieve record crossings of the Atlantic and in May 1885 she improved upon the time taken by the newly acquired Cunarder *Oregon* by making the journey from Queenstown to New York in 6 days 5 hours 30 minutes at an average speed of 18.87 knots. *Etruria* lost the westbound record in May 1887 to her sistership *Umbria* but regained it in May 1888 by achieving a mean of 19.57 knots and retained the Blue Riband until May 1889 when the achievement was bettered by *City of Paris* (2) of the Inman International Line.

Eastbound, *Etruria* gained the Blue Riband from *Oregon* in March of 1887 at 19.75 knots (6 days 4 hours 36 minutes) and kept it until May 1889, losing it again to *City of Paris*.

Apart from some breakdowns mainly due to the overloaded propeller shaft, which included loss of propeller, rudder and part of the sternpost as well as a short spell in dock for modernisation of accommodation, the liner gave excellent service until 1909, when she was sold to shipbreakers.

Umbria

The express liner *Umbria* was completed by J. Elder of Fairfield in 1884 and departed on her maiden voyage to New York in the same year. In May 1887 *Umbria* won the westbound Blue Riband from her sistership *Etruria* with an average of 18.9 knots, crossing from Queenstown to New York in 6 days 4 hours 45 minutes. She lost the record, again to *Etruria* in May 1888.

Umbria also experienced trouble with drive transmission including complete fracture of the tailshaft at sea which, luckily could be repaired by the highly skilled engineers in order to just about make port. However the liner provided regular express service with the Cunard Line on the Atlantic apart from a short spell as troop transport in 1900-1901 during the Boer War. *Umbria* was sold to shipbreakers in 1910.

Campania and *Lucania*

In 1891 Cunard ordered from Fairfield Shipbuilding Company (formerly J. Elder & Co.) a pair of steel-hulled twin screw liners capable of such service speeds as to out-perform all contemporary competition on the Atlantic and at the same time offer superlative comfort and luxury with the paramount and latest facilities.

The liners *Campania* and *Lucania* were 622 ft in overall length by 65 ft beam and at the time qualified as the largest in the world. The power plant of each of the two vessels comprised two sets of triple-expansion, five-cylinder, three-crank engines with the HP cylinders in tandem above the LP units, set at each side of the IP cylinder. Each engine was located in its own engine room separated by a longitudinal bulkhead and the combined output rating for each steamer was 30,000 IHP with the HP mode supplied by steam at 165 psi generated in 12 double-ended smoke-tube boilers equipped with 96 furnaces served by a staff of 132 stokers and trimmers. Combustion air was supplied by means of 12 large fans blowing into the boiler rooms; average coal consumption at full speed on the Atlantic worked out at ca 550 tons per day.

Each of the two liners had a passenger capacity for 550 in the First Class, 280 in the Second and some 1,000 in Third (Steerage). In the First Class the decor style in costly woodwork, stained glass, plush upholstery in velour and brocade as well as luxurious Persian carpets, was equivalent to English baronial good taste and was greatly admired, especially by wealthy American travellers. The two liners were the first Cunarders to be provided with First Class single berth cabins and complete luxurious suites; all principal rooms had ornate coal-burning open fireplaces. Second Class was also of exceptionally high standard, not far short of First Class accommodation encountered on smaller passenger liners on the Atlantic.

Excellent steam heating was provided overall and efficient refrigeration plant catered for all provisions and cargo (meat imports from the United States). Electricity catered for all illumination and power requirements. *Campania* and *Lucania* pioneered wireless telegraphy in 1901 and *Lucania* was the first Atlantic liner to publish a daily newspaper containing up-to-date news received by wireless.

Campania

Completed in 1893, the 12,950 ton express liner *Campania* set out on her maiden voyage from Liverpool to New York in April 1893. In May 1893, eastbound, *Campania* won the Blue Riband from the *City of New York* of Inman International by achieving a mean speed of 21.09 knots between New York and Queenstown with a journey of 5 days 17 hours 27 minutes. She lost this record to her sistership *Lucania* in May 1894.

Campania, *1893/94 Blue Riband express liner. First Cunarder with twin screw propulsion.*

Lucania, *1893/97 Blue Riband Cunard express luxury liner. Sistership to* Campania.

In August 1894, westbound, *Campania* improved upon the record crossing of *Lucania* by averaging 21.49 knots between Queenstown and New York. She lost the record to *Lucania* in May 1894.

Campania maintained the Cunard express mail service until 1914 and then went on a short period charter to the Anchor Line. In 1914 the liner was acquired by the Admiralty and converted into a seaplane carrier. *Campania* had the distinction of having virtually pioneered the aircraft carrier on all oceans. *Campania* foundered in 1918 as a result of a collision with the battle-cruiser *Glorious* in the Firth of Forth.

Lucania

Commissioned in 1893 the *Lucania*, sistership to *Campania*, left Liverpool on her maiden voyage in September of the same year and in October she wrested the Blue Riband from the *City of Paris* of Inman International by crossing westwards from Queenstown to New York in 5 days 13 hours 45 minutes at an average speed of 20.75 knots. In August 1894 she lost the westward record to *Campania* but regained the honour in the same month at 21.66 knots, subsequently improving the performance to 21.81 knots in October 1894 with a journey of 5 days 7 hours 25 minutes. *Lucania* kept the record for this leg until March 1898, then losing it to *Kaiser Wilhelm der Grosse* of the Norddeutscher Lloyd.

Eastbound *Lucania* gained the crossing record from her sistership *Campania* with a mean speed of 21.95 knots and kept it until November 1897, when it was bettered again by *Kaiser Wilhelm der Grosse*.

Lucania remained in Cunard transatlantic service until 1909; she was burnt out at the jetty in Liverpool and subsequently sold to shipbreakers.

Cunard Line Express Mail Liner Lucania – *Engine Room*

Engine Room – Upper Platform.

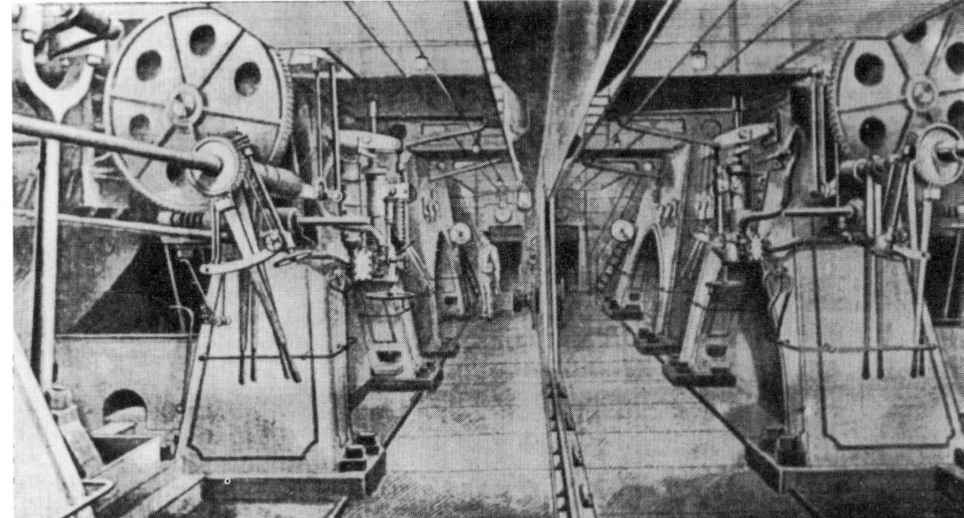

Engine Room – Middle Platform.

Engine Room – Lower Platform.

Blue Riband in the 20th Century

The German Record Breaking Liners

Evolution of the German Merchant Marine

IN ORDER TO APPRECIATE the development of German merchant shipping and overseas trade towards the end of the 19th century, it may be as well to mention a few words related to the history of the German Reich following its creation out of a large number of feudal German-speaking states, the majority of which were landlocked and therefore had originally few natural facilities nor ambitions to fraternise unduly with the rest of the world. Geographically only the states along the coasts of the Baltic and North Sea developed individual sea routes and an outlook directed towards trade with other countries.

Germany and her development into a foremost industrialised maritime trading nation, could possibly trace its origins to the peace table of Vienna in 1813-1815, when sovereign rulers of a decimated mediaeval union of some 30 individual German speaking states paved the way to a future unity. As an intermediate stage in 1848, a loose Confederation was created with a parliament at Frankfurt/Main.

Development of German merchant shipping and overseas trade routes came to be greatly associated with the creation in 1848 of the nearest thing to a unified Navy, which materialised during a period of hostile confrontation with Denmark concerning Schleswig-Holstein, when virtually all shipping trade exits along the coastline were blockaded by a few Danish warships. The Frankfurt parliament of 1848 authorised the formation of a Reich Naval Force and with the help of Hamburg shipowners various ships were acquired and built, to be equipped with suitable cannon. Purchases included such well-proven paddle steamers as the 1839-40 built Cunarders *Britannia* and *Acadia*, renamed *Barbarossa* and *Erzherzog Johann*, respectively, to be classified as frigates. The Reich Navy finally comprised three paddle-frigates, six paddle-corvettes and two sail-frigates. The headquarters of this small new force became Bremerhaven with supreme command delegated to its organiser, Captain (later Rear-Admiral) Karl Rudolf Bromme (known as 'Brommy'), who created a future disciplinary, administrative and logistics framework for Naval developments and functions. 'Brommy' could more or less be looked upon as a German version of Samuel Pepys.

In actions against the Danes, Brommy's flagship was the *Barbarossa* (ex-*Britannia*) equipped with nine cannon and a 200-man crew. It is not clear whether any shots were ever fired in anger but the formation of the Navy appeared to have been considered a great success.

By the end of 1849 with the Danes having been suitably intimidated and all blockades lifted, national fervour and the '1848 Revolution' evaporated and the Reich Government disbanded.

One can but appreciate that the first flagship to wear the flag of the creator of the German Navy was the former *Britannia*, the Cunard pioneering steamer on the Atlantic and virtual perpetrator of the Blue Riband accolade.

During the following three years the 'warships' were laid up, with some passed on to Prussia and others sold off; after the final dissolution of the Reich Fleet any future warlike requirements became the prerogative of the combined fleets of Prussia and Austria.

However, diverse disagreements mainly over Schleswig-Holstein, led to the war of 1866 between the two states and as a consequence of her land victory at Koenigsgraetz in 1867 over Austria and her allied states, Prussia finally annexed Schleswig-Holstein as well as the part of North Sea coast including Kiel and Jade, thus becoming the dominant force and her leadership created the North-German Confederation of 1866 to 1870, with the briskly developing Prussian fleet becoming the Federal Navy.

Following the Franco-Prussian war of 1870-71 in which Prussia was victorious, the whole of Germany came under her aegis and at Versailles in 1871 Kaiser Wilhelm I of Prussia accepted the Imperial Crown of the new Reich. The Navy changed her title to 'Kaiserliche Marine' as the Reich Fleet with Kaiser Wilhelm I as Supreme Commander.

Germany was subsequently greatly aided in her industrial development by a large indemnity from the vanquished France, the cession of Alsace and Lorraine and the acquisition of colonies by Bismarck from 1884 onwards, and began to play an active role among the Great Powers.

The original foundations for overseas trade were laid by the independent Hanse-States along the coastlines of the Baltic and North Seas, with Luebeck, Hamburg and Bremen in the forefront and their flags became well known and respected worldwide. In 1850 the Hamburg shipowner Robert Sloman sent the first German steamship to New York and in 1853 the Bremen firm W. A. Fritze & Co. initiated the Bremerhaven to New York service under the Bremen flag, with the two ex-Reich Navy, ex-Prussian Navy wooden paddle steamers, *Hansa* (originally a frigate built in 1847 as the *United States*) and *Germania* (formerly frigate *Erzherzog Johann* built as *Acadia* for the Cunard Line). These two pioneering paddle steamers operated the transatlantic service, with emphasis on catering for the ever growing emigration until 1857, with one interruption in 1855 for a profitable charter to transport troops during the Crimean War.

Around that time the two most famous German shipping companies were founded. The Hamburg Amerikanische Packetfahrt A G (HAPAG) started transatlantic operations from Hamburg in 1847 and the Norddeutscher Lloyd came into being in Bremen in 1857.

In 1867 the fleets of both companies came under the black/white/red flag of the North-German Confederation.

Even before the outbreak of the Franco-Prussian war the two companies greatly expanded their overseas operations, well beyond the original New York emigrant services; in addition, numerous other shipping interests were materialising and at the time of cessation of hostilities some nine major German shipping companies were trading worldwide.

The 1847 paddler Washington *- a Bremen Atlantic pioneer*

As a result of the 1845 Congressional Bill, tenders were invited in the United States to operate a mail service to Europe by American steamships capable of driving the Cunard monopoly off the Atlantic.

Prior to Collins obtaining the mail subsidy, a contract was allocated to Edward Mills to provide a fortnightly service. Mills failed to obtain adequate funds to finance his first ship and his commitments were taken over by 'Ocean S N Co.' (later called the 'Bremen Line'), newly created by a group of American businessmen who also obtained backing from Bremen investors. The first transatlantic steamship *Washington* of 1,750 tons, was launched at the yard of Westerveldt & Mackay in January 1847 and was scheduled to sail for Bremen concurrently with the *Britannia* of Cunard and in winning this race, assist in the United States supplanting Cunard.

Unfortunately for American publicity, a 'race' did not really materialise, with the *Britannia* arriving at Liverpool some two days before *Washington* entered the channel having experienced all sorts of engine breakdowns and operational complications. *Washington* proved to be a poor seaboat and much underpowered. However she kept on with the Bremen run until the Germans decided to remove their subsidies and provide their own ships for the American service. The US subsidy also ceased and *Washington* was laid up in 1857 in anticipation to sale to other interests.

Norddeutscher Lloyd (NDL)

The Company

THE NORDDEUTSCHER LLOYD WAS founded in 1857 by the prosperous merchant Heinrich H. Maier in Bremen and in 1858 the first service, primarily for emigrants, was initiated by the departure from Bremerhaven of the 2,670 ton screw-propelled steamer *Bremen*, headed for New York with 270 First and Second Class passengers and 400 steerage emigrants. Numerous similar ships were put on this scheduled service and between 1868 and 1871 routes were extended to Baltimore, New Orleans and the West Indies.

Profits from the carriage of emigrants aided greatly to the expansion of the company's interests and the original, Greenock built, robust brig-rigged single screw steamships of ca 2,000 to 3,000 tons and capable of 12 or so knots, were efficiently operated on all trade routes transporting passengers and cargo; the fleet experienced a rapid growth.

In the early 1870's competition from other operators tended to create various trading problems and the West Indies run was discontinued but replaced by going further afield to Brazil and LaPlata, where competition, especially in the carriage of freight, was not excessive and tariffs offered few problems.

By the end of the 1870's, H. H. Maier having retired, new dynamism was introduced by the successor, Johann Lohman. A new type of vessel, the so-called 'Express' steamship of the 'River' class, measuring 4,500 to 5,000 tons and capable of 16-17 knots was ordered from Cairds of Greenock. For the first time in German ships' layout, these ships featured First Class accommodation amidships, similar to that of the White Star 'Oceanic' class and this enabled them to introduce such decor and luxury as not previously encountered on German shipboard. The first of these 'express' liners, the *Elbe* was introduced on the New York run in 1881 and by 1891 11 'River' class liners were operational. These express steamers were a notable success and greatly contributed to placing the Lloyd into an internationally leading position.

By 1885 NDL was operating 40 seagoing steamships aggregating 103,440 GR tons, representing ca 42% of total steamer tonnage of the German Merchant Marine and by the turn of the century the fleet consisted of 104 ships totalling 1,050,000 tons. The 19th century development period saw the Lloyd achieving world leadership.

From 1884 acquisition of colonies resulted in new targets for German Merchant Shipping and in 1886 a Reichspost contract for a subsidised carriage of mail to the Far East and Australia gave NDL impetus for the commissioning of new mail liners and the refurbishment of much of the existing fleet. The 1874 built

Oder initiated the Far East four-weekly service and in the same year the *Salier* departed for Australia.

In 1895 NDL commissioned new liner types to complement the express steamer programme and this 10,000-ton *'Barbarossa'* class was capable of carrying 2,000 passengers as well as a substantial amount of cargo at 15 knots. Originally intended for the North Atlantic, these new ships went into service to the Far East and Australia. To some extent this new large liner came into being in anticipation of the renewal of the mail contract in 1900 and the ships became the largest carriers on the Far Eastern run. The profitable service was operational right up to the First World War, with numerous similar new steamers built during the first decade after the turn of the century. Between 1900 and 1902 the Lloyd also created a substantial network of local services between Australian and Far Eastern ports and at one time some 40 steamships traded in the area. In 1902 a scheduled mail service between Singapore, New Guinea and Sydney was inaugurated.

In the early 1890's a degree of rivalry developed between HAPAG and Norddeutscher Lloyd on the Atlantic and it was becoming obvious that the single-screw Lloyd express liners were getting long in the tooth, thus losing out in the competition with the larger, latest HAPAG twin-screw ships on the prestigious transatlantic run.

Director Lohman died in 1892 and his successor, Heinrich Wiegand, became responsible for future policies of the company. His inheritance offered quite a few problems because of the outmoded fleet but he had the vision and drive to take positive action by placing orders with German shipyards for a new concept of a revolutionary class of high-speed twin-screw express liner intended to surpass not only contemporary HAPAG steamships but, what was even more important, also those of British competitors.

The first of this class, the 14,349 ton, twin-screw *Kaiser Wilhelm der Grosse*, when commissioned in 1897, was the world's largest liner and by wresting the Blue Riband from Cunard in November 1897, the fastest. During the period from 1897 to 1907 the famous 'fourstacker' liners, all built by Vulcan-Werke of Stettin, were the world's fastest and most luxuriously appointed ships and the Lloyd regained its reputation as the leading passenger shipping company by achieving complete dominance of the transatlantic run.

In February 1902 Wiegand formed a 10-year financial agreement with J. P. Morgan's IMMCo while maintaining complete autonomy, and in the long run this proved beneficial to the Lloyd.

Unlike the HAPAG policy of building large medium-speed liners, Wiegand's ambition had always been for the Lloyd to operate fast medium-sized luxury ships on world-wide services but he died in 1909, at a time when a newbuild programme by the Lloyd had to water down his original ideas to suit current demand and to ensure more economical operation in order to compete with other companies' more up-to-date Atlantic liners. In 1909 the 25,000 ton, 19 knot, luxury liner *George Washington*, as well as other 'intermediate' type steamships were added to the fleet, culminating with the 34,000 ton, 19 knot, *Columbus* launched in 1913, which never saw service with NDL because of the First World War, but became the *Homeric* of the White Star Line.

At the outbreak of the First World War, Norddeutscher Lloyd owned a fleet of 124 seagoing ships totalling some 713,300 GR tons and was at the time classified as the second largest shipowner of the German Merchant Marine.

As in the case of all German shipping companies in 1918, the Lloyd lost virtually its entire fleet mainly as reparations, but by 1923 the company started a rebuilding programme with medium-sized passenger and cargo liners destined for world-wide trade, also making good use of the recently introduced and economically favourable diesel engine propulsion. In 1923 the newly completed 32,500 liner *Columbus* (ex-*Hindenburg* on stocks during the war) was commissioned to participate in the rapidly expanding and highly profitable Atlantic trade at the time of American prosperity with the associated requirements for travel and the major exodus of European emigrants in the early 1920's. The fact that the major west European companies operated large elderly and uneconomical liners, mainly of ex-German pre-war vintage, encouraged the German Government, still in the depths of post-war depression, to strongly subsidise the placing of orders by the Lloyd in 1926 for two 50,000 ton pretentious super modern liners to enhance and assert German prestige as well as to employ labour in building the ships capable of creating a source of hard currency.

The modern elegance of the new liners was to be combined with the fulfillment of the ambition to achieve the fastest scheduled service on the Atlantic commensurate with the wresting of the Atlantic record from the aged *Mauretania*.

The two liners *Bremen* and *Europa* were commissioned in 1929 and on her maiden voyage, *Bremen* achieved the Blue Riband; this was followed in 1930 by *Europa*. The pair kept the Blue Riband until 1933/36, losing the honours to the latest liners of Italy and France.

Norddeutscher Lloyd had the misfortune of trying to achieve the dream of becoming the world leader on the Atlantic at a time when, late in 1929, the trade depression and collapse of stock markets engulfed the United States with the consequent reflection upon Europe, thus creating a considerable reduction in Atlantic traffic. However, the American economic recovery after 1933 and the slow but sure return of business confidence in Europe helped the two liners to pay their way, even in competition with the other giant super-liners.

As in the case of most major shipping companies, it made commercial sense to follow government guidelines during the economic depression to reduce national competition and improve operational efficiency by amalgamating the interests of major companies and in 1931 Norddeutscher Lloyd and Hamburg America Line (HAPAG) combined administrative control but the two companies still traded within their particular allocated spheres of interest.

By 1935 Norddeutscher Lloyd was operating some 86 ocean-going ships in its traditional trading areas world-wide and company fortunes experienced a considerable upward trend.

From 1937 development work and planning were initiated by Dr Ing Gustav Bauer of Deschimag Shipyard, Bremen, on plans for a new super-liner of some 80,000 tons to compete with *Normandie* and *Queen Mary* for the Blue Riband honours. The new liner, to be named *Amerika*, was to have turbo-electric propulsion for a speed of 36-38 knots. Apart from Deschimag carrying out tank tests, no further progress was made and the project was abandoned during the Second World War.

The Second World War saw again a virtually complete depletion of the company's fleet including the loss of the two record-breaking liners, which were the last German Blue Riband contenders.

After the war, from 1945 onwards the Lloyd again started rebuilding its shipping, starting with acquisition in 1950 of ships for cargo services and extending same to traditional trading areas. This was followed in 1954 by purchase of various large French and Swedish liners for the then profitable North Atlantic trade as well as by new building of modern diesel-engined medium sized passenger and cargo ships for expanding world-wide services.

In the sixties transatlantic passenger sea travel experienced a rapid reduction in scope because of the major development of jet aircraft and the largest liners reverted mainly to cruising.

In 1971 Norddeutscher Lloyd finally amalgamated with HAPAG (Hamburg America Line) to form the powerful present-day combine 'HAPAG-Lloyd', the world's largest shipping conglomerate with diverse interests including shipbuilding and operation of a substantial fleet comprising giant container liners and bulkers as well as cruise ships and coastal traders.

Record Breaking Liners of the Norddeutscher Lloyd

Kaiser Wilhelm der Grosse

This 14,349 GR ton liner, 627 ft in length (b.p.) by 65 ft beam, was built for the NDL in 1897 by the Stettiner Vulcan Shipyard and represented the first of the famous German four-stack record breaking mail liners on the Atlantic.

The steamship was propelled by twin screws driven by two sets of triple expansion, 4-cylinder engines acting on four cranks, developing 28,000 IHP with steam pressure of 210 psi generated in 12 double-ended and 3 single-ended cylindrical smoke-tube boilers.

Passenger accommodation catered for about 560 travellers in the First Class amidships, 340 in the Second Class in the after end and 1,074 in steerage forward. The First Class especially, enjoyed such

Blue Riband liner Kaiser Wilhelm der Grosse *of Norddeutscher Lloyd.*

spaciousness, opulence and elegance as not yet experienced on the Atlantic, creating considerable competition to the Cunarders and other Atlantic liners of the period. Saloons and other recreation rooms were spacious with high ceilings featuring ornamental decorations and walls adorned with costly pictures, carvings and stained glass. Ostentatious elegance was everywhere in profusion and this applied to suites and cabins with superior furnishings, many mirrors and heavy drapings. Bathtubs were in marble and even taps were gold-plated. The Second Class, located aft, was only slightly less elegant and spacious but the 1,000 or so emigrants were squeezed into the forward end of the ship in company with kitchens, luggage rooms and crews' quarters and had to rely upon 'tweendecks space for leisure and recreation.

The liner could best be remembered in the annals of maritime history as the epitome of German quality, technological prowess and as host to the rich and famous; yet it was the emigrant in his steerage dormitory who provided the shipowner with the maximum profits. But then, this applied to all so-called luxury liners and other Atlantic steamers of the period.

In November 1897 *Kaiser Wilhelm der Grosse* broke the eastbound record held by the Cunarder *Lucania* at an average of 22.36 knots with the ca 300 miles longer distance between Sandy Hook (New York) and the Needles being covered in 5 days 18 hours 40 minutes and completed the Blue Riband return leg to New York in March 1898, in 5 days 20 hours averaging 22.29 knots, again beating the record held by *Lucania*.

In July 1900 *Kaiser Wilhelm der Grosse* relinquished the Blue Riband in both directions to *Deutschland* of HAPAG, but regained the eastbound record in August 1900, averaging 22.89 knots and held on to the honour until September 1900 when this achievement was again bettered by *Deutschland*.

Kaiser Wilhelm der Grosse remained on the North Atlantic service until the outbreak of war in 1914. In May 1914 the Kaiserliche Marine requisitioned the liner and duly fitted out with appropriate guns, she sailed forth commerce raiding. After limited success and having sunk three ships totalling some 10,500 tons, the *Kaiser* was intercepted coaling off Rio de Oro by the RN cruiser *Highflyer* and sunk in August 1914.

When first commissioned in 1897, the good *Kaiser* was to be 'paired' for a record-breaking express service with a second liner, the 1898 completed 12,500 ton *Kaiser Friedrich*, built by F. Schichau of Danzig. Unfortunately for NDL, the *Kaiser Friedrich* could not develop the requisite speed to suit the pairing and after a few trips had to be returned to the makers for numerous modifications which appeared to make little difference, the liner being finally returned to the builders.

The pairing for the North Atlantic run was finally achieved in 1901 when a near-sistership to the *Kaiser*, the *Kronprinz Wilhelm* entered the Bremerhaven to New York service.

Kronprinz Wilhelm

Built in 1901 also at Vulcan Werke of Stettin, the liner *Kronprinz Wilhelm*, of 14,908 tons and 663 ft in length by 66 ft beam, was similar to *Kaiser Wilhelm der Grosse*, but slightly larger and equipped with more powerful machinery to drive her 22 ft diameter twin screws. The powerplant comprised two 6-cylinder quadruple expansion steam engines, each with drive on four cranks arranged from IP x LP/HP x LP/HP x IP cylinders (tandem) and capable of developing some 35,000 IHP with steam at 250 psi generated in 12 double-ended and 4 single-ended smoke-tube

NDL liner Kronprinz Wilhelm *at the Columbus-Quay, at Bremerhaven. Embarkation of emigrants on their way to the 'Land of Unlimited Opportunities'.*

Norddeutscher Lloyd 1901 record breaking liner Kronprinz Wilhelm *arriving at Bremerhaven.*

cylindrical boilers (Scotch) while consuming up to 500 tons of coal per day for a speed of 23 knots. The coal bunker capacity was 4,450 tons.

Six hundred and fifty First Class and 350 Second Class passengers' accommodation was even more elegant and sumptuous than that of her earlier sister-ship and there were four 'cabins-de-luxe' as well as elegant staterooms. Accommodation for the 700 Steerage travellers did not seem to experience much improvement. More modern fitments included much superior kitchens, greater use of electricity, internal telephones and most advanced wireless telegraphy to ensure direct contact with both sides of the Atlantic simultaneously.

In September 1902 *Kronprinz Wilhelm* surpassed the westbound record of *Deutschland* (HAPAG) by the narrow margin of 0.03 knots, crossing from Cherbourg to New York in 5 days 12 hours at a mean speed of 23.09 knots. She held this record until 1904 when it was bettered, again by 0.03 knots by the latest NDL liner *Kaiser Wilhelm II.*

Kronprinz Wilhelm maintained her transatlantic schedule until the outbreak of the First World War, when in August 1914 she left New York without passengers and dodging the Royal Navy blockade, was equipped off the Bahamas by the German cruiser *Karlsruhe* with guns and other requisites in order to act as a commerce raider. Managing to obtain supplies of coal at various neutral ports, *Kronprinz Wilhelm* sunk some 15 Allied ships before being forced to abandon the mission and returning to the United States for internment in April 1915. From 1917 to 1919, renamed *von Steuben*, the liner was used by US authorities as a troop transport. Offered to the Shipping Board after the war, it was found that refurbishment for commercial use of the uneconomical record breaker would be much too costly because of the extent of general dilapidation and she was sold to shipbreakers in 1923.

Kaiser Wilhelm II

In March 1903 an enlarged version of the four-stacker luxury express liners, designed for the Blue Riband and built by Vulcan Werke, Stettin, was commissioned by the Norddeutscher Lloyd. *Kaiser Wilhelm II* was of 18,361 GR tons, 706 ft 6 in in overall length (689 ft b.p.) and 72 ft wide. Her twin screws were driven at 80 RPM by two sets of 2 x 4-cylinder, six-crank quadruple expansion engines installed in two adjacent engine rooms, one for each propeller, and capable of developing a maximum total of 44,000 IHP. Steam at 225 psi was generated in 12 double-ended and 7 single-ended cylindrical smoke-tube boilers (Scotch) fed by 124 furnaces. Bunker capacity was 5,700 tons. The engines represented the largest steam reciprocating powerplant ever used at sea.

The 18,361 ton liner Kaiser Wilhelm II *on the slipways at Vulcan Werke, Stettin. The liner was built in 16 months, during which period materials were assembled at the rate of 513 tons per day on the basis of 26 working days per month.*

Kaiser Wilhelm II *was the last Blue Riband liner to be propelled by twin screws. The two bronze screws were 22 ft-10 in in diameter and weighed 31.4 tons each. Revolving at 80 RPM the propellers enabled the liner to average 23.5 knots between Europe and New York.*

Passenger accommodation catered for 775 in the First Class, 347 in the Second and 770 in Steerage (Third). As in the case of other German express liners, the First Class was equipped on a palatial scale. There were two imperial suites with a private dining saloon, drawing room, staterooms, baths, etc., also deluxe cabins with own sitting rooms and numerous extra large staterooms with private bathrooms. The main dining saloon, extending to the full width of the ship, occupying two decks' height below the promenade deck, was able to seat 600 passengers and had a high central domed roof and two ministrels' galleries. There were huge ornamental columns and rich decorations including large landscape paintings and motifs. An elegant smoking room, located around the funnel casing, was exquisitely decorated and had an ornamental fireplace. As in the other NDL liners, the Second Class was located aft and also featured superior accommodation with wood panelling, brass decor and coloured glass. Steerage quarters showed an improvement when compared with earlier liners, especially as there were fewer passengers to occupy the rather constricted space.

It was interesting to note that Second Class accommodation, as usual being placed aft, was most exposed to the thumping and vibration of the huge reciprocating engines and propeller shafting and presumably the travellers involved did not always enjoy record journeys.

Norddeutscher Lloyd record breaking liner Kaiser Wilhelm II *arriving at Bremerhaven.*

Norddeutscher Lloyd Express Liner Kaiser Wilhelm II.

Top: *First Class Deluxe Bedroom.*

Bottom: *First Class Dining Saloon.*

In April 1904 *Kaiser Wilhelm II* took the Blue Riband from *Kronprinz Wilhelm* by crossing westward at an average speed of 23.12 knots (Cherbourg to Sandy Hook in 5 days 12 hours 45 minutes) and kept this record until October 1907 when it was bettered by *Lusitania* of the Cunard Line.

Eastbound, in September 1906 *Kaiser Wilhelm II* improved upon the record held by *Deutschland* of HAPAG by averaging 23.57 knots between Sandy Hook and Eddystone (Plymouth) in 5 days 8 hours 17 minutes, thus holding the Blue Riband until October 1907 prior to relinquishing it, also to *Lusitania*.

Kaiser Wilhelm II stayed in regular Bremerhaven-Southampton-Cherbourg-New York service until 24th June 1914, finishing her last journey in New York, where she remained because of the threatening outbreak of war. With America joining in the hostilities in 1917, the liner was requisitioned by the US authorities for use as troop transport, in which capacity she covered a huge mileage. In 1917 *Kaiser Wilhelm II* was renamed *Agamemnon* for use by the United States authorities.

After the war *Agamemnon* was handed over to the United States Shipping Board for eventual commercial operation but because of the expense involved in prospective refurbishment, she was laid up in Chesapeake Bay, duly renamed *Monticello*. An offer of sale to the British authorities in 1940 was refused and the very dilapidated 37-year-old, highly uneconomical liner was sold for demolition.

Kronprinzessin Cecilie

In July 1907 the fourth and last of the Norddeutscher Lloyd four-stacker fleet, *Kronprinzessin Cecilie* of 19,360 tons and 707 ft overall length (689 ft b.p.) by 70 ft beam, also a prospective record breaker and equally luxurious sistership to *Kaiser Wilhelm II*, was put into service. The liner was also built by Vulcan Werke of Stettin and had identical powerplant and boilers to her sister.

Although this new luxury liner bettered the speeds of *Kaiser Wilhelm II* during the period 1907 to 1913, by crossing regularly at 23.4 to 23.7 knots, the Blue Riband was already held by the Cunard liners *Lusitania* and *Mauretania*. However, until the arrival of the two Cunard liners, *Kronprinzession Cecilie* had the honour of sharing the record with her sistership.

In company with the other three elegant Norddeutscher Lloyd record breakers, *Kronprinzessin Cecilie* maintained the regular express service between Bremerhaven and New York until the outbreak of war. On 14th July 1914, with clouds of war duly gathering, she happened to arrive in New York and on 28th July departed for Bremerhaven with a nearly full complement of passengers and an important cargo of gold and other bullion destined for European banks. On 31st July, when some four days out of New York, the Captain received a wireless message from the German Government, warning that war was due to be declared and ordering him to avoid capture by the Allied Navies at all costs by returning to the United States. The ship headed back at full speed through thick fog with all lights extinguished and portholes covered. Black bands were painted around funnel tops as a disguise, hoping that Allied warships may mistake the liner for the White Star *Olympic*, a liner twice the size of the fugitive! After a hair-raising journey and with coal running short, the liner finally reached anchorage at Bar Harbour, Maine, where passengers were disembarked and the bullion sent back to US banks – creating much financial consternation and problems.

The liner was escorted to Boston for internment and in 1917 requisitioned by the US Government for conversion as an armed troop transport, duly

Kronprinzessin Cecilie *entering New York harbour.*

equipped with various guns and renamed *Mount Vernon*.

Numerous Atlantic and Pacific crossings carrying vast numbers of troops followed and she was even torpedoed while in convoy in 1918. The liner limped into Brest and after temporary repairs returned to Boston for full restitution, after which she again resumed her duties transporting troops and refugees.

In 1920 *Mount Vernon* finally returned to Boston and was offered to the United States Mail SS Company for commercial service. Because of age, dilapidation and engine wear, the cost of refurbishment would have been prohibitive and the scheme fell through. The liner was again laid up in 1924 and subsequently offered to Britain in 1940 but this offer was emphatically refused and *Mount Vernon* was sold to shipbreakers.

Post World War I – Bremen and *Europa*

After the First World War the Atlantic service between Europe and the United States again became gradually populated by large surviving liners, duly refurbished after the rigours of wartime activities, and included such old hands as *Aquitania, Olympic* and the one and only *Mauretania* which still held the Blue Riband and after conversion to oil firing in 1922, managed to improve upon her pre-war speeds. There was also a vast array of all shapes and sizes of ex-German liners, ceded as war reparations to Allied shipping companies. Some new-built, medium sized steamers appeared on the picture with an eye on economical travel possibilities but the rest were elderly and quickly became functional liabilities.

It had taken Norddeutscher Lloyd and other German companies the best part of a decade to get over the virtually complete loss of merchant shipping; they then had a certain advantage over the Allies insofar as all newly built ships were modern whereas the competition were saddled with well worn and sometimes fairly antiquated ironmongery.

In the early twenties Norddeutscher Lloyd commissioned the 32,565 ton Atlantic liner *Columbus* (ex-*Hindenburg*) as well as a number of medium sized steamers and skillfully organised their trade routes and business activities to gain an important niche on the oceans of the world.

The post-war depression caused Atlantic passenger trade to decline but 'superliners' were being planned and built with considerable subsidies by different governments in order to maintain political prestige and to be able to compete for the developing profitable Atlantic trade on the basis of maximum operational economies.

Encouraged greatly by the German Government, Norddeutscher Lloyd decided that it was economically and prestige-wise feasible to complement the *Columbus* with a pair of larger 'super-luxury' liners to compete for the rebirth of the lucrative Atlantic routes. In 1928 the sisterships *Bremen* and *Europa*, designed for a speed of over 27 knots, were launched in order to bid for the Atlantic supremacy and the Blue Riband.

The liner *Bremen* of 51,656 GR tons was launched on 16th August 1928 at the shipyard A. G. Weser (later renamed 'Deschimag') in Bremen. The sistership *Europa* of 49,748 tons left the slipways of Blohm & Voss in Hamburg on the same date. The two liners differed only in comparatively minor technical details; both had seven decks and *Bremen* was 938.4 ft long overall whereas *Europa* was 940.7 ft; both had a 102 ft beam.

Both liners had quadruple screws driven through single reduction gearing by four 3-stage steam turbine sets, rated at 92,500 SHP for a cruising speed of 27.5 knots and a maximum of 28.5 knots. Although it might have been considered desirable to introduce as much similarity of machinery as possible, broadly speaking each liner's propulsion plant was greatly influenced by the design and opinions of the particular chief engineer employed by the respective shipbuilding firm, with *Europa* coming under the aegis of Dr Frahm of Blohm & Voss, and *Bremen* being championed by Dr Gustav Bauer of 'Deschimag'.

Although turbine drive, engine power, boiler pressure, degree of superheat, etc. were used as design criteria common to both liners, the *Bremen's* turbines were of the builder's own concept, featuring a three casing, three-pinion single reduction gearing per screw, whereas those of *Europa* were built under Parsons' licence with four sets of two-pinion single reduction per screw. The systems of transmitting speed from the four 3-stage (triple expansion) 3-casing turbines to the four screws, differed therefore for the two ships in some detail but achieved the same result in the end. There were also some variations in auxiliary machinery and its drives.

Each of the two liners' boiler plants was designed to generate approximately 500 tons of superheated steam per hour for propulsion and ancillaries at a pressure of 330 psi (23 kg/cm^2) and 350°C (660°F), but again boiler room layouts differed materially. *Bremen* employed 11 double-ended and 9 single-ended water-tube boilers, whereas *Europa* was provided with 24 double-ended water-tube boilers of similar design. Again, opinions of chief engineers in question, resulted in the introduction of different systems of stokehold and combustion air and in different ancillaries being provided. With all, the final desired positive results related to efficient steam generation and utilisation were not materially affected.

Europa – *One set of single reduction, 3-casing two-pinion geared turbines on test bed.*

Europa – *General view of the engine room showing two sets of turbines, engine room telegraphs, controls, etc.*

A novel development in hull design of both liners featured a bulbous bow intended to reduce water resistance at higher speeds. The clean-cut, low and streamlined shapes of the liners were crowned by two short squat funnels which conveyed the impression of speed but had to be lengthened by ca 15 feet after the initial journeys to reduce smut deposits on the promenade and other decks. The liners were also equipped with anti-rolling tanks, as designed by Dr Frahm of Blohm & Voss, in order to reduce excessive lateral movement in rough seas.

Bulbous bow of record breaker Europa *on the stocks at Blohm & Voss, Hamburg, ready for launching.*

Another novel feature on both liners was the provision of an aircraft catapult above the boat deck to facilitate the launching of a small 'Heinkel' seaplane whose duty it was to take off within flying distance from shore for express delivery of mail between Bremerhaven and New York. This postal delivery appeared to have been quite successful at the time but was later discontinued and did not reappear on other Atlantic liners, presumably because a reliable direct transatlantic airmail service had materialised in due course.

Passenger accommodation was similar on both ships, catering for 723 in the First Class, 600 in Tourist and 908 in Third classes. The splendidly appointed interiors, featuring modern, rectangular, clean-cut economy of line gave the impression of functional elegance and introduced new materials in plastics and synthetics, thus departing from the turn-of-the-century 'floating palaces'. The recently introduced 'Tourist Class' comprised a much improved version of the previous 'Second', offering facilities similar to those of First by catering for middle-class travellers. Third Class passengers experienced considerable improvements as compared with pre-war days, with functionally appointed cabins, good service and catering and a reasonable amount of space for recreation and other facilities.

Especially after the depression of the early thirties the two liners gave excellent, punctual and reliable service thus developing a splendid reputation with Atlantic travellers in all three classes.

Bremen

Bremen was the first of the pair to enter the Bremerhaven - Southampton - Cherbourg - New York service and on her maiden voyage starting on 16th July

Express liner Bremen.
First Class Dining Saloon.

Express liner Bremen.
First Class Lounge and Card Room.

1928 record breaking liner Bremen *arriving at New York following her maiden voyage in July 1929.*

1928 record breaking liner Europa *anchored in the Solent in the course of her maiden voyage from Bremerhaven to New York in March 1930.*

1929, she averaged 27.83 knots between Cherbourg and Ambrose Light in 4 days 17 hours 42 minutes, thereby taking the Blue Riband from the Cunarder *Mauretania*, whose last record achievement in September 1909 was to average 26.06 knots, also westbound. *Bremen* lost the Blue Riband to her sistership *Europa* in 1930 but regained it in 1933 at 28.51 knots and kept the record until August 1933, then losing it to the Italia liner *Rex*.

On the return leg of her maiden voyage in July 1929 *Bremen* consolidated the Blue Riband eastbound by averaging 27.95 knots between Ambrose Light and Cherbourg in 4 days 14 hours 30 minutes, again beating the *Mauretania* record set in August 1924. *Bremen's* eastward record was bettered by *Normandie* of Cie Gle Transatlantique in June 1935.

Bremen together with her sistership *Europa* and the *Columbus* maintained a regular transatlantic express service at around their cruising speeds of 26-27 knots, until 1939. At the outbreak of the war, *Bremen* was in New York and on 31st August 1939 escaped during the night, completely blacked out and without passengers, setting out on a course which could be considered quite adventurous, because she steamed over a roundabout route south of Newfoundland to avoid the possibility of meeting Allied warships and after six days arrived in Murmansk on the Berents Sea.

Bremen remained there until December 1939 and with the onset of suitably bad weather, her Captain, Herr Ahrens, risked to resume the journey home and although sighted by RN submarine *Salmon*, managed to give her the slip because of the submarine

Record breaking liner Bremen *at speed. (Extended funnels)*

commander's reluctance to sink the passenger liner. While at Bremerhaven, the elegant liner met its end. On 18th March 1941 a crew member harbouring a grudge, created a fire on board and *Bremen* was burnt out at the jetty with the hulk having to be demolished.

Europa

Europa was intended for delivery on the same date as the sistership *Bremen* but a major delay was caused by a fire on board at the finishing berth, on 26th March 1929. Consequently *Europa* did not depart on her maiden voyage until 19th March 1930, in the course of which she wrested the westward record from *Bremen* by averaging 27.92 knots and completing the journey between Cherbourg and Ambrose Light in 4 days 17 hours 6 minutes. In March 1933 *Europa* lost the record to her sistership *Bremen*.

At the outbreak of the Second World War, *Europa* was in her home port and was subsequently used as a Naval accommodation ship. In 1940 she was brought to Hamburg to be converted for the invasion of Britain but with the event not materialising she returned to Bremerhaven, where new plans for her conversion to an aircraft carrier duly fell through.

The end of the war saw *Europa* being requisitioned by the US Army to be converted as a troop transport 'P 177' and in June 1946 the Allied Reparations Agency ceded the liner to Cie Generale Transatlantique and duly renamed her *Liberte*. Shortly before the start of conversion for commercial service a violent gale hitting the harbour of Le Havre caused the *Liberte* to collide with the wreck of the old liner *Paris*, and badly damaged, she sank to the bottom of the harbour. After salvage on 15th April 1947, *Liberte* was transferred to St Nazaire to be rebuilt and fully overhauled at the Penhoet Yard, with the passenger capacity reduced to comply with French standards for all three classes. Her tonnage was increased to 51,839. A second major fire created further delay in conversion and finally, in 1951 the liner was commissioned on the Le Havre to New York run. In December 1961, with the new superliner *France* coming into service and a permanent reduction in the scope of Atlantic shipping, *Liberte* was withdrawn from service and sold to Italy for demolition.

Sequel:

After the Second World War German Shipping Companies evinced no further interest in Blue Riband records, with transatlantic services becoming related primarily to profitability. The few liners in operation offered excellent travel facilities at economical speeds until they were supplanted by air travel. *Bremen* and *Europa* were therefore the last German record breaking Atlantic liners and can be considered to have been a splendid testimonial to German maritime history.

Hamburg Amerikanische Packetfahrt A.G. (HAPAG) – Hamburg America Line

The Company

The Hamburg America Line or HAPAG, as it is better known, was founded in 1847 by a group of Hamburg merchants in order to operate a line of sailing vessels (or packets) between Hamburg and New York. Between 1848 and 1854 some six 400-600 ton sailing ships, mainly intended for the emigrant trade, were put into service. In 1853, at the instigation of the General Manager, Herr Adolph Godeffroy, it was decided to amplify the service with steamships and in 1854 the first vessels were ordered from Caird & Co. of Greenock and named *Hammonia* and *Borussia*.

The original steamers were profitably chartered for the carriage of troops during the Crimean War; the New York service was therefore postponed until 1856. Further steamers were ordered and the sailing ships, placed on Far East, Australia and Java routes, gradually phased out.

During 1856-70 the New York passenger steamer service via Southampton was consolidated and numerous new 3,000-4,000 ton steamers, also built by Cairds of Greenock, and with extensive accommodation for emigrants, were put into service. By 1872 cargo services to the West Indies and the Caribbean were operated.

In 1875 HAPAG reduced competition following a tariff-battle by acquiring the comparatively new Adler Line of steamers and disposing some of the older vessels. The more modern Adler steamers were operated profitably and carried large numbers of emigrants.

In 1886 amalgamation with the Carr Line which was in partnership with the Sloman-Union Line, introduced the dynamic Herr Albert Ballin into the company invited to become the HAPAG passenger manager. By 1888 Herr Ballin became the Chairman of the Board of Directors and 11 years later he was appointed General Manager. At the time Herr Ballin joined the company, HAPAG as shipowners, ranked 22nd in the world. His leadership brought the firm to the top of the league table.

During 1889-90 the first express passenger service from Hamburg to New York and Baltimore via Southampton was introduced with the 7,249 ton, 19 knot steamers *Columbia* and *Auguste Victoria* built in 1889 by Lairds of Birkenhead and Vulcan, Stettin, respectively. In 1890 there followed two 8,242 tonners, *Normannia* and *Fuerst Bismarck*, both capable of 20 knots. All these 'express' steamers were equipped with twin-screws driven by triple-expansion engines.

Subsequently, during 1890-1898, four medium speed, 12,500 ton passenger vessels, of the so-called 'P' class were introduced on the same service and they catered mainly for emigrants. Services to South America and the Far East were extensively developed and modern newbuilds commissioned.

By the turn of the century HAPAG was operating some 63 ocean-going ships, including large express passenger liners on the Atlantic run and on world-wide services, but never quite achieving the Blue Riband distinction. Due to the efficiency and genius of Albert Ballin, the company flourished and its world-wide engagements were only interrupted by the two World Wars.

By 1900, with HAPAG having become one of the world's most powerful shipowners, Ballin initiated the record breaking express liner, the company flagship *Deutschland* which became the largest liner of the most comprehensive fleet of merchant ships owned by any one company. *Deutschland*, having captured the Blue Riband, created splendid publicity for the company, but unfortunately became expensive to operate because it tended to be mechanically erratic, vibrated profusely and proved a commercial failure. This elegant and at the time much publicised 'white elephant' was the one and only Blue Riband holder of HAPAG.

In 1900 the company also introduced a new 4,000 ton cruising steam yacht *Prinzessin Viktoria Luise* as the latest addition to the recently initiated and most remunerative cruising service; further similar vessels followed within the scope of this sideline.

Also at the turn of the century, the South American service in conjunction with the Hamburg South American Steamship Company was consolidated. A further new venture was the shipment of fruit from the West Indies, for which new liners were built to operate together with the newly acquired Atlas Line of fruit carriers.

Between 1903 and 1909 large 16-18 knot newbuilds of 16,000 to 24,000 tons appeared on the Atlantic and these included the *Amerika* and *Kaiserin Auguste Victoria*, two 18 knot luxury liners of ca 24,000 tons. This was entirely in accordance with Herr Ballin's policy for the future of his passenger services to comprise large, well appointed, comfortable, medium speed vessels. The ultimate ambition to dominate the Atlantic, resulted by 1913-14 in such famous quadruple-screw, turbine driven, 23-24 knot luxury liners as the *Imperator* (52,117 tons), *Vaterland* (54,282 tons) and other great liners virtually monopolising transatlantic services. The third giant, *Bismarck* (56,551 tons), launched in 1914, was completed after acquisition for White Star Line following the First World War.

By the end of the First World War, HAPAG lost all its ships, with the exception of the elderly liner *Victoria Luise* the former record breaker *Deutschland*, but by 1920 resumed its Atlantic services with the co-operation of United American Lines, repurchase of ships and various newbuilds. In accordance with company policy, originating with Herr Ballin, HAPAG concentrated mainly upon North Atlantic 'bread and butter' services and around 1923 to 1925 commissioned four new, typically modest, 21,000-24,000 ton geared turbine driven, twin-screw liners of the 'Albert Ballin' and 'New York' class, capable of transporting across the Atlantic as large a number of passengers as possible with the utmost economy at 14-15 knots in an aura of 'poor relationship' to the greyhounds of the competition. The four steamers were later re-engined up to a more modern and realistic 17 knots, still leaving the prerogative of luxurious high speed to NDL.

Around 1925 the ocean-going fleet totalled 74 ships of ca 450,000 tons. During the 1930's slump HAPAG formed an agreement with the Norddeutscher Lloyd, pooling profits and sharing losses, but there was no amalgamation.

The Second World War saw again the loss of virtually all HAPAG passenger ships through hostilities and as reparations but by 1948 the German Government invested in the company and from 1950 onwards much rebuilding and reorganisation started taking place. In 1955 some 25 ships, including many medium sized diesel engined passenger and cargo liners were in service; by agreement with Norddeutscher Lloyd, transatlantic operation became more or less the prerogative of NDL.

During the late sixties' HAPAG concentrated on large cargo carriers and on the introduction in 1968 of such modern vessels as large container liners.

In 1971 full amalgamation with the Norddeutscher Lloyd was initiated with the formation of the combine 'HAPAG-LLOYD A.G.' Currently the HAPAG-LLOYD Company is the largest German shipping group with many diverging interests and partnerships.

The Record Breaker *Deutschland*

The 16,502 ton express liner *Deutschland*, 684 ft in overall length and 67 ft wide, was built in 1900 at the Vulcan Werke Shipyard of Stettin. She was a twin-screw vessel powered by two quadruple-expansion, 6-cylinder, 4-crank (tandem: MP_1, HP/LP, HP/LP, MP_2) steam engines capable of developing 37,800 IHP at 76 RPM with steam at 220 psi generated in 12 double-ended and 4 single-ended cylindrical (Scotch) boilers fed through 112 furnaces.

HAPAG Blue Riband liner Deutschland *of 1900.*

Deutschland, with her low sleek profile, was at the time, within scope of enthusiastic praises, compared with a greyhound. Her graceful long outline, crowned by four tall funnels in pairs, was not unlike that of contemporary liners being commissioned by Norddeutscher Lloyd, but then these were also built by Vulcan Werke.

Within the graceful 16,502 ton hull of the liner lodged the enormous engines and boiler plant as well as large storage bunkers for some 4,000 tons of coal and in addition, space was provided for a crew of 535 and some 1,750 passengers of which 450 in the First Class were housed amidships in grand luxury, 300 in the Second at the after end and some 1,000 were located in Steerage at the forward end. As in the case of similar liners at the turn of the century, the First Class facilities were of exceptional splendour, created to conquer the Atlantic with beautifully appointed suites, staterooms and cabins, ornate leisure rooms and a huge ostentatious dining saloon capable of seating 450, with an overall ceiling height through three decks, surmounted by a glass dome arising over the boat deck between the two groups of smoke stacks. The total uninterrupted length of the promenade deck was 520 ft. Second Class was also exceptionally well appointed and included a luxurious dining saloon at main deck level and other recreational rooms, all wood panelled and tastefully decorated. Even Steerage passengers were provided with dormitory-type cabins; it is difficult to imagine how 1,000 such travellers could qualify for any other than most elementary facilities for comfort and recreation in the accommodation available.

On her maiden voyage, leaving Hamburg on 4th July 1900, *Deutschland* covered the 3,044 nautical miles between Eddystone and Sandy Hook (New York) in 5 days 15 hours 46 minutes, averaging 22.42 knots and taking the Blue Riband from *Kaiser Wilhelm der Grosse*.

In the course of her return voyage to Hamburg, in July 1900 she completed the eastbound leg from Sandy Hook at 22.46 knots, thus achieving the Blue Riband double and again improving on the previous record of *Kaiser Wilhelm der Grosse*.

During the year following her westbound record, *Deutschland* improved upon her average speeds by small margins culminating with her best journey for the leg, in July 1901 achieving a mean of 23.06 knots. *Deutschland* lost the westbound record to *Kronprinz Wilhelm* in September 1902.

Eastward in August 1900 *Kaiser Wilhelm der Grosse* managed to regain the Blue Riband for one month but then, presumably with the schedules coinciding, the 4th September saw the start of an 'unofficial race', with *Kaiser Wilhelm* leaving New York for Europe at 12 noon and *Deutschland* clearing Sandy Hook at 1.15 pm of the same day and with both vessels sailing the Northern route. On the morning of the second day, *Deutschland* sighted the smoke of her rival, caught up and passed her by the evening. The total passage time of *Deutschland* from Sandy Hook to Plymouth (Eddystone), a total distance of 2,982 nautical miles, was 5 days 7 hours 15 minutes at an average of 23.36 knots. This improved upon her previous best for the leg by 4 hours 7 minutes and by winning this 'race' against her closest rival by 7 hours 40 minutes, *Deutschland* reclaimed the Blue Riband. Subsequently the HAPAG liner improved the eastbound average by stages and finally achieved a mean of 23.51 knots in July 1901. *Deutschland* kept this Blue Riband until September 1906 when the eastbound record was claimed by the newer and larger *Kaiser Wilhelm II* of the NDL.

Throughout her six-year spell as HAPAG's only Blue Riband holder, the liner was an erratic performer and at higher speeds suffered from excessive engine

Record breaker Deutschland *at speed.*

and propeller vibration to such an extent that with the assistance of a severe gale in April 1902 material fatigue caused her stern post to fracture with loss of the rudder. Limping home, the liner spent some six months at the Blohm & Voss yard for repairs and various adjustments, which did not improve matters, especially as the large reciprocating engines tended to be capricious.

During her early years *Deutschland* crossed the Atlantic at near enough her record speeds but after 1902, with passengers tending to view her rather uncomfortable journeys with a degree of pessimism and because the consort ships were quite a bit slower, her schedule speed was reduced to try and hit a happy medium, also introducing some fuel consumption economies.

In 1908/9 two new 16,000 ton medium speed liners were introduced on the Hamburg to New York service and this led to *Deutschland* being withdrawn from the run. In 1910 it was decided that the liner should join the cruise fleet of the company and she was placed with Blohm & Voss for re-engining with new 4-cylinder quadruple expansion engines to bring her speed down for economical operation and for refurbishment as a cruise liner offering First Class accommodation only. The hull was painted white and she was renamed *Victoria Luise*.

Between 1911 and 1914 a successful career included cruising and transatlantic journeys to New York, but at the outbreak of the war in 1914 she was laid up, not being considered suitable for conversion as a commerce raider. After the war *Victoria Luise* was not taken over by the Allies and remained Germany's only passenger liner. In 1920 *Victoria Luise* was again fully refurbished, lost two funnels and duly renamed *Hansa*, converted for emigrant service. By 1922 a

The T.S.S. Deutschland*: Drawing-room.*

The T.S.S. Deutschland*: Dining Saloon.*

further refitting followed and new accommodation catering for 200 Cabin and 665 Third Class created to suit a new service between Hamburg and Canada. *Victoria Luise* was laid up in 1924 and sold to shipbreakers in 1925.

Deutschland: *Corner of Smoke Room.*

Deutschland: *De-luxe Suite, private Dining Room.*

Record liner Deutschland *in the refurbished guise of 1920-21, renamed* Hansa.

Cunard Line after the Turn of the Century

The Company

FROM 1893 ONWARDS, CUNARD had an unbeaten four-and-a-half year spell of Blue Riband custody, but then between 1898 and 1907 there was a monopoly by German record breaking liners. During that period Cunard, having taken delivery of numerous medium-speed 'bread-and-butter' ships of 7,000-14,000 tons, concentrated on making best use of its reputation to consolidate various services and upon developing other routes, such as the Boston run and the Mediterranean as well as the carriage of emigrants, thus improving profitability with increasing sizes and quality of its ships.

During the Boer War many Cunard liners were taken over by the Government for the transport of troops but in 1903, at the time of J. P. Morgan acquiring many transatlantic operators, including the White Star Line, a new agreement was concluded with the British Government for Cunard to keep out of the American 'International Maritime Marine Company' thus remaining British owned. Major loans and subsidies were subscribed for construction of new prestigious record breaking super-liners, which would also be suitable for conversion to Admiralty requirements in case of war.

On the strength of Government backing to replace some ageing tonnage and to offer competition on equal terms to the newest large White Star and HAPAG liners appearing on the Atlantic, Cunard Line commissioned in 1905 two 20,000 ton sisterships *Caronia* and *Carmania*, designed for 18 knots. They had the distinction of being equipped with different power plants in order to act as test ships to prove the efficiency of the new propulsion method by means of steam turbine for major liners, thus confirming the excellent experience of the Allan Line with their 1903 built, 10,700 ton, triple-screw, 18 knot liners *Victorian* and *Virginian* on the Canadian run.

Caronia had twin-screws powered by quadruple-expansion piston engines whereas *Carmania* had three Parsons direct-drive turbines connected to three screws. Experience showed that *Carmania* offered some speed and economy advantages and Cunard therefore decided to opt for turbine drive for the two new Government sponsored super-liners, named *Lusitania* and *Mauretania*, put into service in July 1907 and November 1907 respectively. The *Lusitania* of 31,550 tons was built by John Brown & Company of Clydebank and the 31,937 ton *Mauretania* originated at the yard of Swan Hunter & Wigham Richardson of Newcastle. The two liners, at the time by far the largest in the world, were virtually sisterships and proved to be the most famous Blue Riband holders of all time.

By 1911, two 18,000 ton, 16 knot, comfortably appointed 'intermediate' liners *Franconia* and *Laconia* replaced some aged tonnage to provide improved services via Boston and, as a novel feature for Cunard, were also used for cruising. The pair were the last reciprocating-engined Atlantic mail liners built for Cunard.

To cope with the Atlantic competition introducing ever increasing sizes of passenger carriers on the New York run, Cunard launched in 1913 the 45,646 ton *Aquitania*, a luxurious liner driven by four screws directly connected to turbines. This 24 knot steamship, with no Blue Riband ambitions, served as a running mate to the two record breakers, *Lusitania* and *Mauretania*.

1911-1914 saw a series of medium-speed 'intermediate' liners materialising for the Boston and Canadian services, but during the First World War most of this new tonnage, including the record breaker *Lusitania*, as well as numerous cargo ships, in all totalling 22 vessels were lost through enemy action.

During the early post-war years, Cunard operated the Southampton-Cherbourg-New York service with the *Aquitania*, the record breaker *Mauretania* and the ex-German *Berengaria* (former *Imperator*) which was ceded to Cunard as reparations for the loss of *Lusitania*.

Between 1921 and 1925 Cunard Line also took delivery of 13 large new 'intermediate liners of 13,000 to 20,000 tons, designed for economic service speeds of 16 to 20 knots, to operate on routes from Liverpool to New York via Boston and from Southampton to Quebec and Montreal. During the thirties most of the larger new vessels were also engaged in cruising.

In 1929 Cunard Line started planning two giant express liners to replace the aged trio on the prestigious Southampton to New York route and to create a two-ship weekly service. In December 1930 the keel of the 80,000 ton 'No. 534' (*Queen Mary*) was laid at John Brown's Shipyard of Clydebank. All work stopped in 1931 because shipping was greatly affected by the depression.

In 1933-34 the Government advanced funds to Cunard and this help, which included the completion of *Queen Mary*, was conditional to the Cunard merger with the White Star Line, a company much suffering from duplication of many services since its acquisition from Morgan's IMMC by the Royal Mail S. N. Company just before the depression. Cunard took over the White Star ships but some of the fairly new tonnage had to be disposed of. The joint-company's new name became 'Cunard-White Star Ltd'.

The liner 'No. 534' was finally launched in September 1934 and named *Queen Mary* by the Queen Consort. She was completed during the next two years, sailed on her maiden voyage to New York on 27th May 1936 and captured the Blue Riband in August of the same year. *Queen Mary* as a concept, was designed as a traditionally robust liner with no attempt being made to emulate the German, French or Italian modernistic endeavours to create dashing artistry in the execution of hull and superstructure. Her overall shape, not unlike that of an enlarged *Aquitania*, would not have been out of place in the 1920's and to most travellers she could well have been the epitome of old fashioned conservatism and reliability. With all, *Queen Mary* justified her owners' optimism and she became a great favourite with her passengers whose numbers increased greatly after the slump in the thirties and by 1935 she became one of the few post-1930 liners capable of paying their way.

With a gross tonnage of 81,237 and an overall length of 1,019 ft by 118 ft beam, *Queen Mary* was only 10 ft shorter than the world's longest, the *Normandie*, which was commissioned in May 1935.

Mauretania, *November 1907 on the slipways at Swan Hunter and Wigham Richardson of Newcastle. Ready for launch.*

Cunard liners Lusitania *and* Mauretania.

*Liner No. 534 (*Queen Mary*) on the slipways at John Brown & Company Ltd, shortly before launch in 1934.*

Cunard record breaking liner Queen Mary *at speed.*

Laid down in 1936 as consort to *Queen Mary* and as flagship of the Cunard fleet, giant liner *Queen Elizabeth* was launched on 27th September 1938 at John Brown's Shipyard of Clydebank. Although this superliner of 83,673 tons and 1,029 ft in length (qualifying as the world's largest passenger liner) had a designed service speed of 29 knots, possibly also being meant to be a record breaker, the Second World War interrupted her final completion and she took refuge in New York. Together with all new and old Cunard steamships, the *Queen Elizabeth* subsequently served as a troopship.

Earlier, in May 1939, the second *Mauretania* of 35,739 tons, was completed. Although a 23 knot ship, she was intended to act as a stand-in with the two *Queens* but she was also due to operate as running-mate to the last White Star liners, the motor-ships *Britannic* and *Georgic*. After a few voyages to New York, the outbreak of war saw *Mauretania* (2) laid up in New York prior to conversion for trooping.

During the Second World War all Atlantic liners covered enormous distances worldwide, transporting vast numbers of troops and great quantities of equipment and stores. At the outbreak of hostilities Cunard-White Star owned 18 passenger liners of 434,698 GR tons and by 1945 nearly 2.5 million troops were shipped. The end of the war saw Cunard-White Star with some nine liners left for commercial use and they totalled 345,900 tons. Among ships lost through enemy action were six of the 'intermediate' liners built in the twenties; others returned to company service but some were then ready for early demolition and replacement by new tonnage. Even the 1914 built 45,600 ton *Aquitania*, due to have been taken out of service in 1940, was retained as troop transport throughout the war and upon being returned to Cunard-White Star in 1948, experienced Canadian service until December 1949 and was then sold for demolition in 1950.

In 1947 the Cunard Company acquired the remaining shares of the Oceanic Steam Navigation Company (White Star Line) and by 1949 Cunard assumed full control. 'Cunard-White Star Ltd' thus became simply 'Cunard Line'.

The post-war reconstruction programme included the 1948 purpose-built 34,300 ton liner *Caronia* (2) which was a success at the time but in the course of Cunard rationalisation programme was sold in 1968. Other 13,000 to 22,000 ton liners, capable of 20-22 knots were built in the fifties for Canadian and North American trade and having experienced conversions for cruising during 1963, subsequently spent half their lives transporting tourists between New York and the West Indies. These liners were gradually disposed of during the early seventies mainly in the course of economical rationalisation at the time of the oil crisis.

After 1957 the rapid development of air travel with consequent loss in passenger shipping revenue, decided Cunard to take an interest in aviation and in 1959 the company acquired an interest in the independent airline Eagle Airways. In order to combine sea and air travel, Cunard invested in 1962 to form BOAC-Cunard Ltd, which became quite profitable. However by 1966 financial resources became so strained that the company had to realise its investments in air travel, not without profit.

With the aged *Queen Mary, Queen Elizabeth* and *Mauretania* (2) having to be disposed of in 1966-1968 because of ever growing losses in revenue during the sixties, the present flagship of the company fleet, the *Queen Elizabeth II* was put into service in 1969.

Queen Mary was sold to the City of Long Beach in 1967 and is still in use as a hotel/conference centre. *Queen Elizabeth* was sold to C. Y. Tung of Hong Kong to be converted as a University. During the conversion she was burnt out and scrapped. *Mauretania* (2) was withdrawn from service in 1965 and sold for demolition.

The new liner *Queen Elizabeth II* of 67,139 tons was built by John Brown & Company of Clydebank (Upper Clyde Shipbuilders), launched in 1967 and commissioned in May 1969. This liner was designed specifically for cruising but was also intended to maintain the Atlantic service between Southampton and New York in the summer. After some major and minor teething troubles, *Queen Elizabeth II* settled down to her schedules and became a successful member of the Cunard fleet.

The Cunard company always maintained profitable cargo services, especially since taking over control of such major cargo carriers as T. & J. Brocklebank and the Port Line, running profitable routes to the Far East, Australia and the North American east coast. At peak times cargo shipping accounted for some 50% of the company's operational income and by 1960 ca 60 cargo carriers were operated by Cunard worldwide.

Financial problems related to cargo services arose in the early sixties, mainly caused by rapid development of containerisation which made the most modern and advanced cargo ships virtually obsolete, although tanker and product transportation did not quite feel the pinch. Cunard introduced container ships rather later than other operators and joined two consortia of shipowners working giant container liners with the capacity and ability to handle cargoes far beyond the scope of conventional cargo carriers.

In company with the rest of the shipping world, by 1970 the Cunard financial position became precarious and in August 1971 the concern was taken over by the Trafalgar House Investments Ltd, this acquisition proving of great benefit to both parties. The company's passenger services became organised primarily for cruising with four new purpose-built liners coming into operation to complement the prestigious *Queen Elizabeth II* and by 1983 two Norwegian luxury liners, *Vistafjord* and *Sagafjord* were acquired, together with their owners' interests.

Reference must be made to the fact that Cunard Line contributed four ships to the Falklands campaign in 1982 and these included *Queen Elizabeth II* as flagship of the trooping fleet. It was a great tragedy that one of the ships, the *Atlantic Conveyor* was sunk with the loss of 12 lives, as a result of enemy action.

During the mid-eighties Cunard decided to greatly extend the life expectancy of *Queen Elizabeth II* by major refurbishment and in October 1986 the 19-year-old flagship arrived at the Lloyd-Werft of Bremerhaven to undergo extensive modernisation and complete re-engining; this work was completed (tongue-in-cheek) in April 1987.

Machinery renovation included the complete replacement of the original 120,000 SHP turbine geared propulsion plant by a diesel/electric drive, in the course of which the 66ft funnel was removed, exposing the 4,000 m^2 engine room, where turbines and boilers complete with all auxiliaries were demolished for scrap and lifted out by an offshore crane creating more than enough space for the new installation.

The new propulsion machinery comprises nine diesel engined alternator sets, each rated at 10,620 kW (14,445 HP_m) and driven by nine 4-cycle trunk-piston MAN/Burmeister & Wain engines at 400 RPM. The alternator sets are electrically connected through 10,000 V, 60 Hz switchgear to two 6,500 HP_m electronic synchronous driving motors (voltage transformed to 3,300 V), coupled to two new 84 ton, 5.8 m diameter five-bladed controllable-pitch propellers turning at a maximum of 144 RPM. These propellers replaced the original six-bladed fixed pitch screws. The new powerplant installation is rated at 130,000 SHP for a designed ship's speed of 32.5 knots.

The propellers were experimentally provided with, so called, 'Grim guide-wheels' (diffusers) mounted at the rear of the propellers. The 6.7 m diameter, seven-vane guide wheels, possibly based upon results of wartime research for the Kriegsmarine, are supposed to intercept energy developed by the propeller slipstream turbulence, in order to convert it into additional propulsive effect, thus achieving worthwhile fuel savings. It appears that the Grim wheels disintegrated during the ship's maiden voyage and the anticipated benefits did not materialise.

The operation of the new diesel/electric propulsion was specified for full automation and classified for unmanned machinery room.

It was estimated that compared with the original steam turbine machinery, overall operating costs would be halved thus amortising the new plant inside 4-5 years.

Refurbishment included much upgrading of all accommodation and new public rooms for passengers and crew, increased passenger capacity and provision of additional shops and recreation centres.

Nowadays the Cunard Line is still one of the world's most notable shipping concerns, possibly not in a manner originally envisaged, having become a leading operator of cruise liners, with considerable interest in container as well as other shipping and, by connection with the parent company Trafalgar House, also in hotels and similar facilities worldwide.

Queen Elizabeth II *leaving Bremerhaven after refurbishment in 1987.*

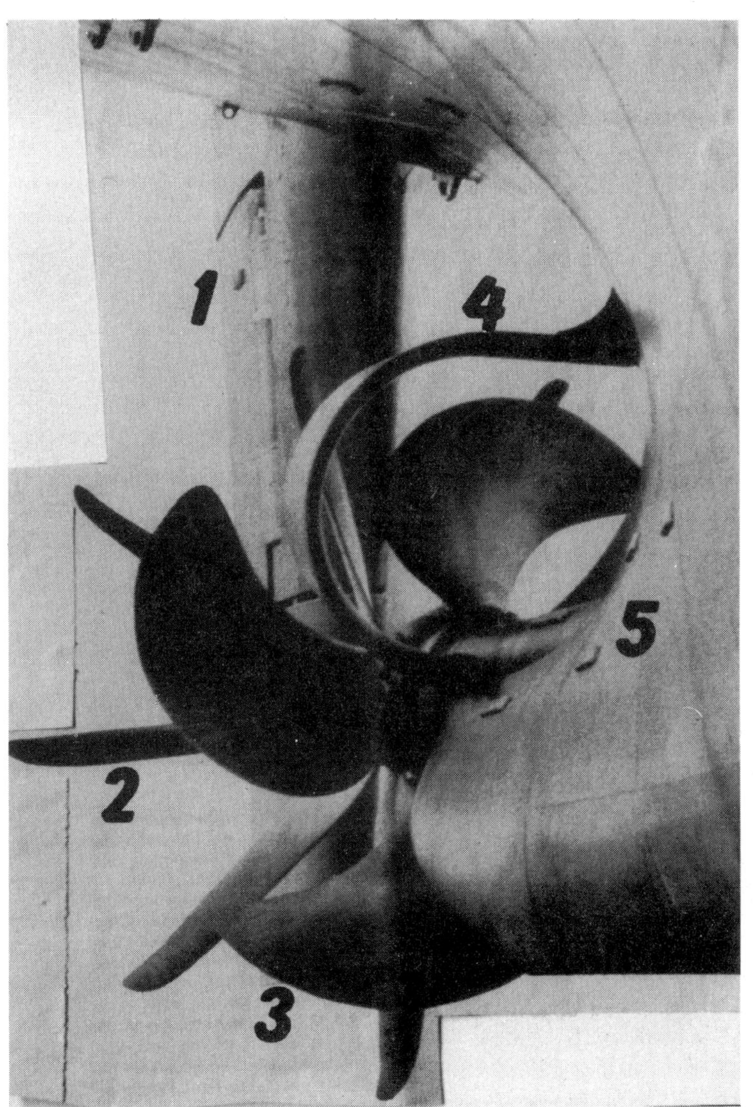

Grim Guide Vanes and other Economy Measures

Illustration depicts a typical application of a nine-bladed free-wheeling guide vane wheel as developed by Dr Grim in order to improve efficiency of propulsion and fuel savings, (2).

Other modern rear-end 'goodies' shown around the rudder (1), but not applicable to the QE2, *include an overall assymetrical design of the ship's stern as developed by Noennecke for the variable pitch propeller (3) and a Schneekluth 'mini-Kort' nozzle (4) aimed at a part of the propeller, or as an alternative to the nozzle, a series of special small spoilers as designed by Grothues-Spork, (not shown here) can be introduced forward of the propeller at (5). Their purpose would be to guide the flow upwards to the upper part of the propeller plane.*

All these designs and appendages have been claimed to reduce water resistance, improve fuel consumption and abolish vibration. Many early developments were carried out by the Naval Research Establishments during the war and at the Hamburg Test Tank. The fuel crises of the seventies greatly accelerated this work and it would appear that many positive results have been obtained with consequent worthwhile propulsive advantages related to long and short-haul ships.

Much as these developments have been encouraged by numerous satisfied customers, unfortunately this cannot be said to apply to the seven-bladed Grim wheels of the Queen Elizabeth II, *as they disappeared without trace fairly early in life.*

Cunard Record Breakers of the 20th Century

Express Liners *Lusitania* and *Mauretania* of 1907

The two liners were the first to introduce propulsion by four screws directly coupled to four Parsons turbines. Two eight-stage high-pressure machines contained in 8ft-0in diameter housings drove the wing shafts and the two eight-stage, tandem low-pressure units, located in 11 ft-8 in casings operated the two inboard shafts. A total of 68,000 SHP could be developed and with the propellers rotated at 180 RPM (190 RPM max) the designed service speed of 25 knots was achieved. It is noteworthy that two separately housed astern turbines were supplied with high pressure steam and were so located as to transmit astern power to inboard propellers through the low pressure turbine drive shafting.

Steam at a maximum pressure of 195 psi was developed in 23 double-ended and two single-ended cylindrical smoke-tube (Scotch) boilers equipped with the Howden system of air pre-heating and experience showed that overall coal consumption worked out at ca 800 to 1,000 tons daily.

The pioneering system of propulsion by turbines with direct drive to quadruple screws at up to 190 RPM needless to say gave rise to some teething troubles. Although engine throb and vibration as created by large reciprocating engines of the past, were obviated by the smooth rotary motion of the new source of power, the high peripheral speed of turbines around 9,500 ft per minute transferred directly to the four propellers, appeared to invoke critical rotational velocities related to particular propeller design. The phenomenon of 'cavitation', not fully appreciated at the time and researched by fairly basic methods, was caused by the speed of revolution of the propeller creating a frontal vacuum into which water entered forcibly, hammering at the propeller blade surfaces with frequency of impulses increasing with speed of rotation. The resulting after-end vibration could become so high that it could be felt throughout the ship, especially at maximum speeds and possibly at certain critical velocities of rotation.

Some improvement was achieved by strengthening the aft-end frames but credit to builders is due for introduction of a reasonable degree of acceptability with redesigned one-piece four-bladed propellers, as fitted in 1909, when the maximum speed of the steamers also increased to around 26 knots. Presumably complete relief from vibration may have been achieved by introduction of present-day technology, such as reduction gearing or variable pitch propellers.

Passenger accommodation was given particular attention in view of the fact that Cunard ships of the 19th century had the reputation of not being up to luxury standards offered by White Star and German liners as well as other rivals. Although the two liners could well be considered sisterships, there were notable external distinguishing variations and their interior decoration was executed by two different architects, representing their particular individualistic approach. Decoration of public rooms on the *Lusitania* was undertaken by James Millar, who was originally involved at the Glasgow Exhibition of 1901 and Harold Peto, well known for his work on interior decoration of country houses, was commissioned to include *Mauretania* on his decor programme.

First Class accommodation for 563 travellers on a scale of comfort and elegance not experienced on earlier Cunarders, included dining saloons built through two decks with domed galleries as well as other lofty public rooms featuring treatment of decor based upon currently most fashionable periods represented by French and Italian period styles of Renaissance and Rococo elegance with the highest

Lusitania *at the Liverpool jetty.*

quality embellishments, finishes and reproduction furnishings, yet completely avoiding ostentatiousness. There were grand staircases, lifts and expansive promenade decks. Special regal suites included private dining rooms, drawing rooms, bedrooms and bathrooms. Staterooms and cabins were equipped with beds and had facilities and decorations of the highest order.

Second Class catering for 460 and located partly aft, also featured rather simpler period decor in a variety of woods, with lofty and elegant public rooms as well as spacious, comfortably appointed cabins of which 34 had two berths and 99 were the four-berth variety.

Third Class, capable of accommodating 1,138 passengers and located on various decks forward, offered rather more utilitarian but comfortable public rooms finished in polished wood and included a dining saloon seating 520. The 31 two-berth and 540 four to eight-berth cabins were rather sparse and not unduly roomy.

The two record breaking liners represented a completely new phase in the quality of Atlantic travel commensurate with size and speed of steamship and virtually pioneered the marine steam turbine for long-haul liners at economically high speeds.

Lusitania

The 31,550 ton *Lusitania*, put into service in July 1907, was at the time the world's largest liner. She took the Blue Riband in both directions from *Kaiser Wilhelm II* in October 1907 by crossing from Daunts Rock to Ambrose Lightship at an average of 23.99 knots in 4 days 19 hours 52 minutes and this was the first ever Atlantic crossing in under 5 days. It must however be admitted that the *Kaiser Wilhelm II* record counted from Cherbourg, a nearly 300 miles longer journey.

The return eastbound leg, on 19th October 1907 averaged 23.61 knots in 4 days 22 hours 53 minutes but this new record was valid only until November 1907, when it was improved upon by the sistership *Mauretania. Lusitania's* westbound record stood until May 1908, it was then bettered by *Mauretania* but in the same year *Lusitania* regained the Blue Riband at 25.01 knots and she further improved upon this speed in August 1908, by crossing the 2,890 miles from Daunts Rock to Sandy Hook in 4 days 16 hours 40 minutes, averaging 25.65 knots. *Lusitania* finally lost the westward Blue Riband to *Mauretania* in September 1909.

When the war broke out on 4th August 1914, *Lusitania* was in New York, from where she slipped out on 5th August and after taking a circuitous route, managed to make Liverpool by 14th August. The liner was not taken over by the Admiralty because of her high fuel consumption and remained on a monthly run to New York. On 7th May 1915, on her way from New York, *Lusitania* was torpedoed without warning by a U20 off Old Head of Kinsale. The liner sank in 40 minutes with the loss of 1,198 lives. This sinking of a defenceless passenger liner created much anger in Britain and with more than 100 Americans among those who lost their lives, became a factor influencing America to enter the First World War. At the time of the sinking Germany had not declared unrestricted submarine warfare.

Royal Mail steamer Lusitania *– 1907.*

Lusitania – *First Class Suite.*

Lusitania – *Lounge and Music Room.*

Mauretania

The 31,938 ton *Mauretania* was also commissioned in 1907 and during her acceptance trials in November achieved 26.03 knots and 26.75 knots over the measured mile at Skelmorlie. She sailed on her maiden voyage to New York on 16th November 1907 but because of stormy conditions just missed topping the Blue Riband record of her sistership *Lusitania*. On her return journey on 5th December 1907, she made her first record breaking eastbound crossing from Sandy Hook to Queenstown in 4 days 22 hours 33 minutes, averaging 23.69 knots, thus capturing the Blue Riband from her sistership. In January 1908 *Mauretania* improved upon her eastbound record with a mean of 23.9 knots and in March 1908 she achieved 24.42 knots.

Late in 1908 *Mauretania* engines were overhauled and new redesigned propellers fitted, with the result that in February 1909 she crossed from Ambrose to Queenstown in 4 days 20 hours 27 minutes at an average of 25.16 knots. In the course of some 3-4 record breaking journeys in 1909, *Mauretania* improved her eastbound crossing times and in June 1909 the best achieved average was 25.88 knots.

Westbound, between Daunts Rock and Ambrose, in May 1908 *Mauretania* had the satisfaction of beating her sistership's record with a mean of 24.86 knots over a 100 miles longer route in 4 days 20 hours 15 minutes, but this achievement was bettered by *Lusitania* in July of the same year. However, in September 1909 *Mauretania* finally wrested the westbound Blue Riband from *Lusitania* by covering the 2,785 miles from Daunts Rock to Sandy Hook in 4 days 10 hours 50 minutes at an average of 26.06 knots. This was only bettered by NDL liner *Bremen* in 1929.

The classic lines of Mauretania *the most famous of all Atlantic liners. Holder of Blue Riband 1909 to 1929.*

Mauretania in Southampton.

The outbreak of war saw *Mauretania* on her way to New York and after returning to Liverpool she made three more Atlantic crossings prior to being laid up until 1915. Instead of being converted as an armed merchant cruiser, *Mauretania* became a troopship and later a hospital ship. In 1916 again a period of trooping followed until she was handed back to the Cunard Line in 1919 and after a suitable refurbishment returned to the New York run with Southampton as her home port. After a major fire on 25th July 1921 in Southampton, the liner was docked and experienced an engine refit in the course of which the boilers were converted to oil firing. Her engine room staff was duly reduced by some 300 stokers and trimmers with consequent major operational savings.

After 1923 *Mauretania* resumed the service between Southampton and New York but was also used for cruising during the winter months. In August 1924 the elderly liner improved upon her previous record crossings by averaging 26.16 knots between Ambrose and Cherbourg and this achievement remained valid for the Blue Riband until July 1929 when the new German liner *Bremen* of NDL took over the honour.

It must be mentioned that the Captain of the *Mauretania* had one last fling in August 1929, averaging 27.22 knots between Ambrose and Eddystone but this speed achieved by the 22-year-old warhorse was still 0.7 knots short of the record set by the super-liner *Bremen*.

Mauretania
Top: *First Class Dining Room.*

Bottom: *First Class Lounge/Music Room.*

After her war service, *Mauretania* in company with the aged *Aquitania* and the ex-German *Berengaria* maintained the Southampton-Cherbourg-New York service, crossing regularly at around 26 knots interspersed with winter cruising. By 1931 her accommodation was modified and refurbished; with her hull painted white *Mauretania* spent most of her subsequent career cruising in the West Indies, with occasional Atlantic journeys during peak periods.

On 26th September 1934 *Mauretania* embarked upon her last transatlantic voyage from New York to Southampton where she was withdrawn from service and sold on 2nd April 1935 to Metal Industries; she departed in July 1935 for Rosythe to be scrapped.

Queen Mary

At the time of her commissioning in 1936, the express mail liner *Queen Mary*, with a gross tonnage of 81,237, an overall length of 1,019 ft and 118 ft beam, was the world's second largest liner, the 1,028 ft long *Normandie* having a gross tonnage of 83,423 thus qualifying for the top position.

Queen Mary was powered by four Parsons impulse/reaction single reduction geared turbine sets driving four screws. Each turbine set comprised one high pressure, two intermediate and one low pressure turbines in series, with each turbine driving a separate gear pinion engaging the main gear wheel of the single reduction gearing coupled to its particular propeller. There were two main engine rooms and two of the four geared turbine sets were located in the forward engine room to drive the wing propellers whereas the inboard screws were connected to the other two geared turbine sets in the aft engine room.

Each turbine set was designed for a service output of 39,500 SHP to each propeller, thus aggregating

Queen Mary *in Southampton.*

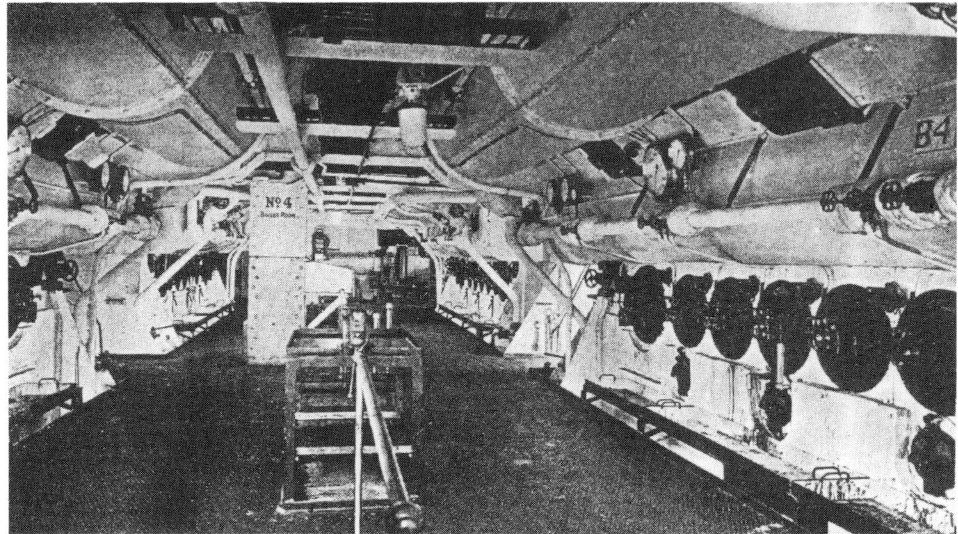

Queen Mary *No. 4 Boiler Room. The water-tube boilers are arranged for firing in fore and aft directions.*

158,000 SHP to achieve a service speed of 29 knots under favourable conditions but the powerplant had ample reserve to ensure economical operation or maintain speeds in the region of 30-31 knots.

Steam for propulsion was generated in 24 five-drum water-tube boilers built by Messrs John Brown & Company under licence from Yarrows and designed to produce superheated steam at 350 psi (400 psi max.) (24.6 AtU and 28 AtU) with a superheat temperature of 700°F (370°C) max.; this steam condition could in no way be considered a strain on the technology of the period. The 24 main boilers were installed in four boiler rooms, grouped in three rows with two boilers per row in each boiler room. A pressurised stokehold draft method was employed.

In addition there was an auxiliary boiler room containing three double-ended 'Scotch' smoke-tube cylindrical boilers to provide superheated steam at 250 psi and 200°F to turbo-generators and saturated steam for other ship's services.

All power plant and auxiliaries were installed in 10 watertight compartments and the total fuel bunkerage capacity amounting to roughly 8,000 tons, was contained in cellular double bottom and wing tanks.

The maiden voyage and subsequent crossings indicated a considerable propensity for the ship to roll in very heavy seas, but by 1937 various modifications lessened the trouble which was finally greatly reduced by the fitting of Denny stabilisers in 1953.

Accommodation for 776 First (Cabin), 784 Tourist (Second) and 579 Third Class passengers was originally provided. Comparing with earlier Cunarders, it appeared that considerable effort was made to improve the Second and Tourist Classes, the latter completely replacing the traditional Third Class in 1947.

Queen Mary: *Forward Engine Room – Telegraphs and indicators on Control Platform. One of the Anemostat air-ventilating ducts is shown at the front.*

Queen Mary: *The After Engine Room – Looking aft.*

Overall the effect of decor showed a complete departure from the 'Pseudo-Versailles' and 'Ersatz-Potsdam' early 20th century syndrome. An attempt was made to provide a spaciously elegant and functional style and to cater for maximum traveller comfort. Depending upon reactions by particular critics, the decor was described as a garish mixture of modern styles with a touch of art-nouveau or just plain functionally modern spacious elegance. But then, to paraphrase Abe Lincoln: 'One cannot please all of the people all of the time . . . etc.'.

Whichever way one reacts to the modernistic elegance and decoration by use of many original paintings and wood veneer panelling in vast saloons, public rooms, galleries, bars, swimming pools, etc., as well as the spacious, well equipped staterooms and cabins in all classes, the utmost comfort and excellent service in pleasant surroundings made the *Queen*

Cabin Class Special Suite.

Two-berth Third Class Cabin.

Queen Mary:
Cabin Class – Restaurant.

Queen Mary:
Third Class – Dining Room.

Queen Mary *at speed.*

Mary a great favourite with her passengers and crew. This was confirmed by the fact that throughout her transatlantic career she was one of the very few express liners to pay her way handsomely and to prove a worthwhile investment for her owners.

Following her maiden voyage in May 1936 and a few subsequent round trips *Queen Mary* embarked upon her record breaking, starting with her sixth voyage.

In August 1936 *Queen Mary* crossed westward from Bishops Rock to Ambrose (New York) in 4 days 27 minutes at an average of 30.14 knots, divesting the CGT liner *Normandie* of the Blue Riband. In July 1937 *Normandie* improved upon this record but in August 1938 the Cunarder regained the Blue Riband by steaming from Bishops Rock to Ambrose in 3 days 21 hours 48 minutes, at 30.99 knots and retained the honour until July 1952, when the ultimate record was achieved by *United States.*

Eastbound in August 1936, *Queen Mary* captured the Blue Riband record from *Normandie* by crossing in 3 days 23 hours 57 minutes, at an average of 30.63 knots. This was the first time the journey from New York to Bishops Rock was made in under 4 days. *Normandie* managed to better this record in March and August 1937 but *Queen Mary* clinched the Blue Riband in August 1938 with a mean of 31.69 knots and this record also remained valid until July 1952 when the Blue Riband was gained by *United States.*

At the declaration of war on 4th September 1939, *Queen Mary* was on her way from Southampton, only a few hours out of New York, where she was then laid up until March 1940 and then commissioned to be prepared for wartime duties. The liner made her way to

Australia for conversion as a troop transport and there she was joined by the new *Queen Elizabeth*, *Mauretania* (2) and numerous other liners. Duly converted, the two *Queens* operated a shuttle service from 1940 onward, carrying Australian troops to the Middle East.

Following Pearl Harbour the *Queens* returned to New York to be refitted for American forces, with their capacity utilised to enable each liner to carry up to 15,000 troops on each journey at a speed of some 30 knots.

The two *Queens* spent the rest of the war trooping mostly on the North American run and much as the German U-boat captains hoped to make use of their torpedoes, the speed of the two liners was such that outside convoys they were able to survive unscathed, with the *Queen Mary* achieving 28 two-way Atlantic journeys and the *Queen Elizabeth* some 34, carrying 869,694 troops eastwards and 213,000 back to the USA; in addition both liners had special reserved accommodation used by such VIP's as Winston Churchill, for journeys across the Atlantic to attend conferences related to pursuance of the war. In October 1942 *Queen Mary* had the misfortune to ram and sink the RN cruiser *Curacao* with considerable loss of life among the cruiser's seamen. The liner suffered some damage to her bows but had to carry on at full speed.

In September 1946 *Queen Mary* was returned to Cunard-White Star Line and together with *Queen Elizabeth* released by the Government in March 1946, was returned to John Brown's Shipyard for a complete overhaul and refurbishment of all luxury in order to initiate in 1947 the two-ship weekly Southampton to New York service. During the next 10 years' peak in transatlantic travel the two super-liners sailed virtually fully booked, thus creating substantial profits and carrying the elitist cream of all rich and famous. Even the catering, amply provided from American sources to counteract British shortages and rationing, became famous the world over.

However, after 1957 the rapid development of Atlantic air travel, especially with the introduction of jet-propulsion, made Cunard realise that the days of Atlantic travel by sea were becoming numbered with the consequent rapidly diminishing financial returns and a major rationalisation of the passenger fleet was indicated. By 1963 it was decided that the ageing *Queens* need to be replaced by new-look tonnage mainly intended for cruising but also able to maintain an Atlantic service tailored to the requirements of the period. After 1963 *Queen Mary* was adapted for summer cruising, but not being equipped for long journeys in hot climates, she was not a great success.

In 1967 the liner was sold to the City of Long Beach, California, to be converted into a floating restaurant, conference centre and museum.

On 27th September 1967, having completed her 1,000th voyage the liner arrived at Southampton and on 31st October she sailed for Long Beach via Cape Horn and this journey with 1,000 American fare-paying passengers (paid to Long Beach) taking 39 days, with *Queen Mary* using two of her four propellers to economise on fuel, proved to be her most exhausting voyage.

The entertainment centre on board opened in May 1971 and at first proved a success but by 1976 there was a subsequent decline in interest.

Queen Mary, now owned by Wrather Port Properties Ltd, is still at Long Beach, serving as an Hotel and Tourist Centre in company with the historical *Spruce Goose* flying boat originally built by the famous eccentric millionaire Howard Hughes.

Queen Mary
Spruce Goose

Italia Societa di Navigazione (Italia Line)

The Company

The Italia Line came into being in 1932 as a result of a merger by three major Italian shipping companies, Navigazione Generale Italiana, Lloyd Sabaudo and Cosulich Line, to form 'Italia – Flotte Riunite'. The 1932 merger was followed in 1936 by virtue of a general re-organisation of Italy's shipping services, by the creation of a new company, the present day 'Italia Line' which started its activities in January 1937. Within the scope of the general rationalisation as valid today, the main Italian shipping services were grouped into four separate traffic sectors, each being assigned to one of four companies, 'Italia Line', 'Lloyd Triestino', 'Adriatica' and 'Tirrenia', which together came to form the 'Finmare' Group.

Major passenger services from Italy to North and South America were operated up to 1975 by the combined fleets of the three original lines and therefore 'Italia Line' embraces the histories of the three companies. The foremost one, Navigazione Generale Italiana was founded in 1881 as an amalgamation of the large number of steamships operated by the Rubattino and Florio concerns, which came into being between 1838 and 1850 and traded from Italy and France to the Americas as well as other parts of the world. Navigazione Generale Italiana dominated the Italian shipping scene for some 50 years and was a major contributor to the efficiency of the Italian Merchant Marine. The company prospered and after the turn of the century absorbed numerous smaller concerns. After the First World War, in order to capitalise on the market situation of 1920-1921 and expanding passenger and emigrant trades, NGI introduced on the North Atlantic their two quadruple-screw prestige liners, the 21,600 ton *Guilio Cesare* and the 24,300 ton *Duilio*. Their success led to construction of the 33,000 ton *Roma* and *Augustus*, also propelled by quadruple screws. All NGI liners were a triumph on the North Atlantic but their speeds, at ca 19-24 knots did not portray Blue Riband ambitions until, with this in mind, the Italian Government provided generous subsidies in 1930-31 for the construction of super-express liners to compete on equal terms with the transatlantic flyers and the first liner to be launched was named *Rex* in honour of the King. This liner became the largest and most luxurious vessel of the Italian Merchant Marine and won the Blue Riband for Italy.

The second company to merge into the Italia Line, Lloyd Sabaudo, was founded in 1906 in Turin and operated passenger and cargo services to North and South America. In 1920-22 as part of Italy's drive to compete on the Atlantic, Lloyd Sabaudo put into service four 18,000-24,000 ton liners of the 'Conte' class which maintained a splendid reputation and contributed considerably to the prosperity of the shipping company. As in the case of NGI, Lloyd Sabaudo planned and built in 1932, with Government assistance, a super-liner similar to the *Rex* but of 48,000 tons and named it *Conte di Savoia*. Originally this vessel was to have been named *Dux* in honour of the Duce, however with Signor Mussolini suddenly developing a twinge of modesty (maybe because the liner was second-largest) the ship's name was changed to *Conte di Savoia*. Although only slightly smaller than the *Rex* and equipped with very similar machinery, *Conte di Savoia* appeared not to have manifested Blue Riband ambitions.

Following the 1932 merger, initiated by the Italian Government to create major economies during the world-wide depression, the fleets of the two companies together with the third large operator, the Cosulich Line founded in 1903 in Trieste, functioned under the flag of 'Italia Line' and included the newly completed *Rex* and *Conte di Savoia*. The three companies were thus able to contribute effectively to the transportation of the more sophisticated type of traveller as well as emigrants especially from Southern Europe, now beginning to form the mainstay of transatlantic traffic following the decline in emigration overall due to restrictive regulations in the United States and to the policy of the Italian Government of the period.

The launch of *Rex* at the S. A. Ansaldo of Sestri Ponenti on 1st August 1931 and *Conte di Savoia* on 28th October 1931 at the shipyard of S. A. Cantieri Riunite del Adriatico of Trieste, took place a few months before the amalgamation of the three above mentioned companies to 'Italia – Flotte Riunite'. The coming into service of the two great liners in order to introduce the express connection between Genoa and New York, created great prestige for the Italian Merchant Marine, the pair being among the most elegant and luxurious in operation during the period between the wars.

In 1939 on the eve of World War II the 'Italia Line' was operating 37 ships totalling 456,442 tons with several new units in construction. The services of the company comprised 11 routes of which 7 carried passengers and 4 transported freight, in all covering some 2.6 million miles per year. On the basis of 1937/38 averages, 200,000 passengers and over one million tons of cargo were carried per annum.

After the outbreak of war, *Rex* and *Conte di Savoia* continued to operate the remunerative service between Genoa and New York by virtue of Italy's continued neutrality until the spring of 1940 when safety and security of shipping could no longer be guaranteed. *Rex* was then laid up in Bari and *Conte di Savoia* near Venice. They both became war losses, together with *Roma, Augustus* and various others.

After the war the company was left some six old liners of which the 1927/28 built, 24,000 ton motorships *Saturnia* and *Vulcania* (ex-Cosulich) were refurbished and re-engined to take up the New York service by the end of 1946. Acquisition of five American 'Liberty' ships between 1946 and 1947 led to resumption of the cargo trade to Central America and the North Pacific.

Subsequent reactivation of the fleet amounted to completion of some ships left on stocks during the war and salvage for further use of some sunken vessels. The extension of the Truman Law on restitution was instrumental in the return to the company of two more old liners, which were put on the South America run after thorough refurbishment.

Between 1949 and 1960 substantial new tonnage comprising 25,000 to 34,000 ton liners and numerous cargo vessels was added for North and South American services.

As late as 1965, two new super-liners *Michelangelo* and *Raffaelo*, each of 45,500 tons and capable of 26.5 knots were commissioned but after a period of profitable scheduled service on the North Atlantic, tended to be relegated to the tourist trade. Unfortunately due to oil price increases, rapid development of air travel and internal labour troubles, the two liners proved unprofitable and after 1971 became a financial liability. Subsidies were withdrawn by the Government and with other passenger vessels having to be sold off, the two super-liners were laid up in 1975. The ships were finally sold to Iran for use as Army barracks. *Raffaelo* was wrecked during the Iran-Iraq war and *Michelangelo* was sold for scrapping in 1986.

All passenger liners were sold off by 1980 but acquisition of large modern container ships consolidated important cargo services to the Americas and the Pacific and 'Italia Societa di Navigazione' became the largest Italian shipping venture.

The Record Breaking Liner *Rex*

The express luxury liner *Rex*, taken into service in 1932 was launched on 1st August 1931 at the Ansaldo Shipyard, Genoa. *Rex* belonged to the post-depression outburst of super-liner construction in anticipation of an Atlantic travel boom and was planned to compete with and outdo the high speed liners in operation and being commissioned by the North European opposition and to entice the travelling elite to experience the luxury offered by the Southern route. Large Government subsidies helped to create this prestigious liner capable of wresting the Blue Riband from the British and the Germans and to be the running mate of the equally splendid and latest Lloyd Sabaudo crack liner *Conte di Savoia*.

Rex was a handsome liner of modernistic concept, possibly not unlike the German Blue Riband holders of the day; unfortunately the rather untidy looking

Express liner Rex.

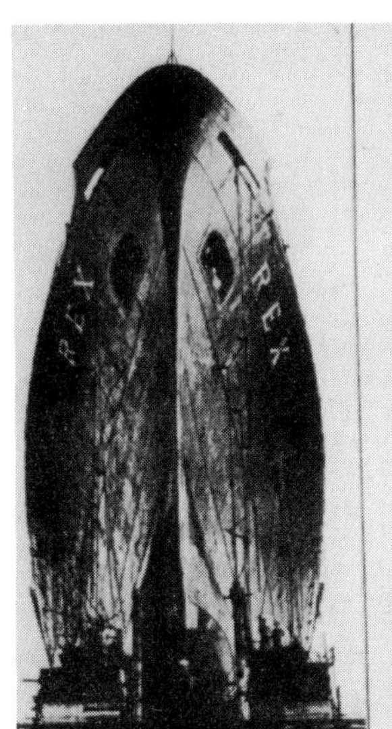

Navigazione Generale Italiana express liner Rex *on the stocks at the Sestri Ponente Yard ready for launching.* Rex *was the largest vessel built at an Italian yard.*

Quadruple-screw express liner Conte di Savoia *built by Cantieri Riuniti del Adriatico for Lloyd Sabaudo in 1932. The liner was of 48,502 GR tons, 814 ft long and 96 ft wide. Four single reduction geared 3-cylinder Parsons turbines drove the four screws and steam was generated in 10 Yarrow water-tube boilers. Machinery produced some 100,000 SHP and during acceptance trials a speed in excess of 29 knots was achieved but although pairing with* Rex *on the transatlantic run was most successful,* Conte di Savoia *never managed a record breaking Atlantic passage.*

Record breaking liner Rex *of the Italia Line.*

forward end of the accommodation superstructure tended to detract from the impressive frontal aspect.

With a gross tonnage of 51,062, *Rex* had an overall length of 880 ft (817 ft b.p.), a moulded breadth of 96.8 ft and a depth to C-Deck of 60.6 ft. The propulsion machinery driving four screws, consisted of four sets of single reduction geared turbines. Each set comprised a high pressure (HP), an intermediate pressure (IP) and a low pressure (LP) engine, with the HP and IP turbines running at 2,500 RPM and the LP turbine at 2,280 RPM in order to drive the main gearwheel and propeller at 230 RPM. The HP turbines were of the combined impulse and reaction type whereas the blading of the IP and LP turbines was entirely of the reaction type. The propelling machinery was capable of generating a maximum of 130,000 SHP for a speed of 28 knots and an overload of 5% was possible if required.

Each turbine set was equipped with three-staged astern turbines acting on the wing pinions to develop some 60% of total power for astern running.

Superheated steam to drive the turbines was generated at 385 psi (27 kg/cm^2) and 716 °F (385 °C) in eight double-ended and four single-ended Yarrow type water-tube boilers. Two auxiliary smoke-tube cylindrical Scotch boilers were provided in a separate boiler room adjacent to the auxiliary engine room and they generated superheated steam at 228 psi (16 kg/cm^2) and a temperature of 608 °F (320 °C).

With a passenger capacity of 604 in the First Class, 378 in the Second and 400 Tourist, the liner could also accommodate some 850 Third Class emigrants. *Rex* was a superbly appointed ship with extravagant decor featuring the best and most elegant of traditional Italian styles with marble columns and mural painted ceilings in lofty public rooms. Staterooms and cabin facilities and furnishings were intended to offer a superior environment to that of other great liners of the period in order to capture a major slice of the international travelling elite. Particularly impressive were the outdoor swimming pools and the 'Riviera atmosphere'.

Super elegant and profitable that both *Rex* and *Conte di Savoia* might have been, they did not really manage to offer serious competition to the latest North European crack liners of the period.

Departing from Genoa on 27th September 1932 for her maiden voyage, the *Rex* experienced considerable mechanical problems and an engine breakdown near Gibraltar which delayed the journey by some three days until appropriate spares were delivered and repairs carried out.

However in August 1933 *Rex* captured the westbound Blue Riband by averaging 28.92 knots while crossing from Gibraltar (Tarifa Point) to New York in 4 days 13 hours 58 minutes. *Rex* kept this trans-atlantic record until May 1935 when the crossing speed was bettered by the Cie. Gle. Transatlantique liner *Normandie*.

Rex was Italy's only liner to achieve the coveted Blue Riband and had the distinction of being the first recipient of the Hales Trophy.

After their last journey following the outbreak of hostilities, *Rex* and *Conte di Savoia* were laid up in safety in 1940 and there materialised plans to convert both to aircraft carriers or alternatively, as troop transporters, but nothing came of the ideas.

In September 1944 RAF bombers attacked the *Rex* with rockets and set her on fire. The liner burnt out and sank after rolling over in the Gulf of Muggia near Trieste. After the war salvage was considered but because of extensive damage the ship had to be scrapped at site.

A similar fate befell the running mate *Conte di Savoia*; she was bombed in 1943, set on fire and sank. After the war the liner's hull was raised but various plans for rehabilitation did not come to fruition and in 1950 she was sold for demolition.

Compagnie Generale Transatlantique (French Line)

The Company

THE STORY OF CIE GENERALE Transatlantique is intimately bound with development of transatlantic trade and the struggle for supremacy between the major shipowners of Western Europe and the United States since the advent of the iron steamship.

By the middle of the 19th century, France as a maritime nation had fallen behind her rivals on the high seas. In May 1855 the Compagnie Generale Maritime was founded to ensure expansion of the French Merchant Marine. At the head of the company came the dynamic brothers Pereire under whose guidance the company prospered and by 1861 paddle steamers were operated to North Africa and European ports in addition to numerous sailing ships involved in the California and Newfoundland trades. Despite this progress, the brothers Pereire set their sights further afield and in July 1861 the company was granted French Government mail contracts to encourage sea trade with North and Central America and the consequent subsidies, also in 1861, helped a major reorganisation, with the company being renamed 'Compagnie Generale Transatlantique' (CGT).

Beginning in 1864 the first large steamships to inaugurate mail, passenger and cargo services from Le Havre to New York were introduced; they were seven large paddle steamers of 3,200 GR tons and capable of service speeds of 13 knots, built in Scotland but also at the Penhoet Yard. These were followed in 1866 by three screw-propelled vessels whose success persuaded the directors to abandon paddles in favour of screw drive.

During the 1870-71 war most of the fleet were on naval duty and subsequently all remaining paddle steamers were converted to screw propulsion with compound engines using higher boiler pressures and at the same time lengthened and modernised. The mail contract was renewed in 1873 resulting in a series of up-to-date newbuilds during the seventies. In 1880 the firm's activities were extended by North African mail contracts, which also stipulated that ship construction at French shipyards rather than in Britain was to be encouraged. In the sixties the company created a new shipyard at Penhoet in order to carry out repairs and some new construction.

CGT was therefore now able to build its own ships within limits of the available facilities. The original mail contract was renewed in 1883 with the proviso that a major proportion of funds be earmarked for weekly sailings to New York at a minimum speed of 15 knots. To fulfil these requirements, CGT decided on the immediate construction of five express liners, the first of which, named *La Normandie*, was built at Barrow. She was a 6,300 ton vessel with 7,000 IHP compound machinery and in July 1885 achieved the fastest ever crossing of the Atlantic by a French liner, in 7 days 23 hours at a mean speed of 16.4 knots.

By the beginning of 1889 the CGT owned 68 steamers totalling 150,063 GR tons in use on the company's world-wide services. In addition, six steamers were in the course of construction, one of which was the modern liner *La Touraine*, a twin screw vessel of 8,429 tons and equipped with 12,000 IHP engines for the New York service. A year after her commissioning in 1891, *La Touraine* achieved the Le Havre to New York journey in 6 days 21 hours, thus bettering all previous French liner crossing times.

Because of special requirements by the Government as a condition for the renewal of the Atlantic mail contract in 1901, the two new mail liners, *La Loraine* and *La Savoie* of 11,372 tons were to be capable of 22 knots; the ships were launched at the Penhoet Yard in 1899 but were not put into service until early in the 20th century because of construction delays.

Early in the 20th century, J. P. Morgan's shipping activities resulted in the formation of the 'International Mercantile Marine Company' and some pressure was applied on CGT to join the ring. The position became speculative but.because of the company's diverging interests and the disapproving attitude of the French Government, Morgan's advances were rejected.

In 1904 M. Charles Roux became president of the company and he commenced a campaign to improve and modernise services by carrying out new extensive programmes to construct new liners for certain services. Between 1909 and 1913 there was a replacement of aged Atlantic tonnage and the new vessels created an improvement in speeds; not actually entering a race for the Blue Riband, most of the fleet was very near the top of the list for high averages. In 1912 the quadruple-screw, 23,769 ton *France* powered by direct-drive Parsons turbines of 42,000 SHP and capable of 25 knots plus, as well as many new 'cabin' class liners, were introduced. Although *France* could possibly have competed for Atlantic records, it is not known whether an attempt was ever made.

After the First World War, fairly heavy losses having been experienced, shipping required much reorganisation and the French Government was committed to replacements, which led to newbuilds including completion in 1921 of the 34,000 ton quadruple-screw liner *Paris* and construction in 1927 of the famous 43,450 ton quadruple-screw liner *Ile de France*. This pair became a byword for French comfort, luxury and cuisine. A number of elegant 'cabin' class liners of 18,000 to 28,000 tons were built for North American, West Indies and Pacific coast services; some 20 passenger ships operated the Mediterranean trade in the thirties.

In 1922 after a lapse of nearly 46 years, CGT made Plymouth a regular port of call for their ships, both on the New York and West Indies runs.

In the mid-twenties the first ideas of a giant liner to become the world's largest and fastest, were being developed in France as an answer to the nationalistic maritime ambitions in Germany and Italy and as a competitor to the British giant coming into being since 1930 on the slipways of John Brown's at Clydebank.

The keel of the new flagship of the CGT fleet of some 100 merchant ships, was laid in 1931 at the Penhoet Shipyard of St Nazaire and the hull of the express super-liner *Normandie* of 83,423 tons was launched in October 1932.

As in the case of other super-liners of the period, this national prestige giant was strongly subsidised by the Government who also contributed greatly to

Normandie

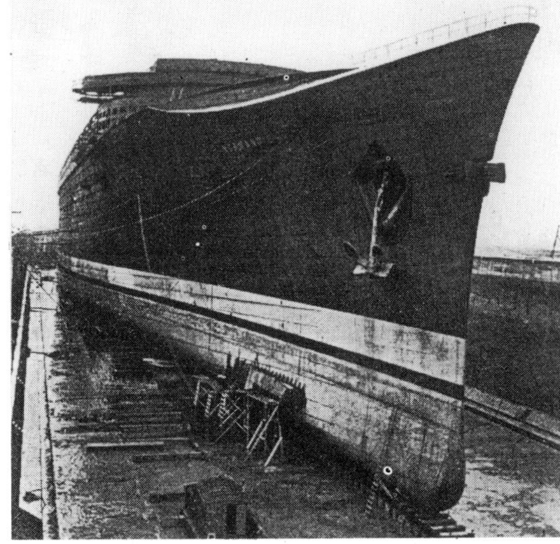

Top: *In dry dock at St Nazaire for the fitting of propellers.*

Left: *In dry dock at St Nazaire. Bow view.*

major modifications to port facilities, such as dry docks and fitting out quays to suit this largest vessel ever built in France.

The fact that in the thirties the world depression was at its peak, created some pessimism with the populace but this was to some extent counteracted by employment of much labour. However as in the case of *Queen Mary*, depression was later instrumental in a temporary halt to the finishing work on the hull, with *Normandie* not being finally completed until 1935. The maiden voyage was embarked upon in May 1935.

Until the outbreak of war in 1939 *Normandie* maintained a second-to-none profitable luxury service, carrying diverse notables and the famous between Europe and New York, in a regular service paired with *Ile de France* and sometimes with 'intermediate' liners stepping in when required. Unfortunately, the third partner, the splendid luxury liner *Paris* was destroyed by fire at the Le Havre jetty in 1939.

During the Second World War, the French Line contributed greatly to the war effort by provisioning the part of the fleet not rendered inoperative in Europe, for the transport of Allied forces and this included the famous *Ile de France*, one of the few survivors. The greatest tragedy was the loss of *Normandie* by fire in New York during conversion.

After the war it was July 1947 before CGT could resume their North Atlantic service with the 'intermediate' liner *De Grasse* of 18,000 tons, originally built in 1924, during the war converted by Germans into a rest centre and subsequently sunk in the harbour of Bordeaux. *De Grasse* was salvaged and completely refurbished at Le Havre prior to re-opening the New York run via Southampton. In 1949 also after major

Nearing completion in 1934.

rebuilding and modernisation, the *Ile de France* joined *De Grasse* and she was followed by the *Liberte*, originally built as the German record-breaker *Europa*, ceded to France as reparations.

Liberte replaced the *De Grasse*, which was duly sold to the Canadian Pacific Steamships Ltd.

Various liners and cargo ships were subsequently commissioned by the French Line in order to consolidate the numerous reactivated services and in 1962 the last real flagship of the company, one of the outstanding liners of the century, and also classified as the last super-liner in regular North Atlantic trade, was put into service. This liner, named *France* (3) bore a degree of similarity to *Normandie* but although her tonnage was 66,350, she was 1,035 ft in length by 110 ft beam and therefore some 6 ft longer than her illustrious predecessor and her hull actually approached the 'longship' ratio.

France was powered by double-reduction geared turbines developing 160,000 SHP to drive four screws and enable her to achieve nearly 35 knots on trials.

This Government subsidised liner apparently never contested for the Blue Riband but became one of the most successful passenger carriers of the post-war era, representing as she did, French culture and the French artistry. *France* offered stiff competition to Britain's ageing *Queens* but she never achieved the economic success originally forecast and by 1972, with

Normandie *at the Finishing Berth.*

increasing competition from air travel and escalating oil prices, French Line sent the liner cruising and in 1974 finally withdrew her from the New York service to be laid up at Le Havre.

In 1979 *France* was finally acquired by the Florida based Norwegian Caribbean Lines, experienced a major refit and conversion and renamed *Norway*. At present the liner still enjoys a splendid reputation cruising between Miami and the West Indies.

Normandie was the only French liner to achieve the Blue Riband. Cie. Gle. Transatlantique is not any more involved in scheduled transatlantic passenger service, having been assimilated since 1972 within the combine 'Compagnie Generale Maritime', operating mainly freight services in conjunction with the former 'Messageries Maritimes'.

Record Breaking Luxury Liner *Normandie*

At the time of her commissioning in 1935, *Normandie*, with a gross tonnage of 83,423 and an overall length of 1,028 ft by 117 ft beam, was the world's largest liner and this qualification applied until the launching of the Cunard liner *Queen Elizabeth* in 1939.

Normandie's graceful hull originated from designs by M. Yourkevich of Penhoet and featured a strongly raked bow with an underwater bulb forefoot as developed in tank-tests in order to minimise water resistance and turbulence. This design feature was not dissimilar to that of *Bremen* and *Europa*.

The main propulsion machinery consisted of the latest development in turbo-electric drive and comprised four 33,400 kW turbo-alternator sets, electrically connected to four propulsion motors, each being capable of developing 32,500 SHP for service speed and 40,000 SHP at maximum overload, to drive the four screws. Superheated steam to the turbine stop valves was generated at 335 psi (325°C) in 29 water-tube boilers of the Penhoet three-drum type. Auxiliary requirements were catered for by four marine Scotch type cylindrical boilers at 143 psi. The *Normandie* propulsion system is described in greater detail in a later chapter.

The original passenger accommodation catered for 58 in the 'Grand Luxe' Class, 806 in First, 654 in the Second ('Tourist') and 454 in the Third Classes. The total ships' crew was 1,345.

Interior decor was a masterpiece of French artistry created by the most prominent architects and artists, introducing in the First Class a style related to the history of Normandy, portrayed on panels and reliefs of exquisite workmanship, much use being made of decorative glass, plaster of paris and marble, with lofty public rooms located above and below the promenade deck. The most imposing room on the ship was the dining saloon, 305 ft in length with a ceiling height of 25 ft and capable of seating 700. This room was panelled entirely in moulded glass tiles with vertical strips of hammered glass. Illumination was achieved by 38 virtical glass brackets, two glass chandeliers and 12 giant glass standards as well as hidden lamps in the gilded ceiling. At each end there were giant bas-reliefs depicting Normandy's wealth and art. Many other items of artistic decor were represented in the dining saloon where exquisite cuisine was offered to the passenger elite of the period.

In addition there were four private dining rooms, each 17 ft x 9 ft, entered by eight ornamental bronze

Normandie – *First Class Main Dining Saloon.*

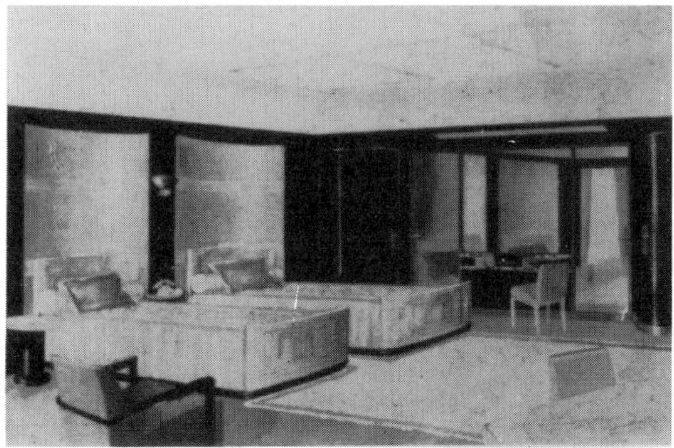

Bedroom of the Rouen Suite.

Drawing Room of Caen Suite with Dining Room beyond.

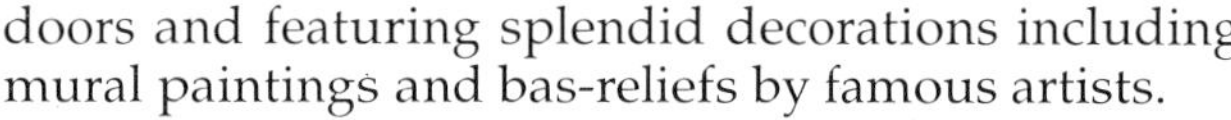

doors and featuring splendid decorations including mural paintings and bas-reliefs by famous artists.

'De Luxe' and First Class suites and staterooms, 24 of which had private verandahs, provided incomparable luxury and comfort. The enclosed promenade deck offered a length of 430 ft on each side of the liner and had sliding windows in special safety glass and access from the promenade deck to all public rooms was provided by double glazed doors.

Other public rooms including entrance halls, chapel, lounges, drawing rooms, smoking room, etc., featured exquisite decor and furnishings, using vast areas of glass, large bronze-framed windows and resplendent giant bas-reliefs and paintings, all beneath 22 ft high decorated ceilings. There was a 75 ft long swimming bath tiled in mosaic and floral patterned walls, a magnificent theatre/cinema seating 380, shaped to give the best possible acoustics and with the general tone of decoration in silver was provided with softly diffused lighting. The artistically laid out winter garden occupied the forward end of the promenade deck.

Tourist Class accommodation aft of the First Class, consisted of many elegant and lofty public rooms and cabins, which although not featuring all the grandeur of First Class, offered exceptionally high standards of space and decor, to a great extent equivalent to First Class facilities on an average 20,000 ton liner.

Third Class at the after end of the ship was designed with particular regard to comfort of passengers and with a part of it convertible to Tourist Class. The accommodation included a 45 ft x 45 ft dining saloon decorated in yellow marble, mahogany veneered columns and a high central dome. Other public rooms such as the lounge and smoking room featured much wood veneer, leather and mural panels with indirect lighting. The two, three, and four-berth cabins offered appropriate facilities for comfortable travel and were located on D and E decks.

Tourist Class Lounge.
With cinema equipment and dancing floors, forms the social centre for Tourist Class. Mural treatment in polished wood and central dome supported by glass pillars.

Typical Tourist Class Stateroom.

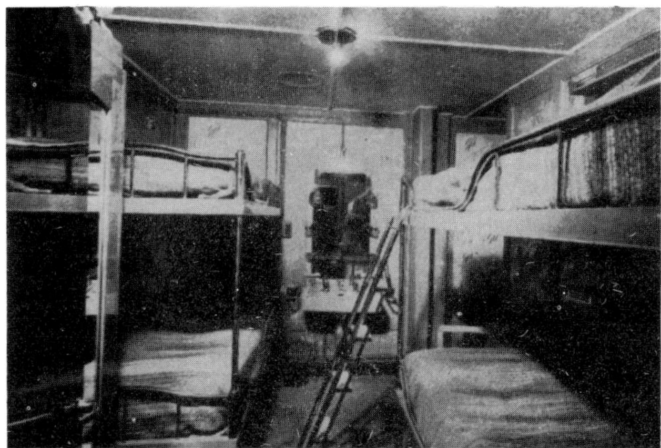

Typical Third Class Cabin.

Third Class Dining Saloon.

The officers' suites and crew's quarters of the *Normandie* were of particular note and to a great extent reflected the quality of passengers' accommodation, being in keeping with the standards prevailing throughout the liner.

The Blue Riband and After

Normandie completed successful trials at which speeds of 30-32 knots were achieved and on 29th May 1935 she left Le Havre on her maiden voyage to New York. The westward run from Bishops Rock to Ambrose Light (New York) took 4 days 3 hours 2 minutes at a mean speed of 29.98 knots and this beat the previous record set by *Rex* of Italia Line in 1933.

On the return leg of the maiden voyage in June 1935, *Normandie* averaged 30.35 knots eastbound in 4 days 3 hours 25 minutes, improving upon the mean speed of the last record holder *Bremen* by nearly 2.4 knots. In the course of her maiden voyage *Normandie* thus achieved records in both directions.

Normandie kept the westbound record until August 1936 and then lost it to *Queen Mary*, only to regain the Blue Riband in July 1937 by crossing from Bishops Rock to Ambrose at 30.58 knots in 3 days 23 hours.

Normandie finally lost the westbound honour in August 1938, again to *Queen Mary*.

Eastward, between Ambrose and Bishops Rock, *Normandie* held the Blue Riband record until June 1936, when it was bettered by her rival, but the CGT liner regained it in March 1937 averaging 30.99 knots and completing the journey in 4 days 6 minutes and in August of the same year improved upon this by her best ever crossing at an average of 31.20 knots in 3 days 22 hours 7 minutes. However August 1938 saw the Blue Riband being finally passed on to *Queen Mary*.

Normandie in company with *Ile de France* maintained her high speed super-luxury service between France and New York until the outbreak of the Second

World War and in August 1939 she was ordered to stay in New York, where she remained 'laid up in safety' by pier 88, Manhattan. However, after Pearl Harbour the liner was requisitioned for the US Navy Department by the American Government and renamed *Lafayette* prior to the start of her conversion, late in 1941, for transportation of troops, with the target date for completion set for February 1942. All work was to take place by pier 88.

The fact that this conversion had to comply with unduly complicated US requirements and sometimes with useless specifications, made it impossible to keep to the two months' target date. In the chaos created by labour troubles, apathy, politics and inferior supervision it appears that red-hot metal from an oxy-acetylene torch ignited some highly combustible stores and rapidly created a conflagration. This disaster has been described in great detail in numerous publications, sufficient to say the liner was ablaze and became a total loss inside the first half hour. The amount of water pumped into the blazing hull in an attempt to quell the flames finally caused *Lafayette* to turn over on her side and resting on the bottom of the harbour to obstruct completely piers 88 and 89.

Lafayette remained on her side for some months before work started to remove her insides and superstructure prior to attempting to right the hulk. By August 1943 the liner's hull was finally floated and removed to the Brooklyn Navy Yard, where it remained for a further three years before being sold for scrapping. Various ideas regarding salvage for further conversion to suit diverse duties were propounded during the righting of the hull but were found to be quite unrealistic.

It was a tragic end to one of the world's finest and most luxurious liners ever built and France's only Blue Riband holder.

United States Lines

The Company

United States Lines as such was formed in 1921 and although it experienced two major reorganisations, apart from the period covering the Second World War, offered uninterrupted North Atlantic passenger services; it was always considered to be one of the more efficient companies in the world.

At the end of the First World War the United States Government was in possession of a substantial fleet of large ex-German liners, interned and kept as reparations. These included two previous holders of the Blue Riband, the *Kronprinz Wilhelm* and *Kaiser Wilhelm II* as well as the *Kronprinzessin Cecilie*, also the 54,000 ton *Vaterland* (renamed *Leviathan*), the 24,000 tonners *George Washington* and *America* as well as a number of smaller passenger and cargo steamers in addition to numerous wartime American built vessels. During the war most of the above mentioned liners were used as troopers and became rather the worse for wear.

Prospective private owners were unable to put the ships into useful service because of the colossal cost of appropriate refurbishment and the fleet was put under the control of the 'United States Shipping Board' a state agency. Funds were finally allocated by Congress to create an American Shipping Company, the 'United States Lines', which functioned as an operational agent for the Shipping Board in order to start up a transatlantic service by means of an American fleet of luxury liners.

Eventually by 1923, *Leviathan* and the other suitable liners were refurbished in full for introduction on scheduled itineraries. *Leviathan* was given particular pride of place by virtue of the fact that her rebuilding and modernisation, which took the best part of three years, was one of the most extensive and costly achievements ever to be performed and created an American 'world's largest' liner, her tonnage having been newly 'remeasured' at 59,950 as a result of rebuilding, compared with the original 54,200 tons.

In addition, the general modernisation and refit of prime movers, as well as conversion of boilerplant to oil firing enabled the liner to achieve over 26 knots on trials (she was originally designed for 23 knots), although this speed could not subsequently be maintained during Atlantic crossings.

Leviathan became the flagship of the American Merchant Marine and from July 1923 she operated the prestigious New York to Southampton service, usually in company with the overhauled ex-German liners, *George Washington* and *America*. Although the United States Lines' ships, especially *Leviathan*, were well liked by the travelling public, they were seldom profitable, mainly because of the prohibition being extended to ships, certain amended immigration laws and the coming of the great depression.

Because of difficulties in making the refurbished fleet pay its way, by 1929 many of the old ships became a great financial liability and the United States Government withdrew subsidies. The company changed hands having been purchased by P. W. Chapman & Company and the trading name became 'United States Lines Incorporated of Delaware'.

After less than three years, with the Chapman organisation not having been able to operate profitably, the Shipping Board foreclosed on the balance of repayments and in 1931 sold part of the fleet to the International Mercantile Marine Group, which then operated under the name 'United States Lines of Nevada'.

Between 1931 and 1935 there came a reorganisation of old and new ships and trading areas and by 1938 *Leviathan* and other uneconomical liners on the Atlantic run were sold to shipbreakers.

Replacements by new modern and economical vessels, including the medium-speed 24,000 tonners *Manhattan* and *Washington*, proved a success and during 1939/40 a worthy replacement to *Leviathan* was commissioned; the 34,000 ton, 22 knot *America* (2), the largest liner to be built to-date in the United States, also qualified as the flagship of the United States Merchant Marine.

The Second World War prevented this new liner from taking on her prescribed employment on the Atlantic and she started her career with some cruising until such time as being called up for wartime duties, duly renamed *West Point*. In this guise the new liner, together with many others was engaged in

Sea Queens in Exile.
Watercolour by R. E. Whitney. 1920-1930 impression of pre-war German liners Kaiser Wilhelm II, Kronprinzessin Cecilie, America *and* George Washington, *laid up at Solomons Island, Chesapeake Bay.*

United States *at the finishing berth.*

transporting many thousands of troops in all parts of the world until cessation of hostilities.

In 1946 *West Point* was duly converted back to *America* at the cost of many millions of Dollars in order to resume her pre-war commercial role on the Atlantic. *America* became one of the premier passenger carriers of the period because of her excellent modern accommodation, American cuisine (as compared with post-war European diet based on rationing backwash), punctuality and efficiency of service during her 18 years on the North Atlantic, in the course of which she made some 290 crossings and carried 476,462 passengers. *America* was sold in 1964 to the Chandris Group for conversion to transport emigrants to Australia, for which purpose she was christened *Australis*. After a subsequent change in ownership in 1972 the liner was again acquired by Chandris for further conversion, this time as a cruise liner, renamed *Italis*.

Wartime maritime experience with operation of the giant Cunard *Queens* and other large liners as troopers, as well as strong lobbying by the eminent naval architect William F. Gibbs, influenced the United States Government to subsidise the creation of a special liner, primarily designed as a high-speed troop transport, to be also used as a luxury express liner in peacetime, operating the transatlantic service in company with the current flagship *America*.

The appropriate subsidies by the US Government having been granted, in 1950 the keel was laid at Newport News Shipbuilding & Drydock Company, to construct the quadruple-screw, 53,329 ton super-liner *United States* designed to the strictest safety regulations, incorporating many 'national defence' features and to have a turn of speed to comply with Navy requirements.

At the time of her completion, *United States* was the third largest steamer in the world and it was claimed the safest by virtue of the fact that fireproof materials such as light alloys were used throughout for the superstructure and any combustible materials such as wood panelling, avoided anywhere on the ship.

United States having established the ultimate Blue Riband records, had an exceptionally successful if short career on the Atlantic paired with *America*. The two liners offered the first serious competition to European shipping, especially during the fifties and into the sixties, *United States* alone having carried some 70,500 passengers in the first year of her operation.

However as in the case of all express luxury liners on the Atlantic, this superb record breaker reached and passed the peak of profitable operation because of the ever growing competition from the airlines and by the late sixties, even without a pairing on the Southampton run, she was becoming a financial liability. The United States Administration stopped the operational subsidy in 1968 and in November 1969 *United States* left Southampton for the last time prior to being 'mothballed' in retirement.

The *Manhattan* and *Washington* scrapped in 1960 and *America* disposed of in 1964, United States Lines' passenger services became greatly curtailed during the seventies, in the main being transferred to branch lines and associated companies, with major container traffic becoming the priority commitment.

Late in 1987 United States Lines Inc. finally withdrew from shipping. Six large freighters and terminal facilities associated with its Pacific trade were sold to Sea-Land Corporation and the South American facilities complete with four ships were acquired by American Transport Lines.

Record Breaking Luxury Liner *United States*

United States was a handsome vessel featuring a balanced design of overall modern concept, with streamlining and shape of superstructure giving the impression of power and speed.

The liner was not launched off traditional slipways but built in a graving dock on horizontal keel blocks and floated in a nearly completed condition, with prefabrication, subassemblies and welding being used throughout her construction.

United States was 'floated' from No. 10 Dock at the Newport News Shipbuilding & Drydock Company in June 1951 and upon her completion in 1952, measured 53,329 GR tons (26,000 net tons), with an overall length of 990 ft (917 ft b.p.), a width of 101 ft-6 in and a 175 ft depth from keel to top of the forward funnel. The liner had 12 decks and catered for ca 2,000 passengers, a crew of 1,000 and a cargo capacity of 148,000 cubic feet with 48,000 ft^3 for refrigerated cargo.

The liner was the most completely welded passenger ship of the period, with the greatest part of the hull prefabricated in shops by assembly into sections. In all there were some 2,200 prefabricated assemblies, a large proportion of which weighed between 35 and 60 tons with many of the largest being as much as 100 tons. Radiographic inspection of welding was carried out at all stages of construction. Aluminium, amounting to some 2,000 tons was used extensively in place of wood but also as substitute for much steel in the superstructure, the mast, funnels and lifeboats.

The contemporarily latest and most complete navigational facilities included two radar scanners on the mast, latest echo sounding equipment and the 'Mariner's Pathfinder' radar display unit on the bridge, duplicated by a repeater unit in the chartroom. Duplicated quick-changeover equipment for practically all navigational aids was provided in the large wheelhouse.

The latest and most comprehensive radio equipment catered not only for complete ship operation but allowed ship-to-shore calls from any of the telephones in the 694 cabins.

Accommodation in this last of the Atlantic greyhounds catered for 910 First Class, 560 Cabin and 537 Tourist Class passengers. The ostentatious luxury and period-reproduction opulence featured in luxury liners of the past decades were absent but the air-conditioned luxury of the new liner offered the highest possible standards of comfort with impeccable functional if ascetic decor, comprising glass, aluminium and synthetics in the 12 First Class and 14 Tourist Class public rooms and the exceptionally well appointed suites and cabins, more on the lines of a modern first-class hotel than a floating palace.

There were three amply proportioned games areas on the sports deck and on the promenade deck, with the rest of the promenade deck occupied by public rooms including observation lounge, ballroom,

The unusual design of the single light alloy mast and look-out cabin is clear from this photograph.

View showing the painting of the funnel. The large sampan tops are distinctive features.

The ultimate record breaking Atlantic liner United States.

cocktail lounge and two theatres. The promenade deck was fully glased in with floor-to-ceiling windows. On C-Deck there was a swimming pool and pavilion as well as a gymnasium and therapeutic baths.

The 694 cabins of all classes were spacious and luxuriously equipped, with numerous high grade fitments, many wardrobes and much drawer space. All carpeting was fitted wall-to-wall and the majority of cabins were provided with private bathrooms and full facilities. A blend of direct and indirect lighting was installed. Only fully fireproof or fire-treated fabrics, upholstery and other materials were used. Very dubious by present standards however, was the fact that reportedly over 500,000 sq ft of fireproof marinite asbestos board pannelling had also been incorporated. The interior architects and decorators developed pleasing American themes and details of decor and leading American artists were employed to design and initiate the work.

The main propulsion machinery comprised four Westinghouse Electrical Corporation double reduction geared impulse/reaction turbine sets driving four screws. Each turbine set was capable of developing 60,500 SHP, thus aggregating 242,000 SHP for a maximum designed speed of 38 knots. Steam was generated in eight Babcock & Wilcox water-tube boilers at a pressure of 990 psi and superheated to 900°F (527°C). For average steaming, six of the eight boilers were in use at any one time. It would appear that the machinery was originally designed for a cancelled conventionally powered aircraft-carrier.

Builders' acceptance trials were successful and no teething troubles were encountered. It was notable that the machinery installation offered a considerable reserve above the specified requirements and did not need undue urging for a speed of 38.32 knots to be achieved.

It was rumoured that at one stage during the trials *United States* actually steamed at 40 knots.

On her maiden voyage eastbound in July 1952, *United States* averaged 35.59 knots despite gale-force winds and covered the 2,949 nautical miles between Ambrose Light and Bishops Rock in 3 days 10 hours 40 minutes, beating the *Queen Mary* 1938 record by some 10 hours over the same distance. In the course of the return leg of the maiden voyage, also in July 1952, the liner steamed the 2,905 miles between Bishops Rock and Ambrose in 3 days 12 hours 12 minutes (again with a nearly 10 hours' improvement over the *Queen Mary* best), achieving a mean speed of 34.51 knots.

This two-way record crossing was considered the ultimate Blue Riband record. The speed may well have been bettered by a destroyer and also by the speedboat *Virgin Challenger II* in 1986, but such crossings since 1952 do not qualify within the Blue Riband concept related to purely commercial shipping.

For 38 years *United States* claimed to be the ultimate holder of the Hales Trophy which was displayed in the American Maritime Museum at Kings Point, Long Island with the British Maritime League, the appointed administration trustees for the Trophy, having decreed that there would be no changes to the rules relating to the Blue Riband, thus excluding all but genuine merchant ships from holding the Trophy.

The covered promenade, showing the square-patterned deck composition and deep side windows.

One of the sets of aluminium alloy lifeboats and davits. Even the side skates are of light alloy.

After a 17-year illustrious career on the Atlantic, a combination of competition from airlines and unions' intransigence forced the super-liner into early retirement at the Norfolk Cargo Terminal where she deteriorated rapidly, various schemes for refurbishment having falled on deaf ears. Late in 1992 the magnificent liner was sold for demolition.

Epilogue and the Future

Postscript

PRESENT-DAY LINERS ARE still sailing between Europe and the United States, but apart from some East European 15,000-18,000 tonners indulging in leisurely trips taking 6-8 days, there are some super-cruising liners making their way across at reasonably economical and unexciting speeds, usually in conjunction with subsequent, possibly scheduled, cruises to American tourist paradises. Some travellers may not fancy flying in 4-8 hours and therefore prefer to make the journey in one of these remaining liners, especially if there is no particular hurry.

On the comparatively empty Atlantic the Blue Riband record of the last scheduled Atlantic liner *United States* could hardly ever be challenged by a merchant ship, primarily because transatlantic sea traffic having experienced the rapid reduction due to the popularity of air travel, the appearance of a one-off liner to suitable specifications would be quite unrealistic, its prime and running costs being in no way compatible with any income derived from the particular service. From that angle, the Blue Riband and the Hales Trophy must be expected to remain in the safekeeping of the *United States* – ad infinitum!

However, competition possibilities on the basis of pure speed on water over the Atlantic is then left as an assignation to any water surface-craft capable of improving upon the crossing time of the last scheduled Atlantic liner, the prerequisite being completion of the journey between recognised Start and Finish points. Commercial shipping having been eliminated by irreversible conditions, the creation of such new record crossings may have to be left to the equivalent of a sporting achievement by privately financed organisations prepared to make the best possible use of appropriate latest scientific and technical developments and provide backing in order to 'further national prestige' and at the same time achieve publicity for particular interests and/or to raise funds for worthwhile causes. Whether the Blue Riband as such and the Hales Trophy could in any way be involved, remains a debatable point.

Virgin Atlantic Challenge

Richard Branson, creator of the 'Virgin Group' which includes the Virgin Atlantic Airways and various other interests in records, videos, clubs and publishing, developed the idea of challenging the Blue Riband achievement of the last record breaker *United States*, between Ambrose Light (New York) and the Bishops Rock Lighthouse. The fund-raising exercise was to finance research into Leukaemia and the Patron was HRH Prince Michael of Kent.

Challenger I

After some five years' planning and development work, a specially designed powerboat *Challenger I* was completed in 1985 for the attempt. The hull was of 'Cougar' catemaran design, 65 ft (19.8 m) in length and the vessel was powered by two 2,000 mHP 'MTU' V-12, turbo-supercharged diesel engines driving twin, surface piercing, four bladed propellers through 'ZF' (Type BW 455) gearboxes. The boat was manned by nine specialist crew members and there were three refuelling ships organised along the Atlantic route. The latest electronic and computer equipment was provided to monitor boat and engine performance and for navigation. Full radio, telephone and telex lines with the shore were installed.

It is now past history that the 1985 attempt proved a disaster when the boat, well on course and only some three hours from the finishing point, hit floating debris and sank. There were no lives lost but many lessons were learnt.

Challenger II

The idea of achieving the speed record was not given up and a new, monohull boat, 72 ft (22 m) in length, was created through a new partnership and built by Brooke Marine, builders of yachts. Similar type of V-12 turbo-charged 'MTU' diesels (Type 396-TB93), each rated at 2,000 mHP, were installed, but this time driving two five-bladed surface piercing propellers fitted inside combined rudder shrouds and engine exhausts, through 'ZF' reverse-reduction gearboxes. The boat was built to the highest standards regardless of cost and with performance as paramount consideration.

Speedboat Challenger II – *Sectional view.*

Challenger II *leaving New York.*

This time the crew was reduced to six expert members and, as in the first *Challenger*, the latest sophisticated equipment was provided to enable full control of the journey to be maintained at all times. Again there were three refuelling points en route.

Even though *Challenger II* lost some 7½ hours on the way because of contaminated fuel having been pumped from a supply ship, the 2,942 nautical miles' journey was completed at an average of 36.54 knots in 3 days 8 hours 31 minutes, thus laying the claim to have improved upon the record crossing of the liner *United States* by a margin of 2 hours 9 minutes and to have earned the Blue Riband.

The dispute regarding the *Challenger II* being entitled to the Blue Riband which originated within the Merchant Marine, may well go on for a long time. Harold Hales, when donating the Blue Riband Trophy, stated that the presentation should be made, as appropriate, 'to the ship making the fastest crossing between Europe and America' and within this context the classification of the 22 m powerboat as 'Ship' in the true sense of the word, can be debatable. Certainly the term 'Merchant Ship' cannot apply.

The Blue Riband arguments were presumably to some extent instrumental in the appointment late in 1990 of new trustees to administer the Hales Trophy and they duly confirmed that 'the original rules regarding the Blue Riband should still apply' and that attempts on the Atlantic record by small high-speed craft are unlikely to meet the terms of the Trust Deed. They also suggested that a second trophy be created to encourage such achievements by the smaller craft.

It would appear that in 1988 two further high-speed crossings of the Atlantic were attempted and although both were not successful, presumably other attempts will be made in the future, as long as man has the competitive urge backed by revolutionary design and scientific developments. It is however most unlikely that such achievements would in any way be related to the Merchant Marine as such.

Catemaran 'SeaCat'

Passage of time did not after all allow the Atlantic Blue Riband to merge into obscurity of past history and by 1989-1990 contemporary developments in sea travel led to further mutation of seagoing craft with ambitions to achieve historical immortality and publicity.

The birth and development of such a vessel was to a great extent accelerated by anticipated maritime short-haul competition with the Channel Tunnel in order to reduce travel times between Britain and the Continent of Europe, while offering the utmost comfort and facilities to fare-paying passengers.

The 'Sea-Containers Group', present owners of 'Hoverspeed Ltd' and operators of five large hovercraft, decided on planning their future contribution to express cross-Channel traffic, that even the largest craft of this type had virtually reached the limit of economical development and of its dubious operational suitability in stormy weather. They placed orders with the International Catemaran Tasmania Property Ltd, for four of the newly developed generation of high speed craft, large catemarans named 'SeaCat', capable of crossing the Channel at 35-40 knots, for operation on various cross-Channel routes.

This vessel type is to-date the largest catemaran built and the first capable of carrying a large number of passengers and cars. The concept of 'SeaCat' features two long narrow hulls for floatation on water and for cutting through waves at speed rather than having to ride over them, by virtue of low buoyancy at the bows. A central main hull is supported by the two wave-piercing floatation hulls and rides high above the waves, thus claiming to be reasonably impervious to excess buffeting and vibration associated with direct wave contact and not experiencing detrimental effects upon passenger comfort.

SeaCat Hoverspeed Great Britain.

Within the centre hull the short-haul passenger accommodation on the top deck consists of a 20m (66ft) wide saloon, bar and observation lounge, offering comfortable seating and facilities for some 450 travellers. Beneath the saloon deck is located the car deck with a capacity for 85 cars. The passenger module is flexibly mounted to further reduce noise and vibration and is fully air-conditioned.

'SeaCat' has an overall length of 73.6m (241ft) and a beam of 26.3m (86ft). Gross registered tonnage has been assessed at 3,000. Although intended for short-haul journeys, for delivery a bunkerage capacity of 200 tons of diesel fuel has been provided and this was equivalent to 4,500 miles at the cruising speed of 30 knots.

The propulsion plant is located in the side hulls and this siting is expected to completely obviate noise and vibration. Within each of the two hulls there are housed two 16-cylinder Ruston RK 270 turbo-charged medium-speed diesel engines, each capable of developing 4,580 IHP (3,600kW) at 750 RPM. The total propulsion power is therefore 18,320 IHP. The revolutionary departure from conventional propeller propulsion was introduced at this juncture. Each of the four engines is directly coupled to a water-turbine system capable of generating a propulsive thrust by suction and forcible ejection of a high-speed water jet beneath the surface of the sea.

Whether the advantages offered by this revolutionary system would ever completely replace the conventional propeller, is a quite impossible conjecture until more extensive experience, research and development has taken place.

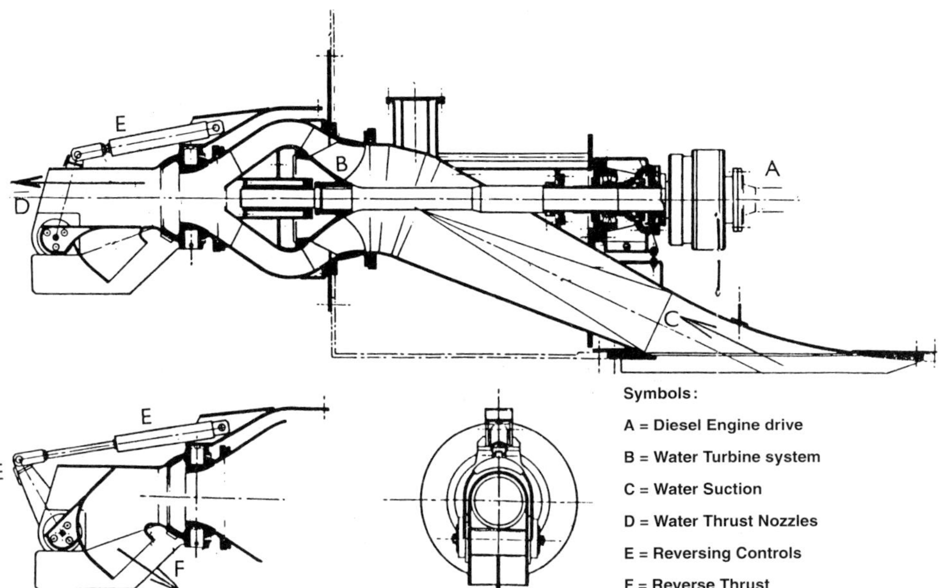

Diagrammatic section of Riva Calzoni Propulsion Water-Jet system.

Manoeuvering and steering of the ships is also facilitated by the water jets, each of the inboard jet outlets being equipped with special steering and reversing nozzles and controls. The two outboard jets are used for ahead full power once the vessel clears the harbour. Highly advanced and sophisticated electronic navigation systems and radars are fitted to ensure safe high speed navigation and positioning.

The first two SeaCats, named *Hoverspeed Great Britain* and *Hoverspeed France* were scheduled to start operation on the Portsmouth to Cherbourg run in 1991, reducing the usual ferry crossing time of 4 hours 40 minutes to 2 hours 40 minutes. With the arrival of further SeaCats, a special Dover terminal would, no doubt, be organised. By the end of 1992 various other ferry services featuring SeaCats, including many seasonal crossings, are to be put into operation in Britain and other parts of the world.

Delivery of the first SeaCat by the builders was made from Tasmania via the Pacific, Panama Canal and New York. This enabled arrangements to be made to promotionally challenge the existing transatlantic crossing record, the Blue Riband achievement by the 53,329 ton *United States* in July 1953, when the 2,942 nautical miles between Ambrose Lightship and Bishop's Rock were covered in 3 days 10 hours 40 minutes, at an average speed of 35.59 knots.

Following a series of acceptance trials at which speeds around 42 knots were achieved, the catemaran departed from the Ambrose Light location on 20th June 1990 and arrived at the Bishop's Rock Lighthouse on 23rd June, having averaged 36.966 knots in the course of a record journey of 3 days 7 hours 25 minutes and improved upon the eastbound crossing by 3 hours 15 minutes in spite of fairly rough seas and 15 ft waves.

The extent to which SeaCat qualifies for the Atlantic Blue Riband might well have been a debatable point in the world's traditional shipping circles. Arguments could possibly have been reduced if the vessel was more fully equipped for the journey to include some passengers and freight. However, apparently conditions for entitlement to the Hales Trophy have been satisfied and interpretation of ambiguities and controversies resolved.

The Hales Trophy has now been relinquished by the US Maritime Museum and transferred to the offices of the Sea-Containers Group.

Developments in Marine Technology from 1840 to the Present Time

Space Occupied by Propulsion Machinery and Fuel

THE PRESTIGE LINER DESTINED to sustain competitively high service speeds, was seldom if ever an economically viable Atlantic carrier unless fully utilised and invariably had to be well subsidised; experience with operation showed that the introduction of particularly rapid and impressive luxury express services was to a great extent intended to cater for a prosperous clientele as a status symbol and to enhance the reputation of a shipping company's fleet, usually comprising more economical, medium speed, 'Bread and Butter earners' of more conventional design but equally well appointed and which, by being equipped with lower rated machinery and having to carry correspondingly less fuel, offered more space for a gainful payload commensurate with lower operating costs.

In addition to often acting as 'loss leaders' for the more profitable trade, record breakers and other 'express' liners played an important chauvenistic role with a major influence upon nationalistic prestige thus qualifying for substantial subsidies. This outlook can be dated back to the 1850's, when the American Government allocated grants for Collins' paddle steamers carrying some 300 passengers in greater luxury than previously experienced on shipboard, while flogging their engines and consuming vast quantities of coal in order to attain record speeds at the expense of discomfort caused by vibration which also led to requirements for excessive maintenance. However, much valuable passenger trade was gained from the Cunard Line, for a short period of time.

With the rapid growth of the Atlantic liner because of cut-throat competition during the 19th century, machinery developments had to keep pace with ship sizes and at each stage of evolution of the reciprocating steam engine, the express liners required the ultimate in power generation from the contemporarily latest machinery, which together with the ever increasing duties required from auxiliary plant, tended to occupy the utmost available space and had to be provided with sufficient fuel to cater for record consumption at record speeds.

The rest of a particular company's fleet, doubtless operated at more conservative speeds, greatly benefited from such developments by utilising de-rated versions of the latest machinery. In order to assess the economics of propelling a ship, it can be assumed on the basis of interpretation of design criteria and tests that power required to give onward motion to a particular ship's hull through water, is proportionate to at least the square of the requisite speed of the vessel.

Whereas the pioneering paddle steamers' machinery and fuel bunkers tended to occupy more or less

45% to 50% of the total hull capacity, introduction of screw-propulsion and of vertical reciprocating engines improved the percentage of payload capacity until demands for power from larger engines to ensure greater speeds for ever increasing sizes of steamships, again showed the tendency to fill the hull at the expense of commercial viability.

As typical 19th century examples can be mentioned the Guion record breakers and the Cunarders *Umbria* and *Etruria*, in which the ultimate economical size of the compound engine was obviously reached and the steamers required a utilisation factor of at least 75% to 80% to pay their way. Such operational economics can well lead to great financial strain especially during politically or otherwise motivated periods of much reduced travel.

The ultimate size in development of triple and quadruple-expansion steam engines for large high-speed liners, was also reached in the case of the turn-of-the-century German twin-screw 21-22 knot 'Fourstackers', where machinery and fuel occupied over 40% of the hull capacity. Economical realism for the companies was introduced after the turn of the century by the commissioning of larger, 18-20 knot luxury liners powered by steam turbines.

The conservatively rated passenger carrier for commercially profitable operation, could have been expected to have a service speed of, say 4-6 knots below that of the contemporary record breaker of comparable size, but provide accommodation for a larger number of passengers and offer equal if not better quality of travel, thus being able to trade without loss even during the lean periods on the Atlantic.

The following illustrations depict longitudinal cross-sections of typical period liners in order to indicate space utilisation within the hulls.

Great Western Steamship Company – 1845

Iron hulled, screw propelled 2,936 ton steamer *Great Britain* – designed by Isombard K. Brunel.

Powered by an inverted 4-cylinder steam engine with speed stepped-up by means of gear and chain.

Steam was generated at ca 5 psi in three 'Box type' double-ended flue boilers each of which was provided with four furnaces at each end.

With a daily coal consumption of roughly 35-40 tons, the total bunker capacity of 1,000 tons was intended to cater for a return Atlantic journey.

Machinery and coal bunkers occupied ca 45% of the ship's hull capacity.

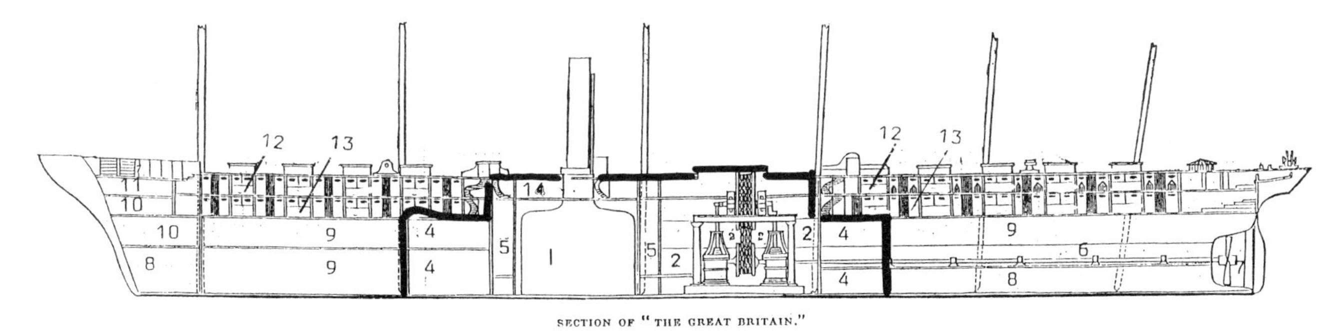

SECTION OF "THE GREAT BRITAIN."

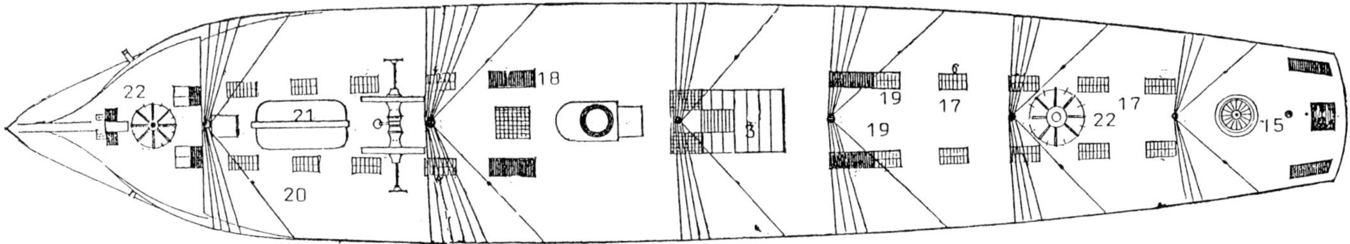

Interior Accommodation – *Great Britain*

1. Boiler Room
2. Engine Room
3. Engine Room Entrance
4. Coal Bunkers
5. Stokehold
6. Propeller Shaft
7. Propeller
8. Water Tanks
9. Cargo Holds
10. Stores
11. Crew's Quarters
12. Promenade Deck and Cabins
13. Saloon Deck and Cabins
14. Galley
15. Skylight
16. Steering Gear
17. Promenade and Saloon Lights
18. Entrance for Cabins and Saloon
19. Entrance to Promenade and Saloon
20. Lights for Cabins and Saloon
21. Lifeboat
22. Windlass

Cunard Steamship Company – 1840-1850

The 1840 'Britannia' class steamer. Twelve pioneering wooden paddle driven Atlantic mail steamers of a similar type category as the original 'Britannia' class but progressively increasing in size with proportionately greater space occupied by machinery and fuel.

Range of technical data:

Tonnage (GR): 1,154 to 2,224.

Hull data: Length = 207 ft to 266 ft.

Width = 34½ft to 40½ft.

Power of side-lever engines = 740 IHP to 2,150 IHP.

Average coal consumption = 37 to 75 tons per day in four boilers.

Coal bunker capacity = 640-900 tons.

Hull spaces:

'A' Engine Room

'B' Coal Bunkers

'C' Boiler Room and Flues

'D' to 'F' Accommodation, Stores and Freight etc.

Machinery and Coal Bunkers occupied ca 45% of the hull capacity.

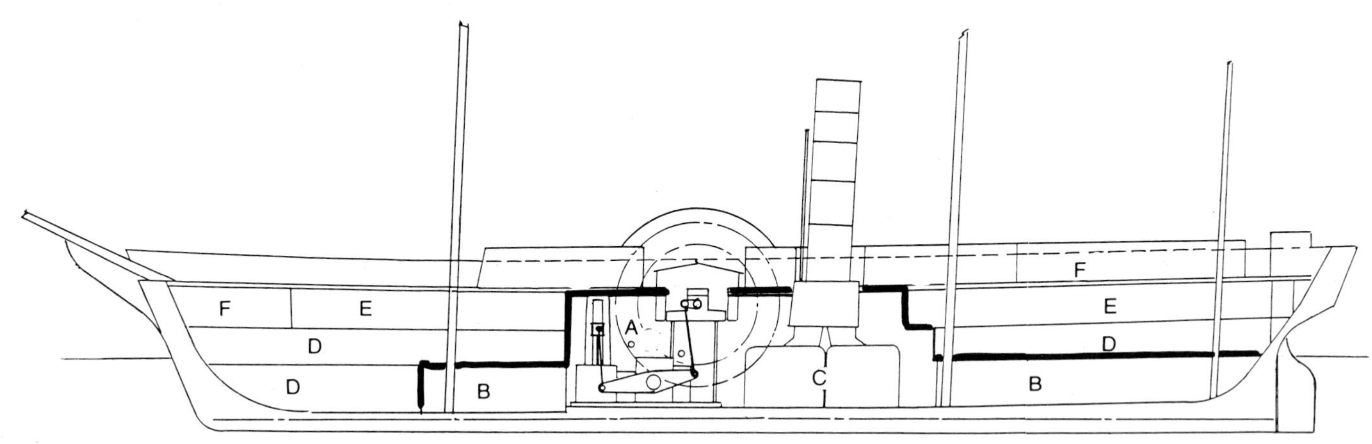

Cunard Line – 1856-1862

Record breaking mail steamers *Persia* and *Scotia* of 3,300 GR tons and 3,871 GR tons respectively, were the last paddle driven Cunard Atlantic liners.

The side-lever engines could develop 4,600 and 4,900 IHP respectively, and in each ship eight tubular flue-box boilers with 40 furnaces consumed up to 160 tons of coal daily, worked by 16 stokers per six-hour shift, to generate steam at 20 psi and achieve average Atlantic crossing speeds of 14-14.5 knots.

Coal bunkers with a capacity of 1,600-1,800 tons were located along both sides of two freight holds, 75 ft long and 16 ft wide by 20 ft high, situated forward and aft of the ships and to some extent acting as part of 'double skin' protection below the water line.

Machinery and coal bunkers occupied ca 43% of the ship's hull capacity.

Location symbols:

'a' Freight/coal bunker holds

'b' Boilers

'c' Engine Room

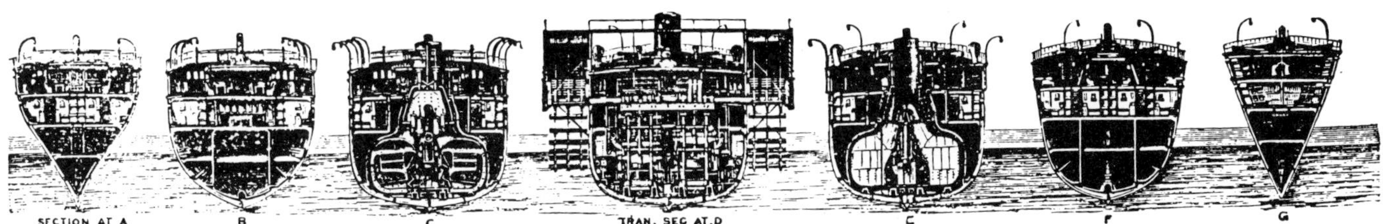

Norddeutscher Lloyd – 1898

First Norddeutscher Lloyd 'Fourstacker' record breaking liner *Kaiser Wilhelm der Grosse* of 14,349 GR tons and an overall length of 649 ft and 65.5 ft width.

Propulsion of the twin screws was by two 4-cylinder, 4-crank triple expansion engines developing a total of 28,000 IHP at 80 RPM.

Steam at 210 psi was generated in 12 double-ended and 3 single-ended cylindrical smoke-tube boilers consuming on average 450 tons of coal daily to achieve a mean of 22.3 knots as a Blue Riband record.

108 furnaces were stoked by a team of some 190 stokers and trimmers. The coal bunker capacity was 4,000 tons.

Machinery and fuel bunkers occupied ca 42% of the hull capacity.

Location symbols:

'A' Propeller shaft tunnel

'B' Propulsion Machinery

'C' Coal Bunkers

'D' Boiler Plant

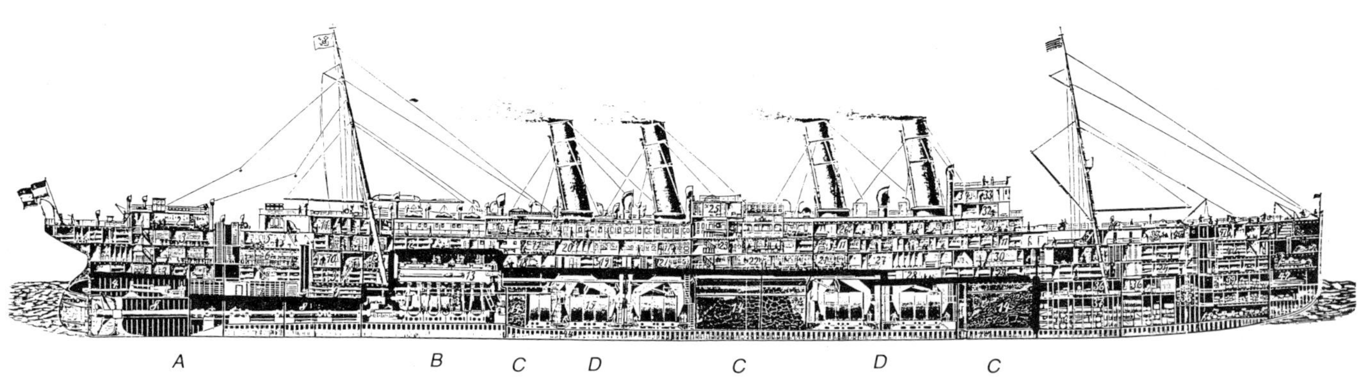

Deutsches Schiffahrtsmuseum, Bremerhaven

Cunard Line – 1907

Record breaking quadruple screw mail liner *Mauretania* of 31,937 GR tons, was 790 ft in overall length by 88 ft beam.

Propulsion of the four 17 ft diameter screws at a maximum of 190 RPM was by four Parsons direct-drive turbines, each developing 17,000 SHP.

Illustration shows *Mauretania* as built, with steam supplied by 23 double-ended and 2 single-ended coal fired boilers with 192 furnaces on Howden draught and developing 195 psi steam pressure. Average coal consumption was in the order of 800 to 1,000 tons daily to achieve service speeds of 24-25 knots during Atlantic crossings.

The boilers were stoked by 324 firemen and trimmers and the total boiler room personnel was 392. The coal bunker capacity was 6,500 tons.

In 1921 the boilers were converted to firing by oil fuel and this reduced the boiler room staff by 300 and introduced considerable saving in fuel costs, gave the boilers a new lease of life and improved the overall efficiency of generation of steam.

When built the machinery and coal bunkers occupied ca 39% of the ship's hull capacity.

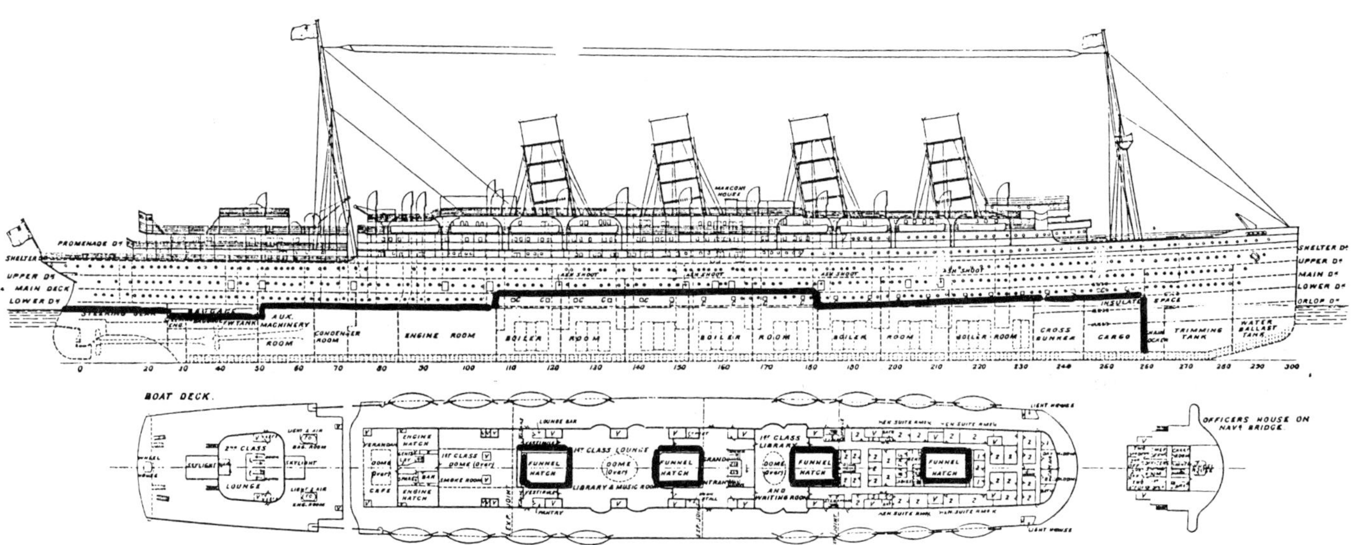

Rex – Italia Line – 1932

Sectional elevation of the luxury record breaking liner *Rex* of 51,062 GR tons and 880 ft in overall length by 96.8 ft width.

Propulsion machinery comprised four sets of three-stage single reduction geared turbines capable of developing a maximum of 130,000 SHP to drive four screws revolving at 230 RPM for a service speed of ca 28 knots.

Superheated steam at 385 psi (27 kg/cm^2) and 716°F (385°C) was generated in eight double-ended and four single-ended water-tube boilers, fired by 'Bunker C' grade oil fuel, bunkered in numerous wing tanks with a total capacity of some 6,100 tons.

Machinery and fuel occupied approximately 32% of the ship's hull capacity.

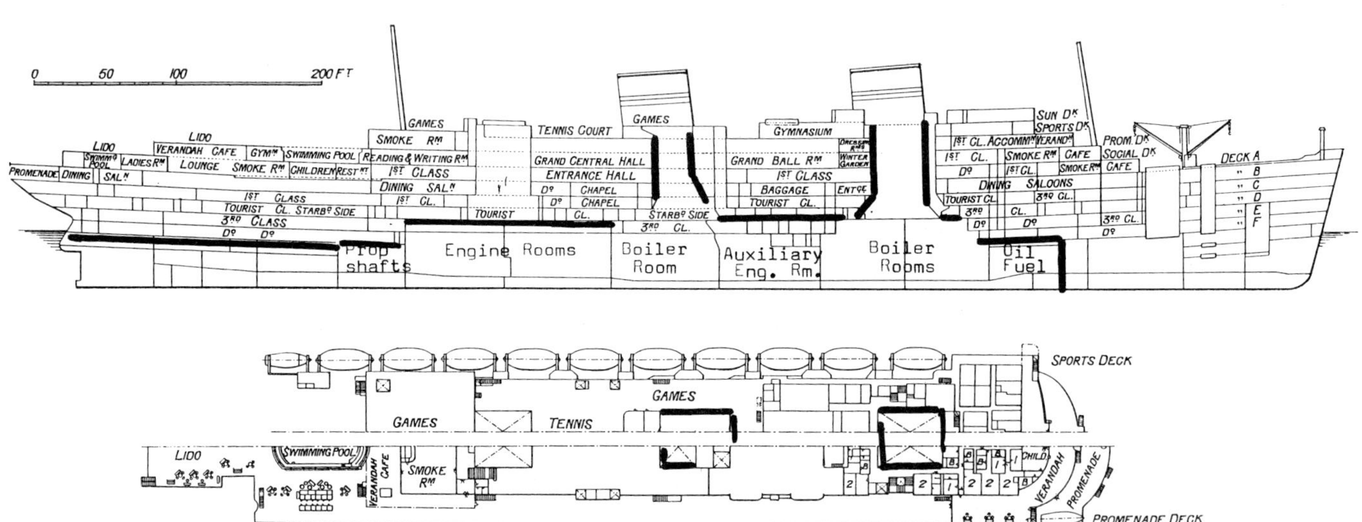

***Conte di Savoia* – Italia Line – 1932**

Sectional elevation of the luxury express liner *Conte di Savoia* of 48,502 GR tons and 814 ft in overall length by 96 ft beam.

Propulsion machinery consisted of four sets of three-stage Parsons single reduction geared turbines developing ca 100,000 SHP to drive four screws for service speeds of 25-27 knots.

Superheated steam for the turbines at 450 psi (31 kg/cm^2) in 10 Yarrow water-tube boilers was generated firing 'Bunker C' oil fuel.

Although paired on the Atlantic run with the record breaking liner *Rex*, the *Conte di Savoia* appeared to have no ambition to emulate the partner's achievement, which was not repeated for the company. The two liners operated their Genoa to New York service at reasonably economical and trouble-free speeds.

Machinery and fuel occupied approximately 26% of the liner's hull capacity.

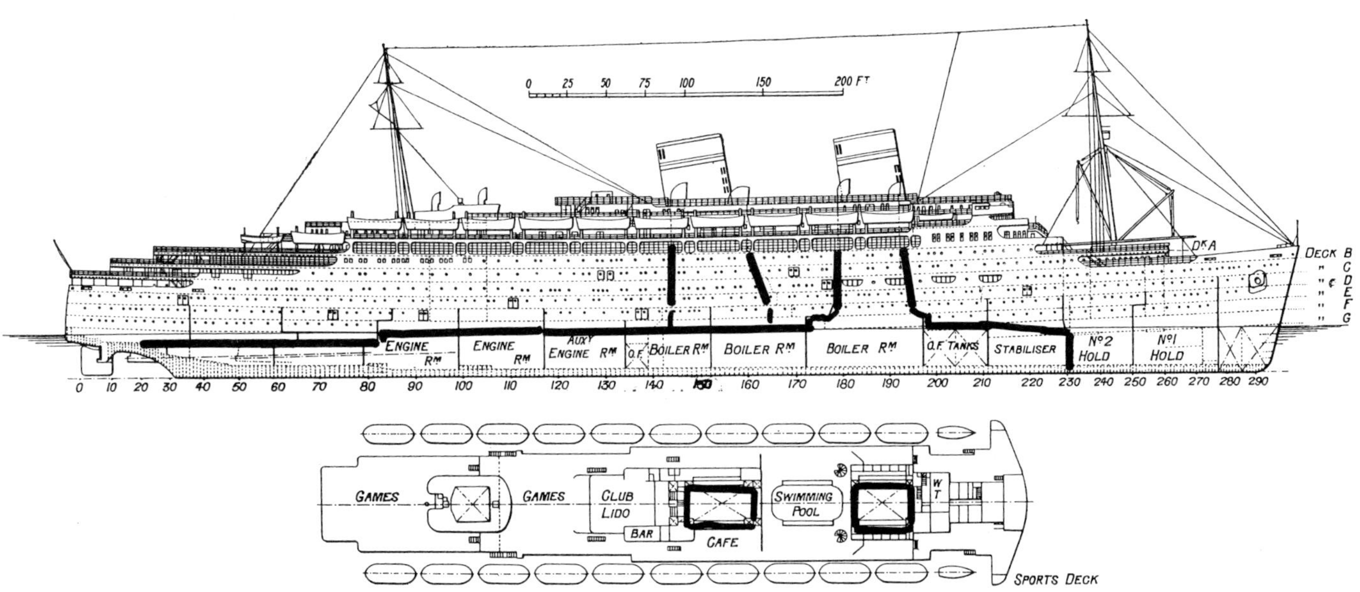

Queen Mary – Cunard Line – 1936

1936-1952 record breaking quadruple screw mail liner *Queen Mary* of 81,237 GR tons and 1,019 ft overall length by 118 ft beam.

Propulsion was by four single reduction geared compound turbine sets, each comprising 1 x HP, 2 x IP, 1 x LP turbines, aggregating 160,000 SHP for speeds of 30-32 knots.

Twenty-four Yarrow five-drum water-tube boilers generated propulsion steam at 400 psi and 700 °F. Two smoke-tube (Scotch) boilers provided domestic steam at 250 psi and 200 °F superheat.

All boilers used 'Bunker C' marine grade oil and overall consumption was around 1,000 tons per day.

Oil fuel was bunkered in cellular double bottom and wing tanks and total capacity was ca 8,000 tons.

Machinery, boilers and oil fuel bunkers occupied ca 30% of the ship's capacity.

Location symbols:

'A' Boiler rooms

'B' Engine rooms

'D' Refr. auxiliary machinery rooms

'E' Propeller tunnels

'G' Generator rooms

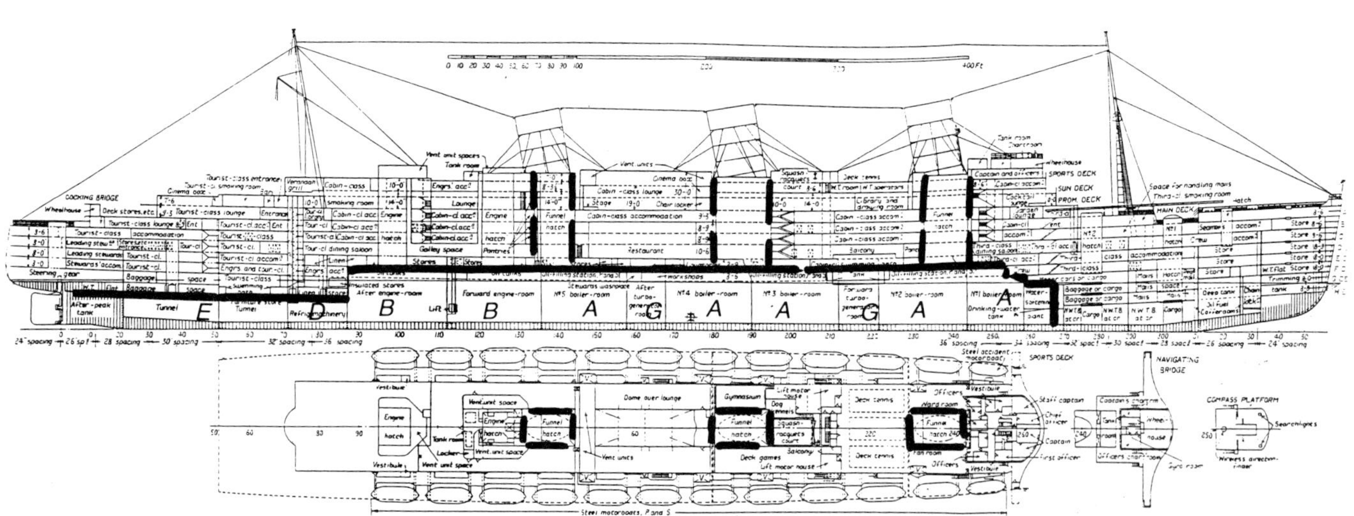

Normandie –
Compagnie Generale Transatlantique – 1935

1935-1939 record breaking quadruple-screw luxury liner *Normandie* of 83,423 GR tons and 1,028 ft in length overall by 117 ft beam.

Propulsion was by four sets of turbo-electric prime-movers capable of developing a maximum of 160,000 SHP to achieve speeds of 30-32 knots.

Twenty-nine Penhoet three-drum water-tube boilers generated propulsion steam at 335 psi (325°C). Auxiliary steam was provided by four single-ended smoke-tube (Scotch) marine boilers at 143 psi.

All boilers used 'Bunker C' marine grade oil fuel and overall consumption was around 1,200-1,250 tons per day. Oil fuel was bunkered in the cellular double bottom and wing tanks with a total capacity of 9,600 cbm roughly equivalent to 9,000 tons.

Machinery, boilers and oil fuel storage occupied ca 28% of the ship's hull capacity.

Location symbols:

'A' Boiler rooms

'B' Turbo generator room

'C' Drive-motor room

'D' Auxiliary machinery room

'E' Propeller tunnels

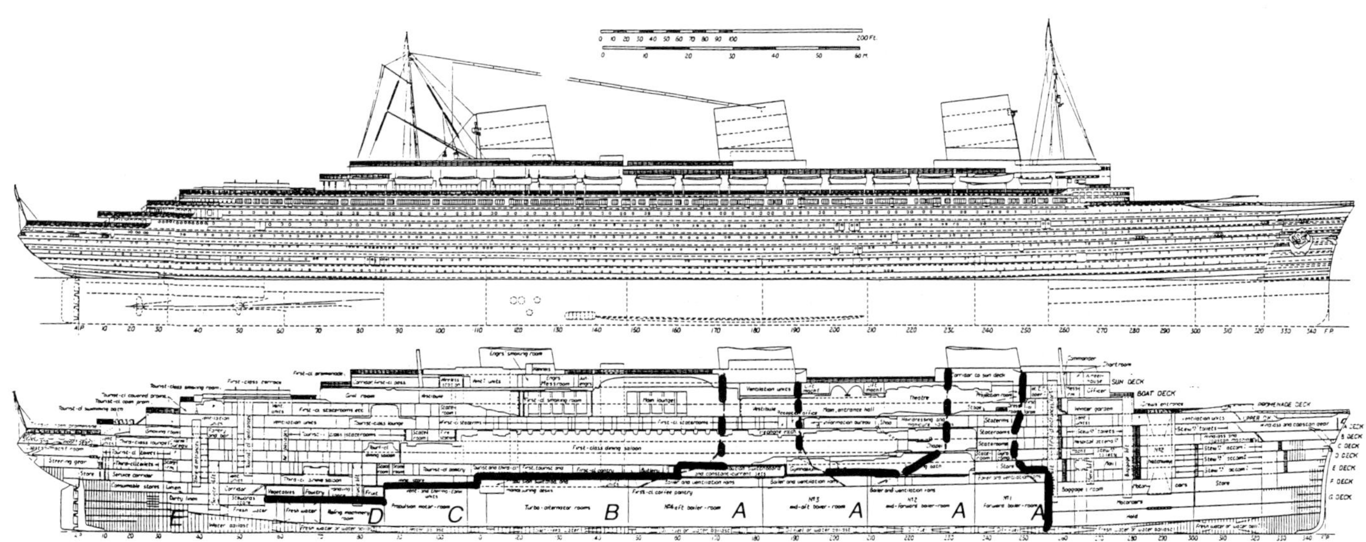

Courtesy of Shipbuilder & Marine Engine Builder

Steam Generation – Marine Boilers

Firing of Ship's Boilers

WITH THE INTRODUCTION DURING the early days of the 19th century of steam as the principal medium for propulsion of ships on the high seas, there materialised a particular breed of seagoing labour called firemen or stokers, whose duty it was to attend to the steam generating coal fired boilers and ensure their proper function. Depending upon the size of ships and numbers of boilers, stokers could possibly have been expected to perform both, coal trimming and firing duties but in the case of large liners, requiring attendance to greater numbers of more sophisticated high pressure boilers, it became important to have separate teams of men shovelling and trimming the coal stocks in the bunkers and transferring adequate amounts to the firemen to feed the boilers.

In Britain most of the labour in these categories of trade appeared to originate in Ireland and they, needless to say, were a tough crew prepared to work in abysmal conditions and when in port, consumed vast quantities of liquid refreshments.

The fireman-stoker usually started his vocation as a trimmer requiring no particular skills or experience but frequently using the job as a pretext for a free journey to skip ship for settlement in 'the land of unlimited opportunities'. However, chosing to remain onboard of ship, the trimmer having gained some experience, could well foresake his original spade and wheelbarrow for the more elaborate tools of the trade, such as the 8-9 foot slice and rake and qualify as a stoker-fireman. Whereas the trimmer's job lay in helping with coaling in port and providing the fireman with barrow-fulls of coal, the stoker's firing skills would include an accurate spreading of 40-50 lbs spade-fulls of coal on the glowing 6-8 ft long firebed of the boiler grate through a narrow firing door which had to be kept open for as short a period as possible to avoid loss of heat, keep the firebed evenly raked and sliced to break the clinker and remove ash and clinker for eventual disposal overboard. All this work had to be executed in an aura of a radiation temperature of ca 300 °C emanating through the open boiler door maintaining a stokehold temperature at 30-40 °C in an atmosphere permeated with coal dust, while balancing on the coal-strewn stokehold floor heaving and lurching with the movement of the ship in all weather conditions.

Regarding numbers employed, a comparison may well be drawn of the last of the Cunard paddlers (*Scotia* of 1856) equipped with eight boilers, each having five furnaces fired by 65-70 boilermen in shifts to maintain a steam pressure of 20 psi, with one of the early 20th century giant coal-fired liners, such as the *Bismarck* of HAPAG, in which 340 stokers and

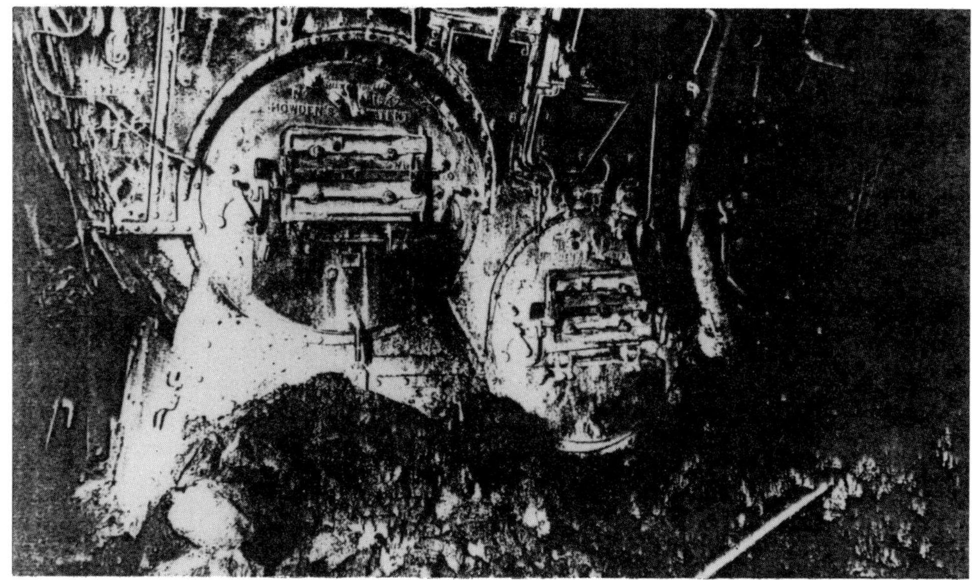

trimmers coaled the 46 water-tube boilers developing a pressure of 195 psi.

Coal as traditional fuel for steam raising, was always in plentiful supply and comparatively cheap. In marine use it was never the ultimate solution, having to be manhandled in constricted spaces thus becoming very labour intensive and also a filthy material for direct handling and utilisation on shipboard, creating exceedingly unpleasant working conditions.

The introduction of oil fuel for steam raising in commercial shipping around the 1920's, completely revolutionised handling and pure economics of steam generation and although on the average more expensive than coal, offered advantages which made it the only realistic fuel for marine use.

The main factors favouring oil can be summarised: (1) Oil having to be pumped, is handled and stored more easily and in a clean environment. (2) Occupying ca 38 cb ft/ton, oil requires much less storage space than coal at 45/50 cb ft/ton. (3) Average higher Calorific Value for oil at 18,500 Btu/lb compared with that for coal at about 12,000 Btu/lb much reduces the equivalent consumption. (4) Oil fired boilers in good condition can operate at 80-85% efficiency whereas coal firing could never improve on 65-70%. (5) Combustion of oil can be much more easily controlled and automated, leading to improved economics. (6) Operating personnel as compared with coal firing is greatly reduced, with firemen and trimmers becoming surplus. Immeasurable improvements in working conditions commensurate with considerable reduction in labour costs, were created. Referring to the example above, when *Majestic* (ex-*Bismarck*) was converted to oil firing, the stokehold staff was reduced from a total of 420 to 70, the firemen and trimmers having become redundant.

Fuel Oils

There are various grades of fuel oils marketed and they can be classified within the context of residue stages of refining operations as distillates derived directly or indirectly from crude. Different oil grades require different burner types and the selected fuel determines type of burner, method of atomisation, type and size of boiler and auxiliaries as well as final operational costs.

The most important difference between different marketed grades of liquid fuels is their viscosity, which helps to classify oils into 'light', 'medium' and 'heavy' grades. In elementary terms, viscosity is a measure of internal resistance experienced by adjacent layers of a fluid in the course of relative displacement and this resistance reduces with the increase in temperature of oil. Therefore viscosity as a characteristic value must be quoted in conjunction with related standard temperatures. In addition to various scientific terms relating to viscosity characteristics, in general practice oils are classified in empirical terms for kinematic viscosity related to time taken (seconds) for the flow of a fluid quantity through various forms of standard tubular viscometer. Three commonly used terms are 'Redwood No 1 secs' (R1) for the UK, 'Saybolt Universal secs' (SUS) for the USA and 'Engler Degrees' (E) for Germany. Whereas 'R1' and 'SUS' reference units relate to direct efflux of standard oil quantity at 38°C (100°F) and 21°C (70°F) respectively, the Engler Degrees measurement represents ratio of viscometer outflow time for oil to that of the same quantity of water. 1°E corresponds to viscosity of water at 20°C. According to viscosity standards, marketed grades of fuel oils vary from 1,000-7,000 R1 secs (also called 'Bunker C') for heavy grades to blends up to 950 R1 for medium oils and 45-200 R1 for light grades.

All heavy oils require pre-heating to ca 100 to 200°F for viscosity reduction to facilitate pumping, filtration and storage and 200-300°F may be required at the burner for atomisation. Even 250 R1 secs medium oils require pre-heating to 50°F for pumping and some 150°F for injection. Most oil burners operate within a viscosity range of 60 to 100 R1 secs.

Based upon operational economics, it is usual practice to fire large marine boilers with 'Bunker C' fuel oil having a viscosity of around 2,000-3,000 R1 secs. All ships' bunkers are then equipped with coils of steam piping to maintain proper storage and atomisation temperatures. When suitably pre-heated, marine grade oils are usually atomised for combustion by 'blast injectors' using steam or high pressure air.

Heavy oil-fired boiler plant in No. 3 Main Boiler Room of the luxury liner Normandie.

Iron Flue Boiler

When Atlantic scheduled services were introduced around 1837 and for a subsequent decade or so, marine boilers of the day were of the iron 'flue' type and were also called 'box' boilers, with flues made up of flat iron plates riveted together to form rectangular passages. There was little progress made during this early period which included the provision of simple expansion engines using steam at 5-20 psi for the side-lever and oscillating machinery propelling Atlantic or other paddlers and screw-driven ships of the era.

The flue-boiler comprised a shell, as a rule rectangular in section, containing the furnaces from which the flues or passages led products of combustion backwards and forwards, twisting in various ways according to the designer's ideas, to terminate at the top of the shell, thence joining the funnel base. Some of the early designs became weird and intricate without necessarily achieving positive results such as permitting higher temperatures but often with alarming results as far as safety of operation was concerned. However, the usual marine boiler of the period remained a comparatively simple apparatus with flues so arranged that the iron plates could be easily cleaned, both on the fireside and the waterside.

Diagrammatic sketch Fig. 1 illustrates a typical three-furnace low pressure marine flue boiler, where 'A' is the ashpit and 'B' the hand-stoked furnaces from where combustion gases pass into the transverse flue 'C' and thence into the lower flue 'D', from which, as indicated by arrows, gases pass through passage 'E' connecting lower flue to upper flue 'F' and then reverse into uptake 'G' to be discharged into funnel. 'L' is the water level.

Other boiler designs may have had a single flue, which would have been as deep as the two flues shown.

Flat plates being used throughout, internal parts were held together by numerous rivetted stays and obviously any attempt at higher pressures would have been associated with danger.

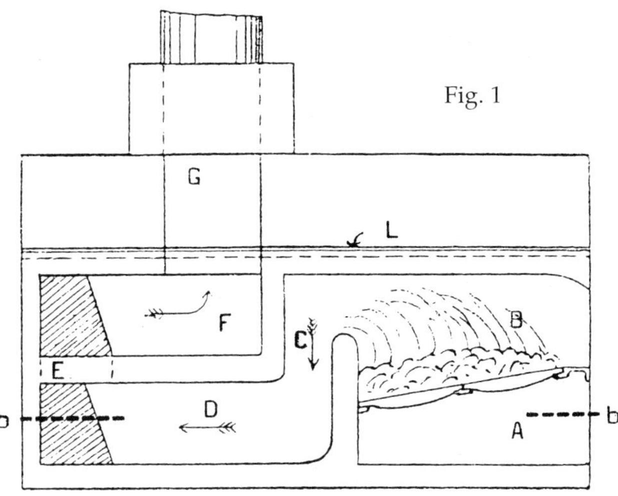

Fig. 1

Section at "a-a"

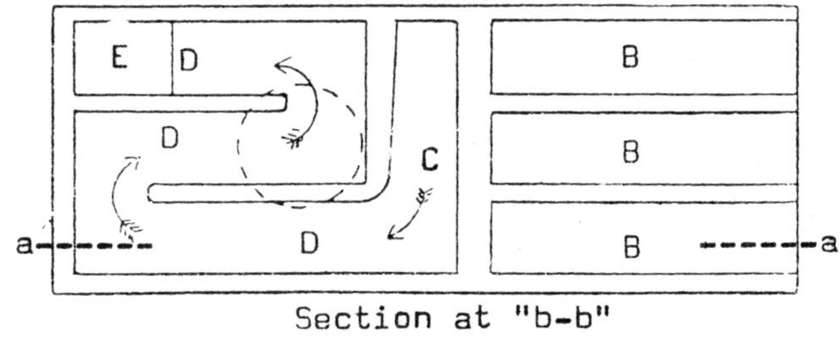

Section at "b-b"

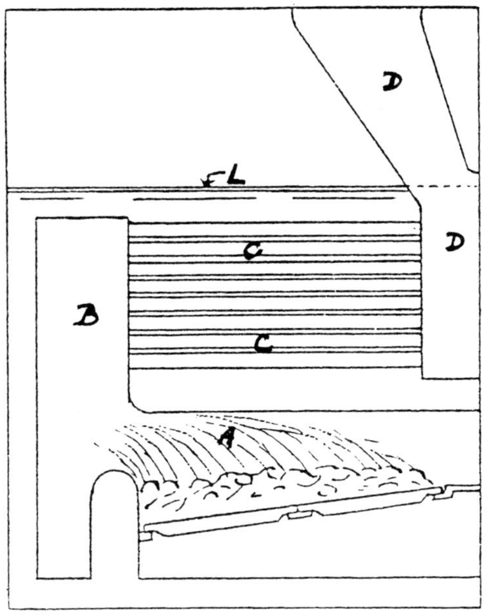

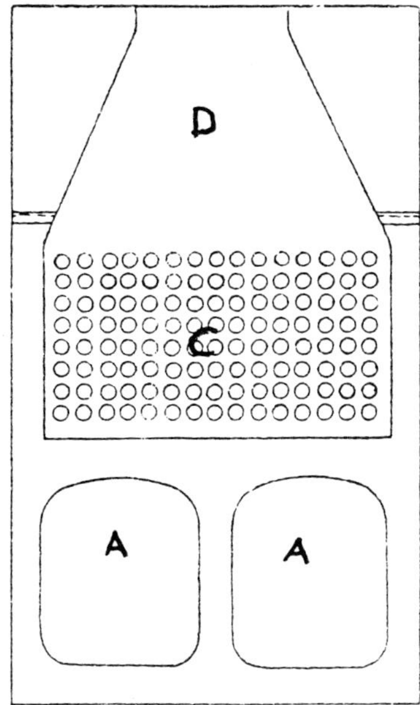

Fig. 2

Tubed iron-flue 'Box' Boiler

A development to allow some pressure increase above the limits set by the flue boiler, resulted in the design of marine boiler being modified by replacing rectangular flues by a large number of small diameter tubes. Diagram Fig. 2 indicates sections through a boiler type similar to that used around 1850-1870 as installed in Cunarders *Arabia*, *Persia* and *Russia* as well as other contemporaries. It will be noted that products of combustion pass into chamber 'B' and from there through smoke-tubes 'C' to the uptake 'D'. As in all box-shaped boilers, any number of furnaces could be introduced, space and size permitting.

Cylindrical Tubular Marine Boiler

Experience showed that even the tubed version of the 'box' boiler permitted only a comparatively small increase of working pressures up to 30-40 psi with safety and therefore when compound engines were coming into general use and steam pressures of 50-60 psi were required, the shape concept of the steam boiler had to be revised. It was appreciated that the strongest shape would be circular shells hence the marine boiler comprising a cylindrical multi-tubular shell and furnaces came into being by 1870-75, completely replacing rectangular and other shapes.

The earliest cylindrical smoke-tube boilers were made of iron throughout, with shell plates generally rolled into the circular form after the rivet-holes were punched. The furnaces were plain flues and had a longitudinal riveted joint. Reliability, strength and lightness were greatly furthered by the introduction of steel plates instead of iron, after a few years' experience with the shape. Steel was at first adopted for external parts but then also furnaces and shells were made of steel. Around 1880 corrugated furnace tubes were introduced and were found to permit higher pressures for multi-expansion engines than was possible with stiffened plain flues.

Sketch Fig. 3 shows typical 19th/20th century marine smoke-tube boiler design, which, if suitably adapted and modernised, enabled steam at pressures up to 220-250 psi to be generated. Usual practice was to have three furnaces per boiler although two furnaces were quite common for the smaller units and four furnaces could be fitted in the larger boilers (Fig. 4).

To save space for large outputs, the cylindrical boiler was also made double-ended (Fig. 5) in which a common combustion chamber was served by two grates, one at each end of the boiler. This reduced the length of the boiler and its weight, but if used with forced draught, required a high brick wall between furnaces or two fireboxes separated the grates. The average design of the cylindrical marine boiler adapted easily for oil firing which became generally accepted since the 1920's because of its undoubted advantages.

Superheating of Steam

Superheating of steam in order to dry it by adding heat was introduced because saturated steam at the related pressure tends to cool off when reaching the engine and cooling further during expansion stages it loses more heat so that eventually the engine would receive a small quantity of condensed water. To prevent this and enable steam expansion to do the maximum useful work, steam generated in the boiler is led through a superheater consisting of tube bundles placed where they receive the greatest possible convection heat from the combustion gases. As steam is led through the superheater tubes it receives a final

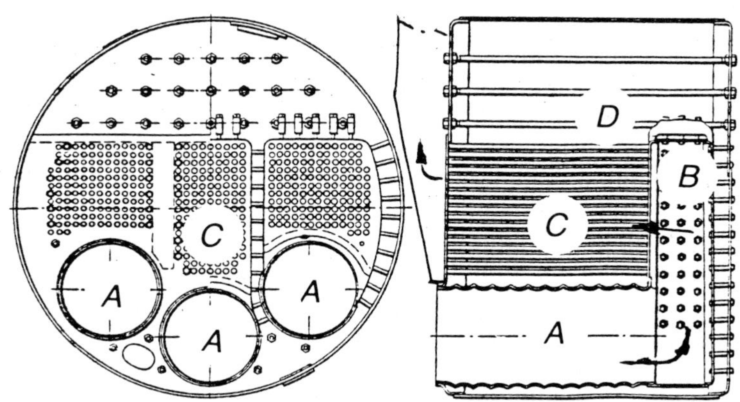

Fig. 3

Sectional view showing the principle of a late 19th century development of the cylindricalsingle-ended three-furnace marine smoke-tube steel boiler.

'A' – Furnace
'B' – Firebox
'C' – Smoke-tubes
'D' – Water/steam

Fig. 4. *Typical turn-of-the-century four-furnace single-ended cylindrical boiler being assembled (shown minus tubes and boiler shell).*

Front view of furnaces. *Rear view of fireboxes.*

heating from the furnace and is raised to a greater temperature before going on to drive the engine.

The reciprocating engine cannot accept temperatures of more than 400°F (200°C) and this controls the degree of permissible pressure and superheat. The turbine imposes no such limit, hence superheating of steam is used mainly for turbine operation which requires dry steam, superheated as per particular design commensurate with the highest obtainable efficiency and reliability.

In principle a superheater for a cylindrical boiler usually consists of a series of loops or elements of special steel tubing inserted in the smoke-tubes and connected to headers placed vertically at the boiler front between the nests of smoke-tubes.

Saturated steam from the boiler stop valve enters the saturated steam header and passing through the elements returns at a higher temperature (superheated) to the superheated steam collector and thence to the engine. The steam elements are therefore in direct contact with the gases flowing from the combustion chamber of the boiler (Fig. 6).

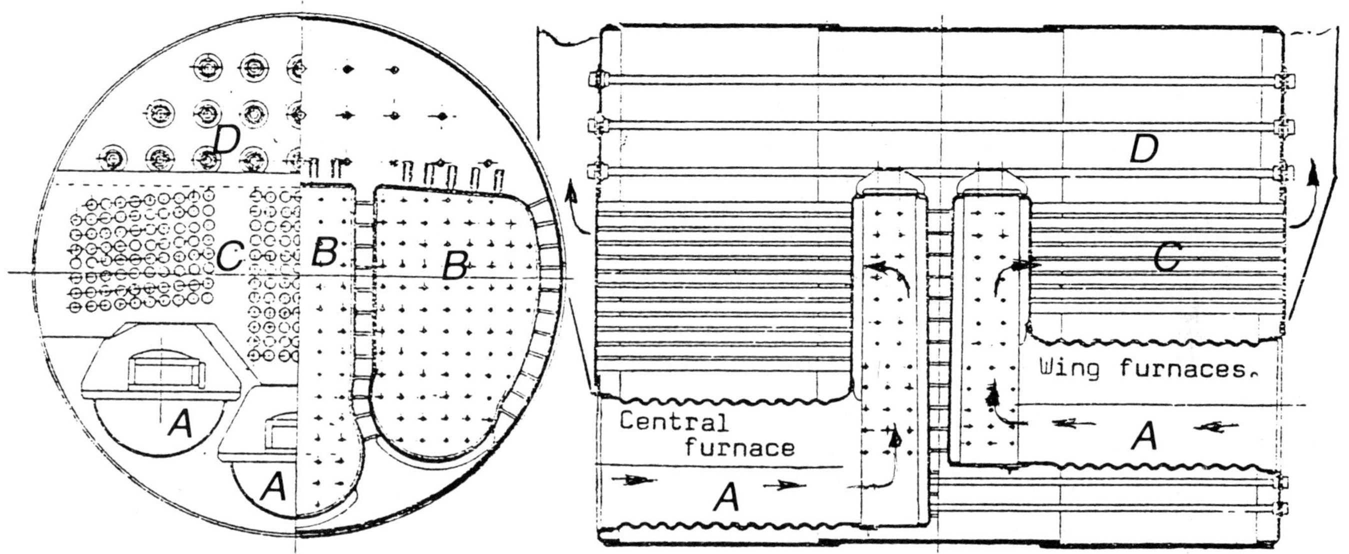

Fig. 5. *Sectional diagram showing turn-of-the-century double-ended cylindrical three-grate boiler.*

'A' – Furnaces   'B' – Fireboxes   'C' – Smoke-tubes   'D' – Water/Steam

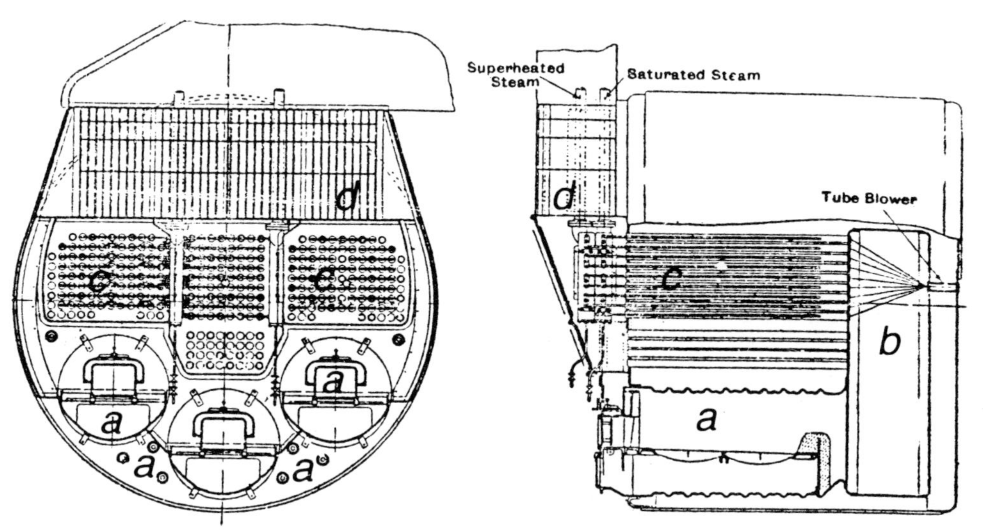

Fig. 6

Diagram indicating typical 20th century marine boiler with smoke-tube superheater.

'a' – Furnaces
'b' – Firebox
'c' – Smoke-tubes
'd' – Superheater

The Water-tube Boiler

Although the cylindrical smoke-tube boiler (also called 'Scotch' boiler in marine use or 'Economic' boiler for land use) has always been comparatively cheap and simple, it is not considered suitable for pressures above 250 psi, the concept as such featuring water and steam contained in the same space. Furthermore for larger marine installations the size and number of single and double-ended boilers as may be required, would tend to occupy undue space.

The water-tube boiler principle had been in various stages of experimental development towards the end of the 19th century but success and reliability was to a great extent achieved with the introduction of suitable materials such as alloy steels and large water-tube boilers were introduced in major power stations and in industry during the first quarter of the 20th century. The German merchant marine virtually pioneered water-tube boilers on the Atlantic with HAPAG introducing Yarrow-type 250 psi steam producers in their three 1913-1918 built 52,000-56,000 ton giant liners, *Imperator, Vaterland* and *Bismarck*. These boilers proved to be efficient steam generators, especially after subsequent conversion to oil firing.

With ever increasing sizes of passenger liners and warships requiring sizeable turbine primemovers operating at elevated pressures of 350 psi to 500 psi (sometimes even to 1,000 psi), different types and designs of the water-tube boiler were introduced for marine use from the 1920's for steam conditions to ensure the highest efficiencies in particular turbine plants.

Four of the 29 high pressure water-tube boilers for working pressure of 400 psi (28 kg/cm^2) and 662°F (350°C) for installation in the 83,423 ton record breaking liner Normandie *of 1935.*

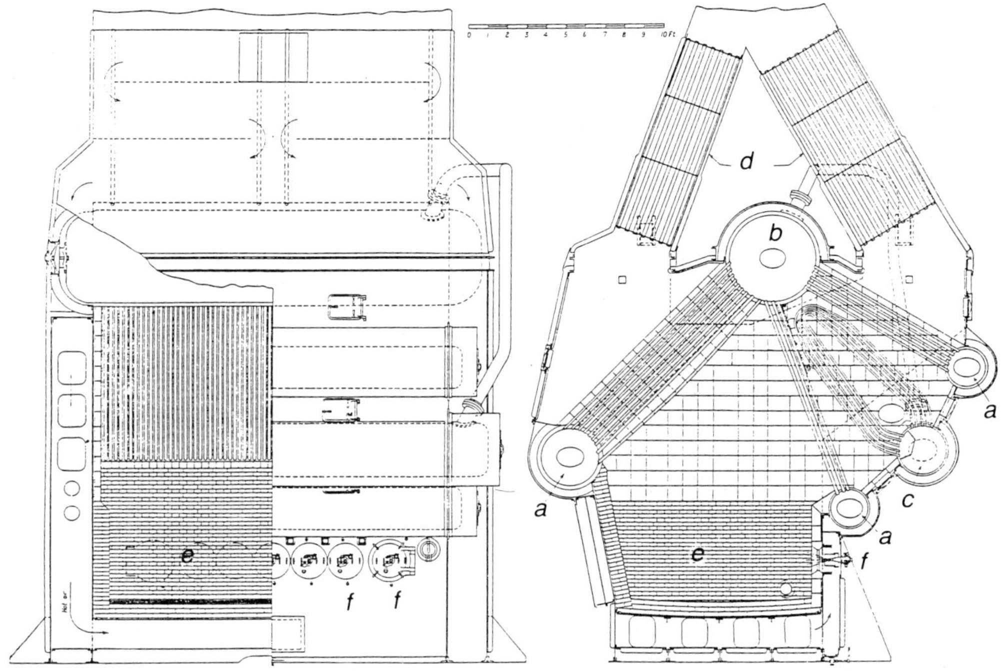

Sectional view of a Yarrow water-tube marine boiler rated at a working pressure of 400 psi (28 kg/cm²) and 700°F (370°C). 24 of these boilers were installed as main steam generators in the 1936 Cunard record breaker Queen Mary. *The boilers were a typical mid-30's design as used in numerous ships of the period.*

'a' – Water drums
'b' – Steam drum
'c' – Superheater drum
'd' – Air heaters
'e' – Furnace
'f' – Oil burners

In the water-tube boiler, water for conversion into steam is made to circulate through small-bore tubes on the outside of which pass the combustion gases from the furnaces. Economiser pre-heated water to be boiled and the steam generated in the tubes are contained in horizontal drums, located at low and high levels respectively. Water from respective drums circulates through the tube banks which are placed in such a manner as to ensure the most effective evaporation by radiation and convection from the heating gases created in the furnace and flowing at right-angles to the tube banks.

Superheaters, which are an essential prerequisite for the water-tube boiler, usually comprise banks of small-bore tubing attached to headers located in the boiler combustion zone in such a manner as to be in the path of heating gases.

The principal advantages of the water-tube boiler as compared with the smoke-tube counterpart include the ability to develop the highest steam pressures, rapidity of steam raising and more rapid circulation, ability to endure greater forcing, reduced weight and space occupied and higher rates of evaporation and superheating. The boiler is also much safer at high pressures because the bursting of one small water-tube would have much less serious results than inadvertant damage to a smoke-tube submerged in water at high pressure.

Marine water-tube boilers are primarily designed for combustion of oil fuel; experimental installations to burn pulverised coal did not offer any particular advantages or savings but gave a lot of trouble.

Numerous types and designs of marine water-tube boilers, having different configurations and location and numbers of drums and water-tube banks, have been produced; Yarrow, Babcock & Wilcox and Foster-Wheeler principles are usually in the forefront.

Water-tube boilers in marine use provide the main high pressure superheated steam to drive the propulsion turbines. For auxiliary and shore use, requiring saturated steam at lower pressures, it has always been normal practice with large installations to provide separate smaller, auxiliary 'Scotch' boilers as may be required. Their total output would amount to only a fraction of propulsion steam and the function would be quite independent.

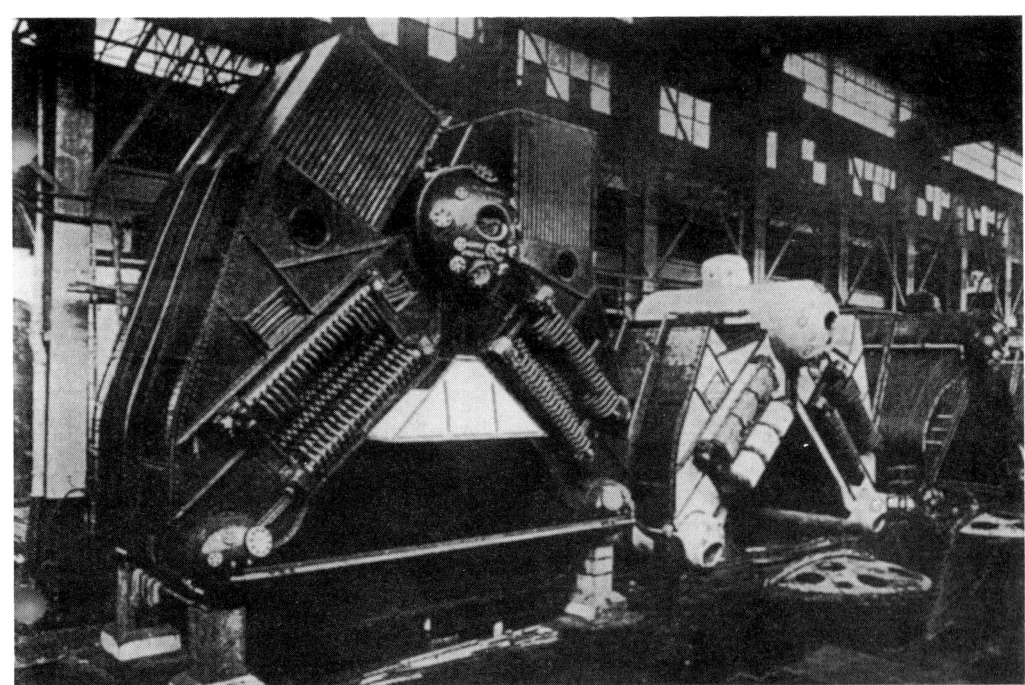

Three-drum oil-fired water-tube boilers in the course of erection for the Italia Line record breaker Rex. *The total installation comprised eight double-ended and four single-ended boilers with a total heating surface of 3,300m², for a steam working pressure of 385 psi at 716°F. Closed stokehold forced draught was provided.*

Ships and their Propulsion

General Remarks

THE RELEVANT PRINCIPLES OF evolution and development of steamships and their propulsion during the Blue Riband period on the Atlantic are explained here, with major changes applying mainly to the 19th century shipping, encouraged by the brisk growth of competition on the Atlantic and other trade routes.

After the turn of the century, with the introduction of the steam turbine, further advances were related more to the detail development and application of this 'ultimate prime mover' and its co-relation with transmission by screw-propulsion commensurate with the higher pressures capable of being developed by modern boilers and the introduction of oil firing. Apart from some general explanations of the relevant aspects, it is not intended to enlarge upon details of such developments. Furthermore the important introduction of the Internal Combustion Diesel Oil Engine as a means of ship propulsion is not enlarged upon because this type of engine, although of extreme significance in connection with marine operational efficiency and economics, was not directly involved in Atlantic records.

The Paddle Steamer

Commencing with the Atlantic pioneers from ca 1830 onwards, the paddle driven steamship ruled the Atlantic routes for more than two decades because the first appearance of screw propulsion required much development and operational experience before it could compete with and completely supplant the paddle wheel. At the inception of scheduled Atlantic travel this was not helped by the fact that the British Government (Admiralty) subsidising the Cunard Mail Contracts, required a regular, reliable all-year service and the company had to comply with Admiralty practices regarding ship construction and propulsion. Cunard was therefore to a great extent inhibited by conservatism in order to follow official directives. Furthermore, the first years of Cunard predominance on the Atlantic, right up to the 1960's, did not produce such positive competition as to create the major financial incentives necessary for extensive improvements to efficiency and towards innovation. One result was that even with competition materialising, Cunard tended to leave it to others to bear the costs of ideas and experimentation until such time as proven reliability and positive results were assured.

The paddle driven wooden steamer persevered on the Atlantic up to ca 1852 during which period the sizes of steamships doubled and propulsive power generated by the same basic type of engine, the two-cylinder side-lever unit, virtually quadrupled. This prime-mover increased in size out of all proportion to an economical power-to-weight ratio and much to the detriment of payload of the ever growing ship sizes. With the introduction of the iron hull around 1852, the last paddle-driven Cunarders *Persia* of 1856 and *Scotia* in 1862, as well as the seven large 3,200 ton paddlers belonging to Cie Generale Transatlantique, featured the ultimate sizes of the side-lever machinery, with cylinder diameter of over 8 ft-4 in (2,540 mm) and a 12 ft-0 in (3,650 mm) stroke. These monoliths were supplied by steam at very low pressures around 20 psi from very large rectangular iron multi-furnace flue-type boilers burning vast quantities of coal.

All this was provided to produce sufficient power for the current speed requirement of some 13 knots but occupied a quite unrealistic amount of space comprising virtually half the ship's hull capacity. This ship type became operationally completely uneconomical and quite incapable of competing with the more advanced steamers and prime-movers being introduced by more forward thinking shipowners.

The Side-Lever Engine

This type of machinery as widely represented on the Atlantic and elsewhere for nearly two decades, was an 1814 development of the various attempts at ship propulsion in America and Britain at the turn of the 18th century and which was based upon the Watt Beam-Engine principle adapted and compacted to drive propulsion paddles. The side-lever system did create a more or less compact and reliable version of the pioneers' efforts by providing a marine engine capable of being built to a standard specification. It replaced the large overhead beam above the cylinder of the Watt principle and the various other complicated and weird alternatives and mutations, by two smaller rocking beams (side-levers) positioned as low as possible by the side of the steam cylinder.

The relevant principle of the side-lever marine engine, usually comprising two vertical steam cylinders, was to connect each of the two upward acting piston rods to the ends of two horizontal side-levers at the base of respective cylinders by means of a crosshead, which operated downward directed connecting rods. The side-levers were pivoted around a fulcrum bearing-pin at about their mid-length. At the other ends of the side-levers a connecting crossbar was attached at its centre to a long vertical connecting rod driving the crank on the paddle drive shaft above; the rocking of the side-levers thus ensured rotation of the paddle wheels. The cranks on the paddle drive shaft were usually set at 90 degrees apart to enable the engine to start from any stationary position. Pumps and other ancillary drives were taken off the side-levers.

The steam cylinders of a side-lever engine were 'double-acting', i.e. steam pressure alternatively forced the piston downwards when given access at the top and upwards with steam entering the lower part of the cylinder.

To maximise useful work from steam by reducing the back-pressure, the side of the piston not subjected to steam had to be made to lose residual pressure by connection to a condenser where exhaust steam was cooled either directly by water jet (jet condenser) or across separating surfaces (surface condenser), thus converting steam back to water for re-use.

Although engines by different firms may vary in detail, the relative positions of cylinder, side-levers and connections for the operation of paddle wheels would usually be as indicated on the illustration on the opposite page.

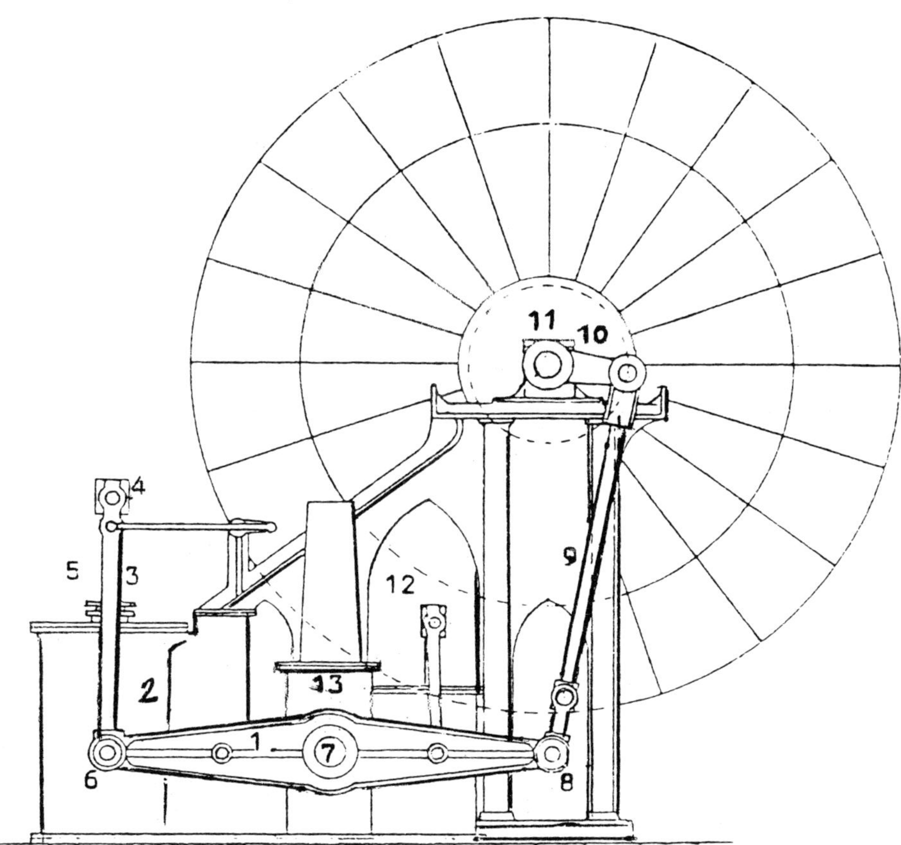

Diagram of typical side-lever steam engine driving a paddle wheel. (Shipping World – *1st September 1887).*

1. Side-levers
2. Steam cylinder
3. Piston rod
4. Crosshead
5. Connecting rods
6. Rocking end of side-lever
7. Side-lever fulcrum pin
8. Side-lever connection to crossbar
9. Driving connecting rod
10. Crank on paddle drive shaft
11. Paddle shaft (14-18 RPM)
12. Air pump worked off side-levers
13. Jet condenser
14. Slide valve worked by eccentric and gab lever

Evolution of the Simple Expansion Steam Engine

On the Atlantic the side-lever engine became redundant virtually with the change from paddles to screw propulsion, which greatly obviated the problems and wasted space associated with levers, linkages and diverse connections. These changes introduced the vertical reciprocating engine as it is known today and made possible subsequent propulsion developments to be directed towards reduction of space occupied by power plant and also towards greater economies of operation, better reliability and increased payload as well as speed of travel.

Higher steam pressures were made possible by the development and introduction by 1870 of cylindrical smoke-tube boilers in place of the very low pressure multi-grate box-type steam generators.

During the period from 1850 to ca 1865 many varying engine designs and configurations were experimented with in order to improve the power-to-weight and power-to-space ratios but until higher steam pressures were achieved and simple expansion engines managed to cope with better utilisation of steam power potential, these ideas met with only limited success although some were put into use, be it to drive paddles or propellers and often proved reasonally effective for the period.

Some designs were the result of attempts to eliminate cumbersome paddle-drive arrangements by placing engine cylinders directly beneath drive cranks. In the 'oscillating cylinder' engine, as per illustration below, cylinders rocked in trunnions supported by the engine frame and piston rods acted

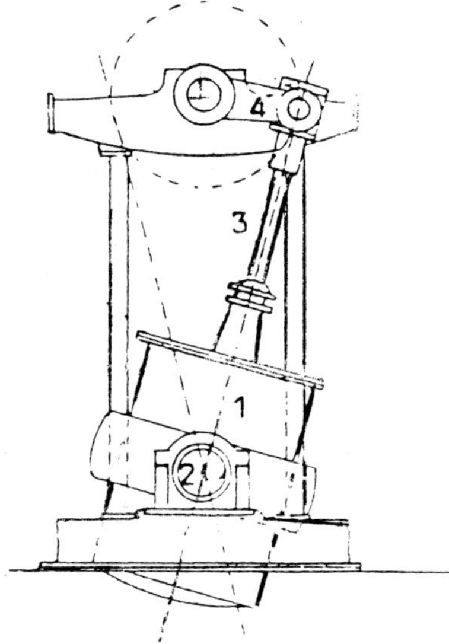

Diagram showing in principle the oscillating cylinder steam engine as fitted in the Cunarder China, *the* Adriatic *of Collins Line and some other companies' screw and paddle steamers during the period 1855 to 1866. The engine type, used for direct drive of paddles or geared-up for screw propulsion, was considered a great commercial success of the period.*

The engine function: Cylinder (1) is supported on its opposite sides on two trunnions (2). The reciprocating motion of the piston rod (3) caused by the piston travel in the cylinder (1) oscillates the cylinder on the trunnions (2) and its top end, engaging the crankshaft pin (4) transmits rotary motion to the propeller shaft. Steam is admitted through one of the trunnions and exhausted through the other to the condenser.

directly on the cranks of the propelling shaft above. This system proved a reasonable development of the simple expansion steam engine used in the early days of screw propulsion for long-haul ships in 1850-1866, but also found favour with small paddlers right up to the turn of the century.

During the first half of the 19th century the simple expansion steam engine, although heavy and inefficient, gave robust service at slow revolutions to suit paddle drives, but with the introduction of the propeller, higher crankshaft speeds were required for more efficient operation and this was achieved through 'gearing-up', using such means as rope drives, pitch chains or toothed wheels. Such geared engines of different configurations were built up to 1850-1860 by which time improved engine design and materials as well as higher steam pressures (around 60 psi) gave rise to higher crankshaft speeds thus allowing engines to be directly connected to screw drive.

It is interesting to note that early engines with pistons operating upwards were called 'vertical' whereas with the advent of screw propulsion and the siting of propeller shaft at low level, engine cylinders were placed above the centre line of the crankshaft and this virtually final form of the reciprocating engine as it is known today, was at the time called 'inverted'.

The Compound Engine

By the mid-19th century the introduction of higher boiler pressures than in earlier practice, led to operational complications and loss of efficiency with simple expansion cylinders, greatly encouraging an accelerated development of the compound system. In an engine of this type, steam is expanded in two stages, leading to improved thermodynamic efficiency, reduced engine size and weight and to lower operating costs. In numerous instances simple expansion engines could be converted to compound working.

The compound engine principle was first conceived by Watt and Hornblower at the turn of the 18th century but the first working marine application was ascribed to John Elder & Co. (later Fairfield Shipbuilding & Engineering Co.), around the mid-1800's. The engine was designed to utilise more effectively the expansive power of steam and fundamentally consisted of two cylinders, of which the first, high pressure (HP) one, smaller in diameter, received steam at full pressure from the boiler and after doing its useful stint and at consequently lower pressure, was exhausted into the second, larger diameter low-pressure (LP) cylinder, where it expanded and did further useful work prior to being finally exhausted to the condenser. The cylinders were so dimensioned and when necessary, steam was so adjusted at entry to the HP cylinder to balance the pressures to ensure that the outputs of the two cylinders actuating the two cranks were as near as possible equal, with their sum amounting to the total engine power.

The application of compounding as compared with simple expansion, resulted in considerable reduction in fuel consumption, ensured higher performance from smaller engines and left more space to be utilised for payload. These remarks of course apply to ship sizes of a particular period and their power requirements.

In the quest for greater outputs, operational improvements and higher crankshaft speeds, configurations with three (one HP and two LP) cylinders and four (two HP and two LP) were built, usually for 'tandem' operation with the HP cylinder placed above the LP, acting on a common crank. Multiple tandem units were also installed for larger outputs but these tended to become rather cumbersome. A typical example was the 1881 liner *City of Rome* of 8,415 tons, a proposed record breaker built for the Inman Line, in which instance six cylinders operated three cranks using the tandem principle.

By 1885, with ever increasing sizes of ships, possibility of higher boiler pressures and perpetually growing demand for speed, the compound engine was reaching the limits of its economic capacity. Furthermore the iron steamer was becoming out of date and with Siemens-Martin high tensile steel being introduced around 1880, steamships could be made stronger and lighter.

An example of large output compound power plant reaching the limits of economic feasibility can be mentioned. The two steel-hulled 1885 Cunard record breakers *Umbria* and *Etruria* of 8,128 tons were equipped with 3-cylinder 3-crank compound engines (one HP and two LP) generating 14,500 IHP driving a single screw for a rated speed of over 19 knots. A steam pressure of 110 psi was developed in nine double-ended cylindrical boilers with 36 furnaces operated by a labour force of 112 men. To all intents and purposes this was the ultimate size for a marine compound engine as far as economics was concerned and enormous in size it exceeded current practice and was very costly to operate, consuming some 300 tons of coal daily.

By 1885 other shipping companies had already appreciated the fact that the compound engine had reached its peak and were solving problems by turning to twin screw operation and to a further major compound development, the triple expansion engine which, using higher boiler pressures for increased ship sizes requiring higher propulsive outputs, had proved as superior to the compound engine as the latter had claimed advantages over the simple expansion system by achieving greater power and economy with notable reduction in size and weight.

The Triple Expansion Engine

The quest for greater economies offered by higher steam pressures and demands for higher power outputs by invariably increasing sizes of steamships during the latter part of the 19th century, gave birth to the development in 1882 by Robert Napier, of the triple expansion steam engine, originally for the P & O Company; meanwhile the Norddeutscher Lloyd introduced this engine type at about the same time.

The design of the triple expansion engine using steam at 120-200 psi boiler pressure, introduced an additional expansion stage to compounding by including an intermediate (medium pressure) working cylinder to function between HP and LP expansion stages. In the basic design, work done by pistons of each of the three expansion cylinders was transposed to separate cranks at 120 degrees to each other for direct drive to the propeller.

The development was a notable success and within some five years, the triple expansion engine, be it of multi-cylinder in line or tandem (e.g. LP cylinders located beneath the HP and MP units with a common piston rod working a separate crank from each superimposed pair) configurations, was in use worldwide and made the largest ships of the period an economical proposition by its degree of design flexibility. The tandem configuration ensured reduced length and weight of engine.

By late 1880 transatlantic liners equipped with twin triple expansion engines driving two screws were becoming commonplace and towards the turn of the century, 10,000-15,000 ton express liners with engines rated at 4,000 IHP to 14,000 IHP, introduced service speeds of 15-20 knots.

Triple expansion three-crank steam engine built in 1881 by A. C. Kirk for a 3,700 ton steamer on the Australian run.

Rated at 1,800 IHP with steam pressure of 125 psi, the three cylinders were: HP = 30 in, MP = 45 in, LP = 70 in Stroke = 54 in.

It was claimed that this engine type consumed 20% less coal than a contemporary compound engine of the same power output.

One of the two four-cylinder triple expansion engines, each rated at 14,000 IHP, as installed in the twin screw, 1897 built, Norddeutscher Lloyd liner Kaiser Wilhelm der Grosse *of 14,349 tons.*

This was the largest triple expansion marine engine ever built.

Typical 4-cylinder, 4-crank medium sized quadruple expansion steam engine on test bed.

One of a pair of engines for a twin screw 12,000 ton liner built in 1909 for the Australian service.

Two 4-cylinder, 4-crank quadruple expansion steam engines on test bed at Wallsend Slipway. Typical medium sized twin screw installation for the 18,100 ton Cunard liner Franconia *built in 1911. Each engine was rated at 6,750 IHP with steam at 210 psi and the steamer was capable of a 17 knot service speed.*

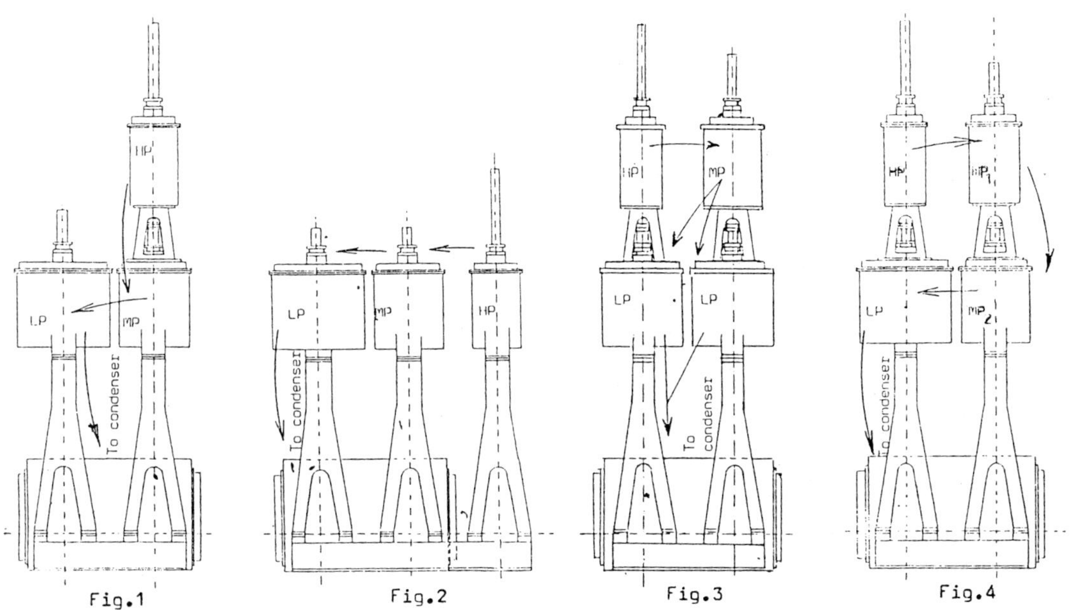

Diagrams showing some typical pressure-staged cylinder configurations of multiple-expansion marine steam reciprocating machinery as evolved since the compound engine era.

Ref. Fig. 1. *Early version (ca 1880-82) of the 3-cylinder triple expansion tandem engine operating on two cranks (alternative was to located the HP cylinder over the LP cylinder). It was designed to save on engine room length for smaller ships. This configuration was found practically impossible to balance for smooth running. It may well be that the original use of this configuration discouraged some shipowners to change from compound working.*

Ref. Fig. 2. *The 3-cylinder, 3-crank in-line triple expansion engine. With certain detail developments in balancing technique this positioning of cylinders found much favour since 1885 because it was easier to balance the cylinder outputs. Increased power requirements at higher boiler pressures (120 to 220 psi) developed the 4-cylinder in-line configuration which offered a favourable power/weight ratio.*

Ref. Fig. 3. *The 4-cylinder triple expansion engine as developed for operation on two cranks using the tandem principle. Offered a well balanced configuration with appropriate saving in engine room length, engine weight and reduction in wear.*

Ref. Fig. 4. *The earliest 4-cylinder quadruple expansion engines were built on the tandem principle on two cranks. With the lightening of engines by using steel the in-line and tandem versions of the quadruple expansion plant became the leading prime mover well into the 1920's.*

During 1893-1897 the twin screw Cunarders *Campania* and *Lucania* of 12,950 tons, equipped with pairs of 5-cylinder, 3-crank (2 x HP, 1 x MP, 2 x LP) triple expansion engines rated at 30,000 IHP with steam at 165 psi, held the Blue Riband of the Atlantic; their coal consumption of ca 400 tons daily compared favourably with the *Umbria* class burning 300 tons.

Operational characteristics of the triple expansion engine enabled it to be used, with periodical detail improvements, as standard power plant for all types of medium speed passenger and cargo ships well into the 20th century period between the wars, when it became completely superseded by the rapid development for marine use of the Internal Combustion Diesel Engine.

The Quadruple Expansion Engine

In the quest for Atlantic records and in order to achieve higher speeds by the ever growing express liners, the quadruple expansion version of the triple expansion power plant was developed towards the turn of the 19th century, introducing the principle of steam expanding in three stages after the HP cylinder, first into the medium pressure (MP_1) and then into a second medium pressure (MP_2) cylinders, followed by a final expansion into the low-pressure (LP) unit. Mean effective pressures at each stage would be so related to the corresponding cylinder areas as to equalise the powers developed on each propulsion crank.

Certain operational advantages were achieved, especially in compacting very large power units while ensuring the best possible exploitation of the expansion potential of steam but economics were not quite of the order anticipated.

One of the first important pairs of engines representing the type was introduced in the HAPAG record breaking liner *Deutschland*, built in 1900. Two quadruple expansion 4-crank engines, each have 6-cylinders, were installed to drive twin screws at 76 RPM and developed 37,800 IHP. Steam was generated at 220 psi in 16 boilers fed by 112 furnaces. The Blue Riband record was achieved by *Deutschland* in 1900 at 22-23.5 knots but due to excessive vibration at high speeds and other mechanical problems, she was duly converted for cruising at more leisurely rates of travel.

The largest quadruple expansion marine engine unit was installed in the Norddeutscher Lloyd prospective record breaker, the 19,400 ton *Kronprinzessin Cecilie*, launched in 1906 and put into service in 1907. She was virtually a sistership to the current record holder *Kaiser Wilhelm II*. The total power plant comprised two enormous quadruple expansion engines, each made up of two 4-cylinder units in a series operating six cranks, for direct drive of twin screws at 80 RPM. The total engine output developed was 44,000 IHP with steam at 225 psi and this enabled the liner to regularly average 23 knots between Eddystone and Sandy Hook. These speeds however did not bring with them the Blue Riband because in 1907 the quadruple screw Cunarder *Lusitania*, equipped with steam turbines, had achieved the distinction.

Although *Kronprinzessin Cecilie* was a super-luxurious and well liked liner, it tended to suffer from strong engine pulsation and throb at high speeds and its daily coal consumption at 700 tons was considered uneconomical. The liner became more a prestige passenger carrier than a commercial proposition.

The quadruple expansion engine was the most represented prime-mover for medium and large passenger liners well into the 20th century being suitable for development to provide appropriate power to suit a good cross-section of steamer sizes of the period, while offering quite a few operational and economic advantages as compared with its triple expansion counterpart. It ensured a reasonably balanced and comparatively efficient power plant to suit speeds around 16-19 knots of the average period liner of 10,000 to 20,000 tons.

However during the onset of the 20th century the state of development of steamship sizes indicated that the technical and economical limits of the reciprocating steam engine for the largest express liners may well have been reached, especially as in the case of chauvenistic requirements for record speeds in excess of 23 knots reciprocating engines were liable to introduce such enormous reciprocating and revolving masses in developing necessary power to revolve huge crankshafts at some 80-100 RPM, as to create unavoidable major vibrations affecting the whole ship.

Fortunately for the shipowner an alternative power source represented by the steam turbine was already appearing on the scene, mainly through the inventive genius of Charles Parsons.

The largest quadruple expansion steam marine power plant ever built.

Norddeutscher Lloyd twin-screw liners Kaiser Wilhelm II *and* Kronprinzessin Cecilie *of 1903-1907.*

A pair of 4-cylinder, 3-crank quadruple expansion steam engines, series-connected to form one 8-cylinder unit with six cranks, capable of developing 22,000 IHP to drive one propeller.

The cylinders are so arranged that the cranks can secure the advantages of the 'Schlick' system of balancing to minimise vibration. The 37½in diameter HP cylinder is in tandem above the first intermediate (IP_1) 49¼in diameter to act on the first crank. Second crank is operated by piston of the IP_2 74¾in bore cylinder and the third crank is actuated from the 112¼in LP cylinder. A piston stroke of 70¾in revolved the crankshaft.

Steam Turbine for Marine Propulsion

The Steam Turbine

The operating principle of any turbine is that impinging jets of high velocity steam or other fluid are directed onto peripherally mounted blades or vanes on a rotor shaft, thus revolving the shaft which is connected to a particular drive. The basic steam turbine consists of two parts, a casing receiving high pressure steam from the boiler into stationary nozzles or blades mounted inside the casing and in which steam is expanded, as well as a rotor which is made up of discs or wheels carrying peripherally mounted blades receiving high velocity jets of expanded steam, whereby the heat energy of steam is converted into kinetic energy. The shape of the blades causes a change in direction and velocity of the steam jet thus creating the force rotating the bladed wheel.

Like any steam engine, the steam turbine converts energy stored in high pressure steam into mechanical work but unlike the process in the reciprocating engine, this work is converted directly into rotary motion and therefore offers such advantages as a smaller machinery unit for equivalent output hence a more favourable power/weight ratio, a complete absence of forces causing vibration and reduced maintenance. Furthermore, the steam turbine, which is also universally used as primemover for power generation, can be designed for the largest ratings that may be required for marine propulsion.

The steam turbine has been experimented with in various forms and for various duties both in Europe and the USA, since the middle of the 19th century and its first practical application by DeLaval in 1883 was to drive an electrical generator. DeLaval introduced the principle of the 'Impulse' turbine, in which expansion of high pressure steam takes place almost entirely in the fixed nozzles of the casing and gains velocity at the expense of pressure until all available heat energy of steam is converted into kinetic energy of high velocity steam jets issuing from the nozzles and directed into the blades through a constant area of steam path with the consequent change in direction of flow creating an impulsive force doing work on the rotor by acting in the direction of rotation of the blades.

In 1884 Sir Charles Parsons developed the multi-stage turbine of the 'Reaction' type, in which steam pressure drop is divided between blades (vanes) fixed in the casing, into which steam is first directed, and the 'moving' blades attached to the wheels of the rotor shaft. The blades are of a shape to offer a narrowing steam path thus making them act partially as nozzles and causing a greater relative velocity of steam at the outlet of blades than at the inlet. The reaction associated with this higher leaving velocity causes additional work to be done on the moving blades. In the normal form of reaction blading, the heat drops over moving and stationary rows of blades are equal and therefore blade profiles can be the same for both rows but reversed in direction.

In a steam turbine the combination of a row of fixed blades or nozzles and a row of moving blades constitute a turbine stage. In a single stage, velocities of steam are very high and the rotor and moving blades would be expected to produce speeds at which centrifugal forces would be excessive.

Single stage turbines are therefore used only for small high-speed machinery. Large output steam turbines must be of the multi-stage type consisting of impulse or/and reaction stages, as described. The total heat drop is then divided within the various stages so that steam speeds in the individual stages are more acceptable and the blade velocities required for most favourable efficiency are reduced to practicable values.

Diagrammatic portrayal of turbine blading.

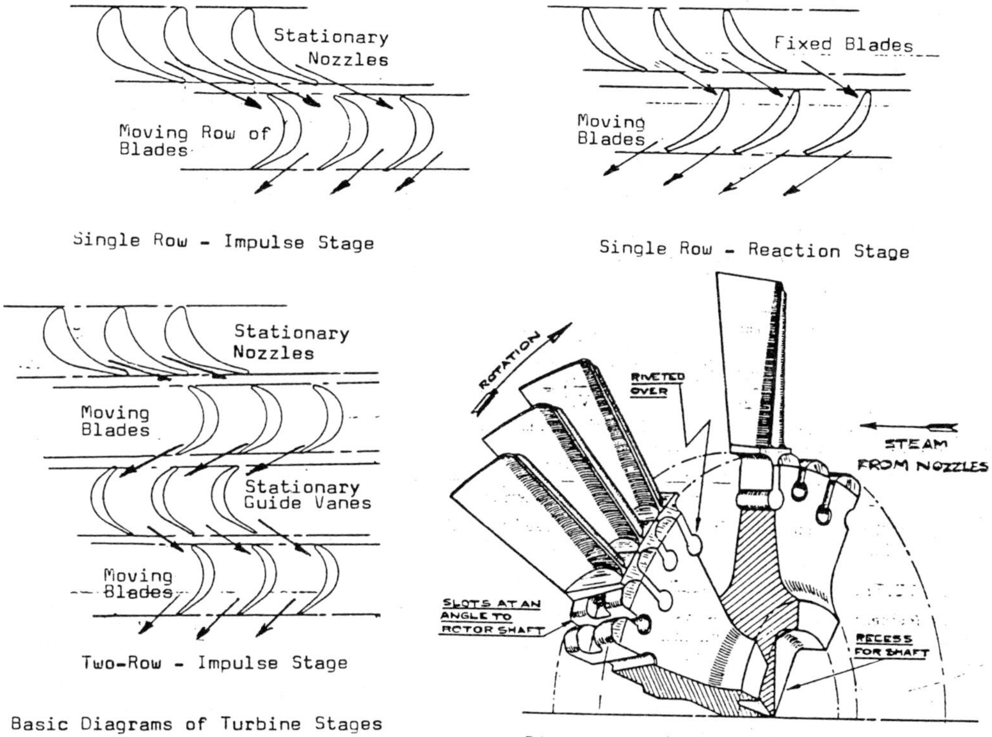

Single Row - Impulse Stage

Single Row - Reaction Stage

Two-Row - Impulse Stage

Basic Diagrams of Turbine Stages

Diagram showing principle of a small Impulse Wheel.

In marine application it has been usual to 'cross-compound' turbine propulsion units from high-pressure and low-pressure multi-stage turbines contained in separate casings, called 'cylinders', each providing a separate drive to respective propellers, either direct (as in the past) or through appropriate gearing. Single turbine units would be more suitable to drive generators but were also installed for propulsion of smaller, high-speed vessels, such as cross-Channel steamers.

Very large prime-movers such as featured in *Queen Mary* and *Queen Elizabeth* comprised four compounded multi-stage turbine units consisting of one high-pressure, two intermediate-pressure and one low-pressure cylinders, each unit providing drive to one propeller through its single-reduction gearing.

Sir Charles Parsons started the development of the marine steam turbine around the end of the 19th century in order to apply it to ship propulsion thus creating competition with contemporary steam reciprocating machinery and apart from wishing to achieve economy in the use of steam, he foresaw the system as suitable for the generation of much higher powers than was economically possible with reciprocating engines and at the same time offering great operational advantages.

In 1894 Parsons built his experimental test launch *Turbinia* and demonstrated it in a blaze of publicity by steering it at 34 knots between various warships at the Naval Review at Spithead in 1897.

Since 1896 other inventors developed marine steam turbine engines and took out patents for turbine designs and these included Curtis (USA), Rateau (France), Zoelly and AEG (Germany) and others; in all cases the designs were based upon the basic principles of impulse and reaction blading and featured a variety of stage and wheel configurations.

The Royal Navy took great interest in this new propulsion method, two test-destroyers were built and from about 1905 turbine machinery was accepted by the Admiralty for newly built capital-ships and other vessels with direct drive to propellers starting with the famous *Dreadnought* of 1906. Around 1916 geared transmission was introduced.

Direct Drive by Steam Turbine

The application of turbine drive for large passenger liners was to a great extent based upon experience with the triple-screw, direct driven 20,000 ton Cunarder *Carmania* built in 1905. In 1907 the two famous record breakers *Lusitania* and *Mauretania* were each equipped with four compound direct-drive (2 x HP and 2 x LP) Parsons engines developing 68,000 SHP to drive quadruple screws at 180-200 RPM with turbine peripheral velocities around 9,500 ft/min.

Three other famous liners, built for HAPAG in 1913/18, at the time and until 1936, the largest in

1907 quadruple-screw turbine liner Mauretania *of the Cunard Line. Low-pressure turbine rotor prior to installation into 11 ft-8 in casing drum for connection to drive one of the liner's inboard propellers.*

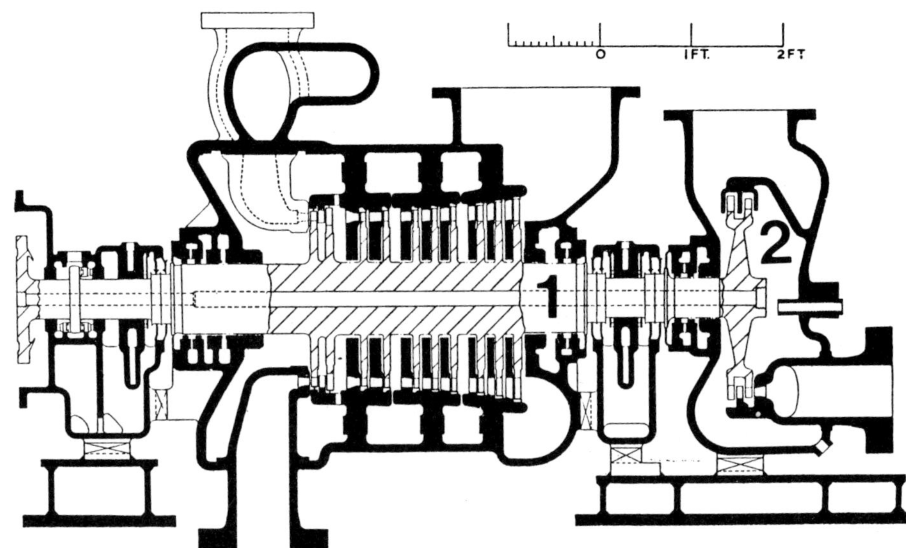

Arrangement of high-pressure turbine, part of a typical set of compound turbine machinery, HP and LP turbines for twin screw liner aggregating 45,000 SHP.

Diagram shows a 2-row Curtis impulse stage followed by 8 single stages. An overhung 2-row Curtis wheel is fitted at the forward end of the HP ahead turbine (1) to form the astern turbine (2).

the world, were *Imperator* (Berengaria), *Vaterland* (Leviathan) and *Bismarck* (Majestic) were ceded to the Allies after the First World War. Each of these three liners was equipped with four compound (4 x HP and 4 x LP) turbine engines of the Parsons and Curtis/AEG type with direct drive to quadruple screws.

In marine practice the higher acceptable power outputs per turbine for direct drive of a propeller were considered to be ca 15,000-16,000 SHP. Early marine turbines were designed to operate with high pressure steam at around 200 psi as compared with 250-300 psi of the contemporary steam piston engines because of pressure loss through clearances between working parts. Against that, maintenance of high vacuum at the condenser allowed steam to expand more than was possible with the piston engine. In the search for higher overall efficiencies however and the use of reduction gearing, steam pressures and temperatures (superheated) have increased up to the limits set by the use of materials and machining limits subsequently developed.

One drawback of turbine propulsion was that the turbine is not reversible and therefore separate turbines are required for astern power. A single astern turbine with a series of reverse-pitch blading was usually located within the LP ahead casing but for higher steam pressures and larger engine units, separate HP and LP astern turbines may be required. A noteworthy example was the machinery of the *Mauretania* where two separately housed astern turbines, supplied with HP steam, were located so as to transmit power to inboard propellers independently.

In early practice the astern turbine (2 or 3 wheels) was kept small thus limiting astern power and restricting manoeuverability of the ship.

Combined Turbo/Reciprocating Machinery

During the early years of turbine development, a combined propulsion system was developed by Harland & Wolff, comprising multi-expansion reciprocating engines and turbine drive. The piston engine was not really suitable for obtaining efficient work from steam expanding to very low pressures owing to practical difficulties associated with large cylinder diameters and port areas required for the greater volumes of steam. A turbine was therefore included as part of the overall powerplant to make use of the low pressure exhaust steam from the reciprocating engines in conjunction with vacuum at the condenser.

The overall marine installation onboard ship therefore consisted of a pair of triple expansion reciprocating engines driving two wing propellers of a triple screw arrangement with the low pressure turbine turning the centre screw. Operational advantages were achieved by improving fuel consumption and better manoeuverability due to good control at slower ships' speeds using the reciprocating engines for more positive reversing. However the efficiency of propulsion obtained with the fast revolving centre propeller driven by the turbine was low at service speeds of the vessel.

The period 1910-1920 saw a number of large liners equipped with the combined propulsion system and notable installations included the three White Star 45,000 to 48,000 ton sisterships of the 'Olympic' class, built by Harland & Wolff.

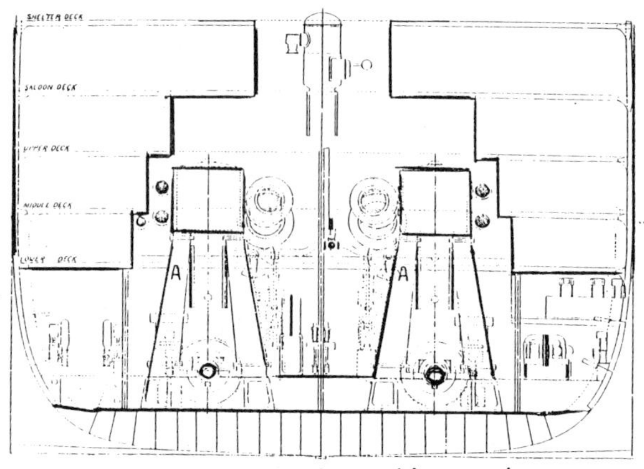

Section through reciprocating engine room

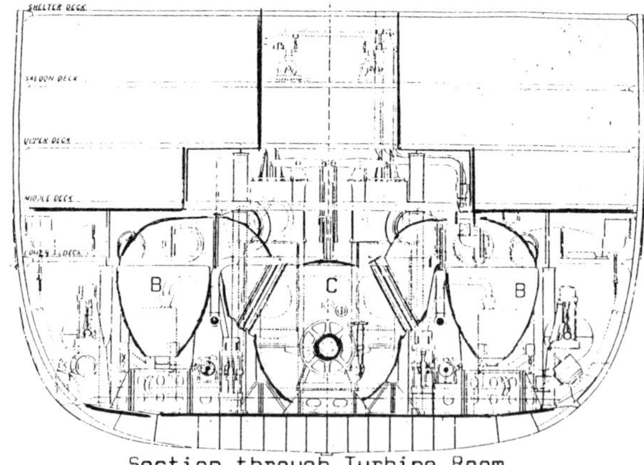

Section through Turbine Room

Cross-section through reciprocating and turbine engine rooms of the 1912 White Star Line triple-screw 21-knot liner Olympic *of 45,324 GR tons, built by Harland & Wolff, with machinery developing 45,000 IHP. This combined triple-screw system was also installed by the makers in the* Titanic *and* Britannic *(2), the two sisterships of the* Olympic *as well as some 12 16-knot, 15,000 to 19,000 ton liners for the International Mercantile Marine Company and other shipowners. The Combined Turbo/Reciprocating machinery was not installed in any Atlantic record breaking liners.*

'A' – Pair of triple expansion steam engines *'B' – Condensers* *'C' – Low pressure steam turbine*

Geared Turbine Drive

In the early days of ship propulsion by steam turbines with the engines directly coupled to propeller shafting, the high turbine revolutions necessary in order to obtain suitable peripheral blade speeds for economical operation and therefore requiring large turbine diameters, were incompatible with keeping propeller velocities so low as to avoid possible blade cavitation (120-200 RPM) and consequent loss in efficiency.

After the First World War, designers turned their attention to such drives as turbo-hydraulic and turbo-electric transmission but the more practical engineers of the period concentrated on the development of mechanical gearing as pioneered by Parsons. Introduction of suitable gearing between turbines and propellers allowed designers of such machinery to select revolutions most suitable for their individual purposes so as to ensure the maximum efficiency of turbine and propeller respectively.

Between 1920 and ca 1947, single-reduction gearing for turbine drive was adapted in both merchant and naval practices. Notable installations included such record breaking liners as *Bremen* and *Europa* as well as ocean giants *Queen Mary* and *Queen Elizabeth*. Most of the world's warships of all types were also being equipped with single-reduction gearing for their steam turbine machinery and although this practice persevered well beyond the Second World War period, during the early thirties numerous ships were also being equipped, sometimes experimentally, with double-reduction gearing drives. The late forties and early fifties saw this development as a rule rather than exception, various problems associated with suitability of materials and manufacturing having been resolved.

The elementary concept of single-reduction gearing drive is that the turbines of a particular turbine set are connected through sliding couplings, comprising toothed and sleeved members, to respective helical gear pinions which in turn mesh with the double-helical teeth of a large gearwheel coupled to the propeller shaft. The numbers of teeth on the pinion and those of the gearwheel create the ratio of desired velocity reduction.

With single-reduction gearing it was customary in merchant practice to have two turbines' pinions driving one gearwheel/propeller shaft in smaller ships where propeller revolutions could be fairly high, but in the case of large liners it was usual to connect three or even four expansion-staged turbines per shaft, with steam passing in a series from one turbine to the next.

In the case of double-reduction gearing a more elaborate arrangement introduces a high-speed or primary gear train as an addition to the single-reduction unit with each turbine drive. This arrangement allows for greater flexibility and more effective reduction of high turbine velocities to suit propeller revolutions. During the post-1948 period double-reduction gearing was developed into a highly efficient and reliable drive; even for ships requiring fairly low propeller shaft revolutions it was usual to employ two series-working turbines per shaft, higher blade speeds being made possible with associated high overall efficiencies and reduced sizes and weight of machinery. A notable example of double-reduction geared turbine machinery was the propelling power plant installed in the ultimate record breaker *United States* and capable of developing 240,000 SHP.

Single-reduction gearing as installed in the Cunard Line record breaker Queen Mary. *Illustration shows one of the high-speed double-helical pinions, as coupled to the turbine, and the main gearwheel to drive the propeller shaft.*

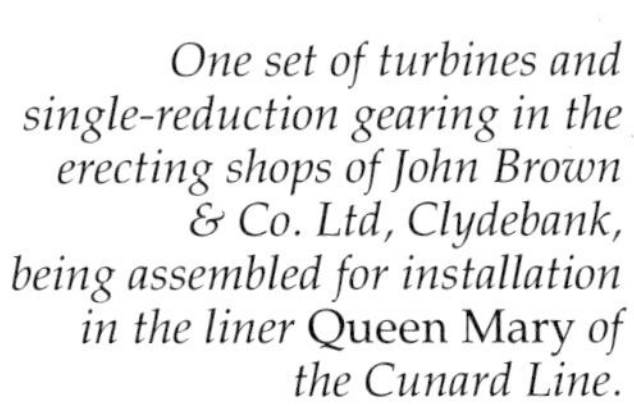

One set of turbines and single-reduction gearing in the erecting shops of John Brown & Co. Ltd, Clydebank, being assembled for installation in the liner Queen Mary *of the Cunard Line.*

A typical 'Four-Square' single-reduction geared turbine set, transmitting 14,000 SHP for a medium speed 20,000 ton Atlantic liner.

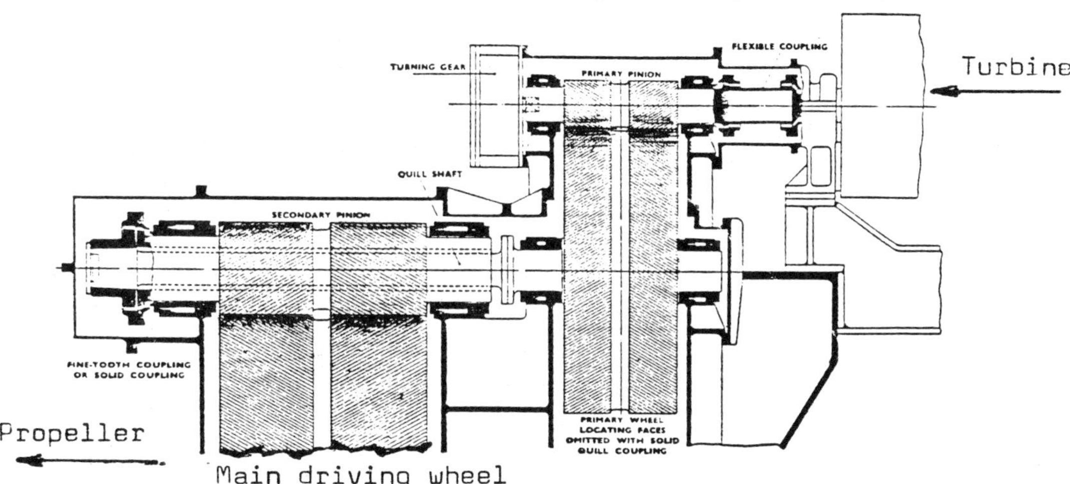

Sketch showing the principle of a typical simple double-reduction gear train (articulated). The high-speed double-helical pinion taking drive from the turbine, engages a primary gear wheel which in turn drives a secondary pinion meshing with the main driving wheel coupled to the propeller shaft.

Turbo-Electric Transmission

This method of propulsion has been developed at roughly the same time as mechanical reduction gearing drive and offered a notable advantage by eliminating the astern turbine while ensuring availability of full astern power without altering the direction of turbine rotation, thus introducing the utmost manoeuverability of a vessel and facilitating full control in heavy seas. A worthwhile degree of flexibility of installation was also introduced insofar as propulsion motors could be located at the after end of the ship, thus considerably shortening the propeller shafting.

During the early days of reduction gearing various manufacturing problems tended to arise and in operation, vibration and noise were sometimes in evidence at certain gear loading or at certain speeds. The positive operational features of turbo-electric propulsion such as complete quietness as well as the earlier mentioned advantages were somewhat negated by the space having to be made available for electrical machinery and its weight, this being particularly applicable to the driving motors.

Development of turbo-electric propulsion as an alternative to mechanical reduction gearing originated mainly in the USA and Germany and a few notable installations materialised. The US Navy utilised turbo-electric propulsion in numerous major warships of the 1920-1929 period and some medium sized passenger ships were also equipped. By 1935, however, the US Navy accepted the advantages offered by geared turbines because of the not inconsiderable bulk of electrical machinery involved with electrical transmission and its succeptibility to damage in case of warlike activities.

Apart from some American and German merchant ships, the British P & O Line made use of the system in some of their liners trading in the Far East during the 1929-1932 period, but then reverted to improved designs of mechanical gearing until in 1961 their flagship, the 45,270 ton *Canberra* again featured turbo-electric propulsion; it appears that *Canberra* was the last major liner so equipped.

The principle of turbo-electric propulsion consists of an alternating current generator (alternator) directly driven by the high speed turbine, electrically connected to an AC motor designed for a suitable speed rating, which in turn is directly coupled to the propeller shaft. Also required is a direct-current exciter or an auxiliary generator and appropriate switching and control equipment. The whole thus comprises a reduction gear having the ratio of reduction determined by the relative number of poles of the generator and motor.

AC motors driving the propellers are usually of the self-starting synchronous (constant speed at all loads) type, offering simplicity of construction, a high power factor and good efficiency.

Normandie

The largest and most famous turbo-electric marine power plant was installed in the 1935 built, 83,423 ton French Line record breaking liner *Normandie*, designed for a service speed of 29-31 knots. The machinery was capable of a total power output of 130,000 SHP on four shafts for a propeller speed of 225 RPM and had an overload rating of 160,000 SHP, i.e. 40,000 SHP per shaft for a velocity of 243 RPM.

The four main drive compound steam turbine (HP and LP) sets were of the Zoelly multi-stage impulse type, each driving a three-phase 5,500 volt (6,000 V max), four-pole air cooled alternator rated at 33,400 kW. Frequency at 1,750 RPM was 58⅓ C/S and 81 C/S at 2,430 RPM.

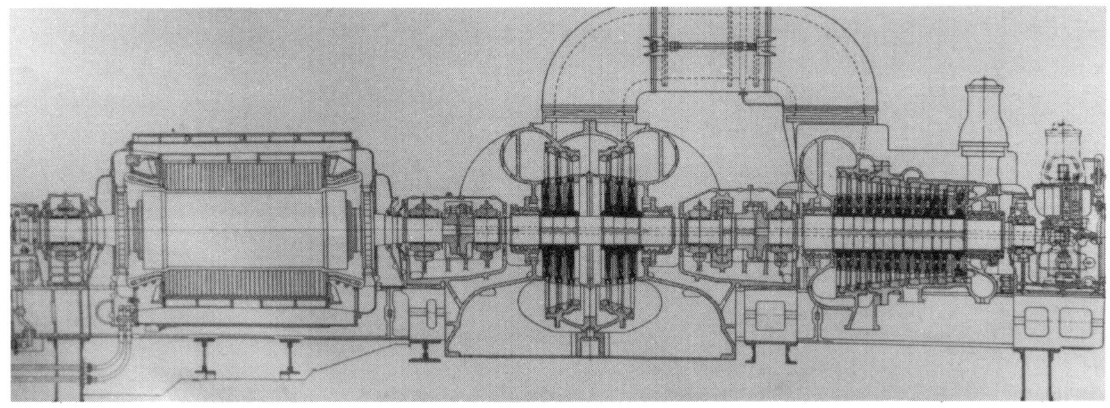

Quadruple-screw liner Normandie.
Sectional arrangement showing one of the four 33,400 kW (at 2,430 RPM) turbo-alternator sets. In the Zoelly multi-stage impulse turbine steam expansion takes place in the fixed blades and the moving blades are mounted on stage-wheels rotating in separate compartments. The turbine set consists of two casings, with the HP cast-steel casing containing 13 stages and the second, LP double-flow casing in special cast iron, housing three stage-wheels in each flow.

Quadruple-screw liner Normandie.
Propulsion turbine/alternator set rated at 33,400 kW. In the course of erection on the Als-Thom testbed.

Normandie.
Central passageway in the turbo-alternator room, with control board in the background.

Normandie.
One of the four Als-Thom three-phase 40,000 SHP propulsion motors as coupled to the propellers and electrically driven from the turbo-alternator sets. These main propulsion motors were noteworthy for their large dimensions, each measuring 21.3 ft (6.5 m) in height, 26.2 ft (8 m) in length and 19.7 ft (6 m) wide.

The four propulsion turbines were supplied with superheated steam at 335 psi (23.5 kg/cm^2) and a temperature of 325°C, generated in 29 water-tube boilers rated at 400 psi (28 kg/cm^2) and 350°C maximum.

The four propulsion motors were of the three-phase synchronous type with salient poles, for a service tension of 5,500 V (6,000 V max.) and each motor was capable of a 40,000 SHP maximum output. Frequency was variable at 0-81 C/S and the number of poles was 40. During normal connection in synchronism the ratio of speed reduction between the four-pole alternator and relevant propulsion motor was therefore fixed at 10:1. The propeller revolutions were thus controlled by the speed of the generator, i.e. in accordance with the speed governing of the turbine. During normal running each turbo-alternator fed one propulsion motor only but it was possible to supply the motors of the two line-shafts on one side by either turbo-alternator on that side thus ensuring better efficiency at reduced power.

Five 120 kW at 150 V rotary-converter excitation sets (four working and one standby) were installed for the propulsion motors and turbo-alternators.

Most elaborate and modern sophisticated switchgear and controls ensured great operational flexibility and manoeuverability at all speeds and under all conditions.

Considering the size of the liner and the exceptionally large, unusual and sophisticated power plant, the behaviour of *Normandie* at speed and performance trials was eminently satisfactory, achieving speeds of over 32 knots with great operational flexibility and smoothness under all conditions. Furthermore, excellent fuel consumption figures were obtained at all speeds and only minimal adjustments were required.

During the subsequent maiden voyage *Normandie* achieved a westbound average of 29.98 knots and the eastbound mean was 30.35 knots; thus Atlantic records were broken in both directions.

It may be of interest to compare the 1935 *Normandie* power plant with a similar one installed in 1961 in the 27.5 knot, 45,270 ton liner *Canberra* built for the Peninsular & Oriental S N Company by Harland & Wolff of Belfast.

In this instance twin screws are driven by two propulsion motors of 42,500 SHP each, electrically connected to turbo-alternator sets, each rated at 32,200 kW at 6,000 V. In this instance three Foster-Wheeler water-tube boilers develop steam at 750 psi (53 kg/cm^2) and 960°F (515°C).

Canberra was built in 1961 for the Australian trade and is nowadays in operation as a cruise liner. After some teething troubles during her early life, the machinery functioned well and the liner gives excellent service which also included operation in 1982 as troop transport in the South Atlantic during the Falklands War.

Present-Day Merchant Ship Propulsion

Since the mid-1960's to-date, with shipping lanes occupied exclusively by enormous bulkers, container ships and tankers as well as giant ferries and cruise liners, the turbine drive is hardly ever used, even for particularly large vessels. Overall operational economies have been instrumental in the rapid development of the Marine Diesel Engine, originating with the first ocean-going motorship, the 7,400 ton *Selandia* of 1912, to become the present-day virtually universal method of ship propulsion.

Slow and medium-speed marine diesel engines of the four and two-cycle type, invariably turbocharged, sometimes equipped with reduction gearing or even for diesel-electric propulsion and making maximum possible use of automation in order to reduce operating personnel, feature to the exclusion of all other propulsion methods in virtually all modern ship types, with the term 'Steamer' having become obsolescent in favour of 'Motorship'.

Terminology and Measurements

Interpretation of Maritime Tonnage Ratings

THERE ARE DIFFERENTLY BASED tonnage measurement ratings, some applicable to all merchant vessels and others with particular reference to ship types. Tonnage is one of the most involved subjects associated with shipping mensuration and only a brief description can be given here.

Size comparison of merchant ships is usually based upon 'Gross' and 'Net' Registered tonnages and in the regulations which govern such measurement of ships, this 'tonnage' relates to volumetric capacity and bears no direct relation to carrying capacity (Deadweight Tonnage) or the ship's weight (Displacement Tonnage). Such measurement tonnage regulations originated with the Merchant Shipping Act of 1854 and were later embodied in the Act of 1894, various modifications and amendments then being introduced at different times to bring the Act up-to-date.

Gross Registered Tonnage (GRT)

'GRT' is a standard everyday definition used for the legal measurement of ship sizes as applicable to merchant ships of all types. It is a mathematically calculated volumetric measurement, assuming in broad terms that every enclosed space below the upper deck plus enclosed spaces above the upper deck strictly required for carriage, are filled with 'cargo' which measures 100 cubic feet per ton (2,832 litres/tonne). Obviously no ship could possibly be so filled and therefore the measurement is quite artificial but it gives a consistent yardstick for comparison of merchant ship sizes with reference to volume and is the usual 'tons' term used in describing for universal statistics the size of any merchant ship as well as for the purpose of ship's registration, pilotage charges and dry-dock dues.

Net Registered Tonnage (NRT)

Associated with Gross Tonnage, the term 'Net Tonnage' may be mentioned and this is the basis upon which canal and port dues and ship clearance at ports are paid. The measurement amounts to calculation for 'Gross Tonnage' with areas not comprising payload capacity, i.e. machinery, bunkers, crews' quarters, ballast spaces, etc, being excluded.

Displacement Tonnage

Displacement Tonnage of a vessel is the quantity of water displaced by the fully loaded ship afloat and is usually expressed in tons weight but sometimes by volume. If a ship is floating freely in water, the weight of water displaced is then exactly equal to the weight of the ship in sea-going condition and with everything onboard. It is usual to take 35 cubic feet of sea water as weighing one ton and fresh water at 36 cb ft/ton. Density of sea water however can vary slightly.

'Displacement Tonnage' is also applicable for measurement of warships although it is the criterion of total weight of a merchant ship and is also used for estimating the value of a ship when she is being sold to shipbreakers.

Deadweight Tonnage (dwt)

In the case of merchant ships, displacement (or total weight) of a vessel is made up of 'Lightweight' (displacement light) Tonnage plus 'Deadweight' Tonnage (dwt).

Lightweight Tonnage of a ship is defined as its weight when ready for sea, but excluding fuel, feed-water, fresh water, stores, temporary ballast, passengers and cargo.

Deadweight Tonnage (dwt) is the only tonnage rating of a ship bearing relation to its carrying capacity and is the weight which can be loaded into the ship before she settles in water down to the Plimsoll load line, as marked on her side for safety. The dwt tonnage measurement is particularly applicable for the assessment of vessels carrying mainly or entirely cargo.

Mensuration and Glossary

Linear Dimensions

In marine practice there are various methods of linear measurement. According to 'Moulded Dimensions' the length of a ship is quoted as 'length between perpendicular', which is a horizontal measurement along the summer load line between points of intersection with the stem and the aft sternpost (or rudder stock). This 'moulded' length is usually referred to by the builders and is quoted in this book unless sizes are qualified as 'overall'. Length 'overall' is the greatest length of a vessel from extreme fore end to extreme after end.

Velocity

The speed of a ship is universally denoted by 'Knots' (Kn). 1 knot = 1 nautical mile per hour = 1.1515 statute m/hr = 1.853 km/hr.

Steam Pressure

The expression 'psi' denotes 'pounds per square inch' (Imperial unit) and refers to pressure as indicated on the boiler gauge or other steam gauges.

14.22 psi = 1 kg per square cm (1 kg/cm^2) = 1 Atmosphere (Metric) Conversion to 'SI' (post 1970) metric units: 1 Bar = 14.5 psi.

Steam pressure identification symbols: 'HP' = High Pressure stage. 'MP_1' = Medium Pressure first stage. 'MP_2' = Medium Pressure second stage. 'LP' = Low Pressure.

Engine Power

For a reciprocating piston engine, be it steam or oil fired, the term 'IHP' denotes 'Indicated Horse Power' which is the unit related to the power developed by the engine, but is higher than the useful power available at the propeller shaft on account of frictional and other losses. The driving power is then denoted as 'Brake Horse Power'.

On the basis of Imperial (Foot-Pound units) measurements, IHP is obtained for a steam engine cylinder by the formula:

$$IHP = \frac{PxLxAxN}{33{,}000} \quad \text{where:}$$

'P' is the mean effective pressure on the piston as measured from the indicator apparatus, in lbs/in^2.

'L' = Piston Stroke in feet.

'A' = Area of the Engine Piston, square inches.

'N' = Number of piston power strokes per minute.

One Horse Power equals 33,000 ft.lb/minute.

For a double-acting steam engine cylinder, the horse-power result from above formula is multiplied by two.

The horse-power of a compound or multiple-expansion engine will be the sum of IHP's of the individual cylinders as calculated by above formula.

The Brake Horse Power (BHP) of an engine, as available for useful drive, can be measured by means of a friction or electrical brake dynamometer.

The Mechanical Efficiency of a reciprocating engine is interpreted by the ratio of BHP/IHP and depending upon period type, size and speed of the engine, can be anything from 70% to 100%.

In the case of a steam turbine, 'SHP' stands for 'Shaft Horse Power', as delivered by the turbine to the propulsion shaft and is virtually the same as 'Brake Horse Power' quoted above. 'SHP' is also measured by means of a brake dynamometer.

Conversion data: One 'HP' (Imperial) = 1.04 (Metric)
= 0.7457 kW.
One 'SI' (post 1970) unit = 0.7355 kW.

Sources for Reference

Bibliography and Further Reading

Bathe, B. W., *Seven Centuries of Sea Travel.*

Bonsor, N. R. P., *North Atlantic Seaway, 1955-1975.* Stephenson.

Brayard & Miller, *Fifty Famous Liners* (Vols. 1-3). Stephens.

Coleman, Terry, *The Liners.* Penguin.

Cornwell, E. L., *Illustrated History of Ships.* 1970. New English Library.

Deeson, A. F. L., *Illustrated History of Steamships.* 1975. Spurbooks.

Griffiths, C., *Brunel's Great Western.* 1985. Stephens.

Griffiths, C., *Power of the Great Liners.* 1990. Stephens.

Grant, Kay, *Samuel Cunard.* 1967. Abelard Schuman.

Hansen, H. J., *Die Schiffe der Deutschen Flotten 1848-1945.*

Haws, Duncan, *Merchant Fleets in Profile.* 1979 (Vol. 2). Stephens.

Hoverspeed, *Official Challenge for the Hales Trophy.* 1990.

Hughes, T., *The Blue Riband of the Atlantic.* 1974. Stephens.

Hyde, Francis A., *Cunard and North Atlantic 1840-73.* 1975. McMillans.

Johnson, H., *The Cunard Story.* 1987. Whittet.

Kempe's Engineer's Yearbook.

Maber, John, *Cross-Channel Packets & Ocean Liners.* 1985. Conway.

'Normandie', *The Shipbuilder & Marine Engine Builder.* 1935.

Plagemann V., *Uebersee.* Becks, Muenchen.

Rentall, P., *Historic Cunard Liners.* 1986. Atlantic Transport.

Rentall, P., *Historic White Star Liners.* 1987. Blue Water.

Rowland, L. T., *The 'Great Britain'.* 1971. David & Charles.

V. D. I. Nachrichten, *Magazine of Verein Deutscher Ingenieure.*

Vernon-Gibbs, C. R., *British Passenger Liners of the Five Oceans.* 1963. Putnams.

Virgin Transatlantic Challenge. 1985. Suzanne Fields.

Virgin Atlantic Challenge. 1986. Virgin Books.

Subject Index